Praise for

THE ANTI-ROMANTIC CHILD

"Rapturously beautiful and deeply moving, profound, and marvelous."
—Andrew Solomon, author of *The Noonday Demon*

"A fantastic memoir. . . . I loved this book."
—KJ Dell'Antonia, lead blogger for the *New York Times*'s
Motherlode blog

"*The Anti-Romantic Child* is beautiful, poetic, and heartfelt. It's more than a mother-child story; it's a journey of self-discovery. It's a book every parent should read."
—Kathryn Erskine, bestselling author of *Mockingbird* and winner
of the 2010 National Book Award

"Every parent should read this luminous book to absorb or absorb again the truth that every child is a surprise—a revelation—to be uniquely learned and understood as well as loved. Gilman's passionate engagement with her son's learning and emerging strengths, in the face of a developmental disorder, persuades us of the complementarity of emotion and intellect, never to be set aside in service to test scores and labels."
—Mary Catherine Bateson, author of *Composing a Further Life:
The Age of Active Wisdom*

"[Gilman] crafts a beautifully sinuous and intensely literary celebration of the exceptional, unconventional child."
—*Publishers Weekly* (starred review)

"A lovely, thoughtful memoir."
—*Boston Globe*

"Priscilla Gilman's lyrical narrative is profoundly moving and ultimately joyous. It eloquently touches the universal."

　　—Harold Bloom

"Priscilla Gilman's account of confronting the fact that her beloved child Benjamin is not the child she had dreamed of in romantic fantasies of motherhood is a very moving personal story. . . . I was immensely touched by Priscilla's journey to joyful acceptance."

　　—Tina Brown, *Newsweek*

"A riveting and original book about love."

　　—Ann Beattie

"A striking celebration of the bond between a mother and son."

　　—*Kirkus Reviews*

"What a glorious book Priscilla Gilman has written. Lively, eloquent, straightforward, and insightful, *The Anti-Romantic Child* deftly delineates and negotiates the complex crosscurrents of a life of the mind and a life of the heart."

　　—Sandra Boynton, children's book author and illustrator

"*The Anti-Romantic Child* is such a profoundly moving book I could hardly bear to read it. It is so riveting I couldn't stop. It is rich, informative, and gorgeously written. If you don't love it as much as I did, you must have left your heart in the taxi cab."

　　—Andre Gregory, theater director, writer, and star of *My Dinner with Andre*

"*The Anti-Romantic Child* is remarkable. This haunting and lyrical memoir will be an invaluable and heartening guide to all who find themselves in similar situations and indeed anyone confronting an unforeseen challenge."

　　—Marie Brenner, writer-at-large for *Vanity Fair* and author of *Apples and Oranges*

"Priscilla Gilman movingly describes how her son's struggle with hyperlexia put her in touch with her 'deepest sense of what's truly meaningful.'"

—Andrew Sullivan, the *Daily Beast*

"A meditation on both the 'passionate work' of motherhood and the wonderment of childhood."

—Vogue.com

"[Gilman] explores the complex emotions of parenting and the ideals and illusions that must live alongside the reality. Throughout, she quotes extensively from Wordsworth as she confides her own disappointments and triumphs in the midst of ongoing hope. Gilman is at once lyrical and deeply analytical as she explores the complexities of parenthood and the need to embrace the unforeseen."

—*Booklist* (starred review)

"Profoundly moving."

—*American Way* magazine

"*The Anti-Romantic Child* is about parental humility . . . and coming to terms with the child you have as he exists and not as you imagined him in your romantic poetry class. . . . A wonderful book."

—Hanna Rosin, "Coffee Talk" endorsement, *DoubleX Gabfest, Slate*

"Poignant and poetic."

—*MORE* magazine, "The Latest Crop of Incredible Memoirs"

"A first-rate writer . . . courageous and irresistible."

—Barbara Jones, the *Progressive Reader*

"Tender, smart, and full of wonder, not quite like any book I've ever read on motherhood."

—Michelle Richmond, *New York Times* bestselling author of *The Year of Fog* and *No One You Know*

"Full of moving moments. . . . [Gilman is] a writer of prodigious gifts. . . . a lovely work. In this memoir, Gilman succeeds wildly at letting us into the family that produced this unique and wonderful boy, Benjy."

—Marie Myung-Ok Lee, "*DoubleX* Book of the Week," *Slate*

"*The Anti-Romantic Child* is one of the most thoughtful and powerful available accounts of being the parent of a child with developmental disabilities, and it deserves to be widely read for many years to come. It's a work of originality and inspiration that could help not only parents, but also teachers, clinicians, and policy makers."

—*Metapsychology* online reviews

"This is a book for parents of all children, conventional or not, for teachers, and for lovers of literature. . . . A true test of the scope of this memoir's audience can be made by reading the quotes of praise on the jacket—you'd be hard-pressed to find another book with advance praise from both a serious academic, Harold Bloom, and a famed children's writer, Sandra Boynton. That is the kind of thoughtful and joyous work this is."

—Girlfriendbooks.com

- An *NPR Morning Edition* "Must-Read"

- A Best Book of 2011, *The Leonard Lopate Show*

- Top nonfiction pick in "Suggested Summer Reading" by *The Sisterhood of the Jewish Daily Forward*

- Nominated for a Books for a Better Life Award for Best First Book

THE ANTI-
ROMANTIC
CHILD

A Memoir of Unexpected Joy

Priscilla Gilman

HARPER PERENNIAL

NEW YORK • LONDON • TORONTO • SYDNEY • NEW DELHI • AUCKLAND

HARPER ● PERENNIAL

A hardcover edition of this book was published in 2011 by Harper, an imprint of HarperCollins Publishers.

Grateful acknowledgment is made for permission to reprint from the following:

"Fern Hill'" by Dylan Thomas, from *The Poems of Dylan Thomas*, copyright © 1945 by The Trustees for the Copyrights of Dylan Thomas. Reprinted by permission of New Directions Publishing Corp.
Excerpt from the poem "One Art" from Elizabeth Bishop's *The Complete Poems*, originally published by Farrar, Straus and Giroux in 1983.
"In Memory of W. B. Yeats," copyright © 1940 and renewed 1968 by W. H. Auden, from *Collected Poems of W. H. Auden* by W. H. Auden. Used by permission of Random House, Inc.

HarperCollins books may be purchased for educational, business, or sales promotional use. For information, please write: Special Markets Department, HarperCollins Publishers, 10 East 53rd Street, New York, NY 10022.

FIRST HARPER PERENNIAL EDITION PUBLISHED 2012.

Designed by William Ruoto

The Library of Congress has catalogued the hardcover edition as follows:

Gilman, Priscilla.
   The anti-romantic child : a story of unexpected joy / Priscilla Gilman. — 1st ed.
     p. cm.
   Includes bibliographical references and index.
   ISBN 978-0-06-169027-3 (hardback)
   1. Gilman, Priscilla. 2. Motherhood—United States—Biography. 3. Mothers—United States—Biography. 4. Literature teachers—United States—Biography. I. Title.
   HQ759.G499A3 2011
   306.874'3092--dc22
     [B]
                                    2010043148

ISBN 978-0-06-169028-0 (pbk.)

12 13 14 15 16   OV/RRD   10 9 8 7 6 5 4 3 2 1

For Benj

O dearest, dearest boy! my heart
For better lore would seldom yearn,
Could I but teach the hundredth part
Of what from thee I learn.

  —*Wordsworth, "Anecdote for Fathers"*

To begin with, let us take the following motto . . .
Literature is Love. Now we can continue.
　　—*Nabokov*

THE ANTI-
ROMANTIC
CHILD

"A POEM . . . BEGINS," Robert Frost once wrote, "as a lump in the throat, a sense of wrong, a homesickness, a lovesickness . . . It finds the thought and the thought finds the words." Frost evokes the tensions between feeling and thinking, experiencing and knowing, loving and understanding, which have been so central to my life as a student and professor of Romantic poetry, a writer, and a mother. This book began as a lump in the throat, as a homesickness for the magical world of my childhood and for the home life I was looking forward to with my child. It began with a sickness of love for a child I adored but did not understand, a love searing in its intensity, overwhelming in its sense of longing and vulnerability, a love I feared would never be reciprocated, and worst of all would never make an impact. It began with a pining for contact with the spirit or essence of my child, a wrenching fear that perhaps everything I did and said was in vain because he was unreachable and unimpressionable, a fierce devotion to a child I would do anything to save.

This is a story of the relationship between literature and life, the ideal and the real, of poetry versus science, magic versus measurement, honoring mystery versus unraveling it. And at its heart, this book is a love story: a story of two very different people learning to accept and affect and make space for each other in mysterious and powerful ways.

A FEW WEEKS AFTER my first child, a boy named Benjamin, was born, a box arrived in the mail from a beloved former professor. The box contained two tiny blue onesies from Old Navy with the phrases SEER BLESSED! and MIGHTY PROPHET! stenciled across the chest in thick white paint. These phrases were quotations from one of my favorite poems, the great Romantic William Wordsworth's "Ode: Intimations of Immortality from Recollections of Early Childhood":

> Thou, whose exterior semblance doth belie
>   Thy Soul's immensity;
> Thou best philosopher, who yet dost keep
> Thy heritage, thou Eye among the blind,
> That, deaf and silent, read'st the eternal deep,
> Haunted for ever by the eternal mind,—
>   Mighty Prophet! Seer blest!
>   On whom those truths do rest,
> Which we are toiling all our lives to find;
> . . . .
> Thou little Child, yet glorious in the might
> Of heaven-born freedom on thy being's height . . .

This gift could not have come at a better time. Several months prior to Benjamin's birth, I'd accepted an assistant professorship in the English Department at Yale, where I'd first encountered Wordsworth in this same professor's class nine years earlier. In the weeks

leading up to my son's arrival, I'd been working hard on a dissertation chapter on Wordsworth. Slightly nervous to be returning as
a faculty member and a bit concerned about how I would be able
to balance motherhood and an academic career, I was grateful for
the reassuring message implicit in this present: that my personal and
professional lives need not be entirely separate and that my roles as a
teacher, a scholar, and a mother could be mutually enriching rather
than at odds.

These familiar lines were also a moving articulation of what
I most looked forward to in welcoming my new baby. I had always bought wholeheartedly into the romantic idea that young
children possessed special wisdom—that children were "prophets"
and "seers" who could give us immediate access to truths that we'd
been "toiling all our lives to find," and that childhood was a time
of unself-conscious exploration, "heaven-born freedom," and joy.
Indeed, one of the primary reasons I had fallen so deeply in love
with Wordsworth as a college student was that he gave eloquent and
poetic voice to my own most cherished (and admittedly somewhat
romanticized) beliefs.

I first encountered Wordsworth in the second semester of Major
English Poets, the year-long required course for English majors at
Yale. I had never really read or studied any Romantic poetry before
college. My only previous memory of Wordsworth were a few poems
in a children's poetry book. In my high-powered feminist all-girls
private school, Romantic Poetry was considered the weak, wimpy
poetry elective, because it was, as we liked to say, "about flowers and
children." But as a college junior, reading Wordsworth's "Tintern
Abbey," the "Intimations Ode," and his book-length autobiographi-
cal poem *The Prelude*, I was transported.

At the same time that Wordsworth is the great poet of childhood,
he is the great poet of loss: the loss of childhood innocence and bliss,
the loss of parents, the loss of children, the loss of emotional imme-

diacy, authenticity, and joy as we grow older. The first stanza of the
"Intimations Ode" epitomizes this stance of impassioned yearning
and irrevocable loss:

> There was a time when meadow, grove, and stream,
> The earth, and every common sight,
> To me did seem
> Apparelled in celestial light,
> The glory and the freshness of a dream.
> It is not now as it hath been of yore;—
> Turn wheresoe'er I may,
> By night or day,
> The things which I have seen I now can see no more.

I had always had an unabashedly romantic attitude toward children and childhood, and idealized what I saw as my own romantic
childhood. My father was a drama critic, professor at Yale Drama
School, and author; my mother a literary agent; and their friends were
highly creative people—artists, actors, writers, directors. I grew up
in a rambling prewar rent-controlled apartment on the Upper West
Side of Manhattan in a family that encouraged me and my sister to
revel in our creativity and the freedom of unstructured play, to be
physically exuberant and affectionate, emotionally and imaginatively
extravagant. We were not allowed to watch television other than PBS
or listen to pop music other than the Beatles, and we spent countless
hours reading, drawing pictures, writing stories and songs, dancing
and singing and making up creative games and little plays we'd put
on for any older family members willing to watch. We climbed and
sledded down the hill behind and waded through the stream in front
of our weekend/summer house in Connecticut. We threw ourselves
into imaginative play with our dolls and stuffed animals.

My dreams of romantic childhood were primarily formed, inspired, and fostered by my father. Forty-seven when I was born, with a failed conversion from Judaism to Catholicism and a failed first marriage behind him, and with a strained relationship to his son from that first marriage, I think he saw in this second marriage and especially in his second chance at fatherhood an opportunity for redemption, for finding that place of transcendence and bliss, of uncomplicated and pure happiness, that had proved so elusive. And he committed himself to fatherhood with fervor and joy.

My very first memory is a kind of Wordsworthian scene, but one in which my father, the nominal adult, helped me, the young child, to see as a child ideally should. It was a summer night in Spain, I was a little over three, and an especially dramatic thunderstorm woke me, terrified, in the middle of the night. The memory begins with my father's voice in my ear and the two of us gazing out into the night. Framed by the large window, the scene before us was like a little theater: the familiar garden strangely unfamiliar, the sky an indigo blue lit periodically by silvery flashes. Narrating the scene, my father sounded like a madcap sportscaster. "There's a big lightning! There's a little one . . . oh a big one again!" he exclaimed as he held me firmly with one hand and gesticulated skyward with the other. I remember something disorienting becoming something glorious. I remember feeling so safe not because he protected me from fear but because he helped me to confront it. He didn't tuck me back into bed; he took me to the window. I remember asking him, "When is the thunder going to come again, Daddy?" and him telling me, "I don't know, Sidda (my family nickname), but that's part of the excitement, isn't it?" My father reassured me that it was all right not to know, to remain in a state of awe and mystery. He gave what could have been a nightmare "the glory and the freshness of a dream."

That same enthusiasm, energy, zaniness, and plunging into life he exhibited on the night of the storm in Spain informed his larger approach to parenting. My father was dedicated to giving me and

my younger sister, Claire, a childhood characterized by transforma-
tions of the common into the extraordinary, freshness of perception,
spiritual intensity, and ardent dreaminess. He participated fully in
our imaginative life and shared our passions. He looked forward to
watching *Sesame Street* as much if not more than we did, and could
have read to us from *The Wizard of Oz* series into the late hours of
the night if my mother had allowed it. He not only respected, he
also almost seemed to share our belief that our Paddington Bears
were not just well-loved stuffed animals but living, breathing members of our family; he asked them questions (which Claire and I answered in squeaky, little-boy voices), brought our baby clothes out of
storage and gave us his old glasses and ties for us to dress them in,
and offered them bites of his toast or sips of his juice. He immersed
himself in the world of our imaginary friends Tommy and Harry
Tealock—"What did Tommy Tealock do at school today?" he'd ask,
and once at the beach he cried, "There goes Harry Tealock!" while
gesturing to no one in particular across the waves. When I began to
devour *Hardy Boys* and *Nancy Drew* books after he introduced me to
them, he and I would compare notes on which plots were the twisti-
est, which titles were the spookiest (*What Happened at Midnight* and
While the Clock Ticked), and which denouements the most satisfying. He'd drive us to the library every weekend and help us pick
books, read them to us over and over again, and engage in animated
discussions about them with us. He'd plan expeditions to a dollhouse
store and share our rapture at the tiny *Life* magazines and miniature
Coke bottles. As the Reverend Gilman, he officiated at the numerous
weddings of our stuffed penguins and bears to our Mme. Alexander
dolls (humorous because Protestant is the one denomination he never
was). As Director Gilman, he visited the auditions Claire and I held
for all–stuffed animal/doll productions of *West Side Story* and *Oklahoma!*; he'd assess the vocal talent of Kanga and agreed that Horsie
was perfect for the role of Judd Fry. And as Maestro Ricardo Gilman,

he conceived, directed, and served as ringmaster of a circus my sister, our dear friend Sebastian, and I put on in Sienna, Italy, the summer I was seven. Our best "trick" was the "clown car": in a snaking rotation, we would all cycle through the backseat of our tiny Italian car, and on the last go-round my father, who had lain unseen on the back floor the entire time with me, Claire, and Sebastian scampering over him, would rise from the floor and emerge, grinning triumphantly, from the impossibly small space.

My sister once aptly described what fatherhood meant to Daddy:

> Fatherhood spoke to the core of who Daddy was as a person. It resonated with his basic faith in creativity. His love for the life of the mind. His deep imagination. And his quest for spiritual enlightenment and beauty. My father BELIEVED in childhood. And he infected my sister and me with this belief, leading us to develop the rich, imaginative life that we had as children . . . My father understood that imaginative creations were not secondary to real life but fundamental to a rich and fulfilling existence. Throughout his life, my father sought something higher, something beyond the dross of the everyday . . . My brother, sister, and I provided him with that. We were more than just his children. We represented all that was good in the world.

My father's magical combination of solidity and ebullience, fierce protectiveness and playful charm, made him both the most exciting and the most reassuring parent imaginable. He was known in our family as the Great Finder, who could elevate a mundane search for a lost bus-pass or library book into a thrilling hunt complete with clues, retracing steps, and suspects, with my father in the role of the wise, witty, and unflappable Hercule Poirot, Sherlock Holmes, or Perry Mason (all great heroes of his). On a nursery school outing to the Bronx Zoo, my father scooped up a young rapscallion who'd been bothering me, held him above his head, and said with a mischievous grin: "I think it's feeding time, and if you don't stop pestering my daughter, it's into the lion's den for you!" But as anyone who knew my father well would attest, he was a person who himself needed a good deal of reassurance; he was an extraordinarily sensitive and vulnerable man. Perhaps it was for that very reason that he knew especially well how to recognize and honor vulnerability in others, and that children and animals universally adored him.

Retaining that childlike intensity of feeling and capacity for wonder, that acute sensitivity as it blended into vulnerability, however, had attendant with it certain risks—for my father and for the daughters who learned to love as he did: with the entirety of our beings. When you love like that, you can get your heart broken, even by a football team. My father frequently told the story of how, the day after he and I sat through a devastating Giants loss, I saw a photo in the *New York Times* of the linebacker Harry Carson sitting in dejection on the bench, and wrote him a consoling letter. "You mustn't be sad. You're a great player and a wonderful man," I wrote. "We'll all be happy again. I love you. Priscilla Gilman, age 9." Just one year after I sent the letter to Harry Carson, I found myself uttering much the same words to my father as he was faced with the devastating loss of our family in the wake of my mother's decision to end their marriage.

> What though the radiance which was once so bright
> Be now for ever taken from my sight,
> Though nothing can bring back the hour
> Of splendour in the grass, of glory in the flower;
> We will grieve not, rather find
> Strength in what remains behind.
> —Wordsworth, "Intimations Ode"

•••

MY BLISSFUL CHILDHOOD IDYLL ended abruptly with my parents' bitter separation when I was ten and a half. Of course, it hadn't ever really been a paradise. Most of the time, my father was hilariously funny, warm, and attentive, but he was prone to outbursts of volcanic anger, usually directed at somewhat obstreperous Claire (he couldn't tolerate her ear-shattering crying as an infant or her tantrums as a little girl, and he'd scream at her for spilling her milk) or at my mother. My mother rarely smiled; she was tense and overworked. And I never sensed any real intimacy or trust between my parents. Although I was a famously happy baby and an effervescent, outgoing little girl, looking back at photos of myself as a child, I am often struck by how pensive and wistful I look, always reaching both arms around my parents to bring them together, lovingly cradling my father's hand in mine or tucking my arm through his, or with a protective arm around my sister's shoulder.

Perhaps the paradise for me was childhood itself—an iconic childhood—one that existed in the children's books I devoured and that I approximated in the endless play with my sister. This was a place of freedom and imagination, unmarred by poisonous secrets and resentments, unshadowed by complex adult desires and disappointments. I think I must have read so avidly in some way to escape or transcend the reality of my riven family: the tension and lack of affection between my parents, the friction between my father and sister, my father's professional insecurity, the sense of some fundamental instability and unhappiness lurking just beneath the surface. Literature was always my solace.

With my parents' separation, the house in Connecticut was sold, and my father's magical presence in our lives was greatly diminished. And in the months immediately after the separation, it became clear to me, because of letters I found, conversations I overheard, and things my mother and some of her friends told me, that my father had had another side, another life, a secret life of affairs and indulgence in drugs and hard-core pornography even as he was playing the role of the good family man and daddy who watched *Sesame Street* with me and presided over my innocent imaginative world. My father never told me anything about his relationship with my mother and never acknowledged his affairs, but on the night they announced the separation to us he told me through heaving sobs, "Oh Sidda, I don't want this, this is your mother's decision, I don't want to lose our family!" and cried in anguish another night, "I'd kill myself if it weren't for you girls." Both of my parents took me into their confidences, shared their pain with me, and then said sternly: "Don't tell Claire; she can't handle it." Claire was only fourteen months younger than I was, but they deemed her the "little one"; they felt they had to shelter and protect her, but that I could take it. It was a big responsibility for a little girl, one I took very seriously and never questioned until many years later.

My father was plunged into a nearly suicidal depression after the split, primarily because he was so heartsick at losing daily interactions with my sister and me. He had no real home for the first year or so, and Claire and I only saw him at lunches and movie outings. His grief and despair shadowed our every interaction with him, even the supposedly most lighthearted. I missed my father terribly: his presence in my daily life, the buoyant and funny, reliable and reassuring dad he'd been before. He was childlike, but in a different way: suddenly, achingly vulnerable, helpless, unmoored, deeply wounded, struggling to make sense of what had happened and to figure out what was to come.

My father once wrote that "being a fan means practicing a form of sympathetic magic, by which you suffer with, draw strength from, and generally share in the vicissitudes and personas of modern day champions and heroes." He had always been my biggest fan and I his, and as I had drawn strength from him, now I suffered with him, as I had basked in his sympathetic magic, now I shared, wholeheartedly and without qualification, in his vicissitudes. Claire and I drew on everything our father had taught us about how to comfort, reassure, and love. I learned as a young child that my role was to be cheerful, optimistic, and energizing for others.

With the advent of adolescence, I was urged by my parents to focus my energies on my studies, to buckle down and excel at school. From my teenage years on, the two things my parents agreed on were that I should not follow my passions for acting, singing, and creative writing into a career and that instead I should get a PhD in the humanities. They insisted that the life of a performer or writer was too unstable, too uncertain, and not compatible with being the kind of mother I wanted to be. They also told me that I wouldn't be sufficiently intellectually challenged in the world of the performing arts and that the life of a professor was a rich and rewarding one. Achieving academically was one of the ways I both pleased my parents individually and brought them together. The best way to make my father feel better, always, was for me to do well in school, especially to write essays on works of literature he loved. The one thing I can ever remember my parents discussing in a reasonably friendly tone of voice after they separated were my academic successes.

Each of my parents was living out a dream through me. My father was an adjunct professor at Yale Drama School but he not only had no advanced degree, he'd never even finished his BA (although he kept this secret from most people). Daddy said he felt like a fraud when he went to speak at universities and conferences and in front of him was a placard that said DR. GILMAN. He'd forged an idiosyncratic career path, on his own terms, and it seemed wonderful to me, but he'd always felt insecure and uncertain. My mother, whose undergraduate degree had been in the performing arts, had always wanted more education, especially in literature and philosophy, and she often explained her marriage to my father in terms of her desire to have him educate her. I felt guilty having any negative feelings at all about my studies, because my mother would have killed to have had the opportunities I did.

But when I arrived at Yale for my sophomore year, I'd felt both adrift and burned out after a very intense first year of college, during which, despite academic success, I'd felt empty and dissatisfied. I dropped out of school after two weeks, went home to New York City, and spent the year teaching aerobics (to get out of my own head), reading all of Proust's *Remembrance of Things Past* in French (both of my parents adored him), and in intense psychoanalysis to confront the pain of my parents' split. Going deep into my childhood trauma and my sense of a lost innocence with an analyst primed me to respond to Wordsworth on my return to college. Wordsworth's poetry of nostalgia and longing appealed to me in part because of my feeling of a life before and after my parents' split, of a paradise lost.

Wordsworth's loss of his childhood (and of his parents), the sense of an unclosable gap between his childhood and adult self, his longing for the unspoiled innocence of childhood, all this spoke to me as a college junior with urgency and power. And in his idea of "abundant recompense" (what John Milton called "the paradise within, happier far"), Wordsworth both captured the trauma of loss and gestured toward the possibility of its healing. On the first day of class, my professor, the same one who would give me the onesies many years later, wrote these famous lines from "Tintern Abbey" on the blackboard and told us that this could be the course's theme:

> —That time is past,
> And all its aching joys are now no more,
> And all its dizzy raptures. Not for this

Faint I, nor mourn nor murmur; other gifts
Have followed; for such loss, I would believe,
Abundant recompense.
  —"Tintern Abbey"

This notion of a gain greater than the loss that preceded it, the mature pleasures of adulthood more than making up for the loss of childhood's "giddy bliss" was both intriguing and comforting to me. Most of all, in addition to the sheer beauty of the poetry, Wordsworth's vivid evocations of the unparalleled bliss of childhood, the refreshing honesty and authenticity of children, the intensity of feeling in and about children struck deep chords in me.

But eight years after I first encountered Wordsworth, finishing my dissertation, these qualities of emotional immediacy and intensity, simplicity, and authenticity were precisely what I felt were missing in my academic studies. Indeed, soon after beginning graduate school, I'd discovered that passion for literature was often left far behind in the pursuit of arcane arguments and cutting-edge theories. To an idealist and humanist like myself, it was a profound and painful disillusionment. But I felt a strong pressure from my parents and from my husband, a fellow Yale graduate student in English and American literature, to stick it out and get the PhD. And I couldn't figure out another career that would enable me to combine my two passions: teaching and literature.

As I became increasingly dissatisfied with the dryness and coldness of academia, I turned to Wordsworth for reminders of what was truly important. And what was most important to me, and always had been, was having children. As a young child, I had presided, as Mrs. Gilman, over a brood of close to 150 stuffed animals and dolls, and even as I always had ambitions of pursuing a major career, I planned to be a young mother of three or four children. Even though, or perhaps because, I was a child of divorce and a city girl through and through, I had always been especially attracted to stories of happy families, especially *Little Women* and its sequels, the *Betsy Tacy* series, and *Little House in the Big Woods*. I wanted that little home in the woods, a burrow, a nest, that cozy pioneer family spirit. My marriage to Benjamin's father had been predicated on our mutual love of poetry and our mutual desire to raise a storybook family as a compensation, an "abundant recompense," for the many losses and sorrows of our own families.

> My heart leaps up when I behold
>   A rainbow in the sky:
> So was it when my life began;
> So is it now I am a man;
> So be it when I shall grow old,
>   Or let me die!
> The Child is father of the Man;
> And I could wish my days to be
> Bound each to each by natural piety.
> —Wordsworth, "My Heart Leaps Up"

RICHARD AND I MET on the first day of graduate school at Yale. He'd been two classes ahead of me at Yale when we were undergraduates, but I never laid eyes on him until we both entered the PhD program in English and American literature. At the orientation meeting and during those first few weeks of grad school—Richard and I just happened to sign up for all the same courses—he struck me as a remarkably intelligent and guarded person. Extremely tall and almost painfully thin, but handsome in an Abraham Lincoln–esque way, he rarely smiled, and looked stern, even forbidding. His eyes were virtually hidden under heavy black brows and enormous glasses with thick lenses.

Intellectually, he was formidable. I learned that as an under-graduate he had won the senior essay prize and another prestigious writing prize. I heard that the professor who'd later give us the onesies considered him one of the most brilliant students he'd ever taught. The sentences that infrequently came out of Richard's mouth were always exquisitely formed, studded with huge words and convoluted turns of phrase, and unfailingly grammatically and syntactically perfect. He knew Greek and Latin, not to mention German and Spanish, and could spot any and all allusions, even the most obscure. Within the first month of graduate school, he wrote a book review for our Renaissance Lyric Poetry class that stunned everyone in the class into jealous, worshipful silence—he could write circles around us all.

But he wasn't in any way pretentious or aggressive with his bril-liance. He wouldn't throw around jargon for the sake of it, and he didn't make his comments for effect, to impress, to intimidate. Every time he spoke, other students sprang to attention and assiduously took notes, but he didn't even seem to notice. And he passionately loved the literature. This I could tell by the way his voice caught in his throat as he read aloud an especially beautiful line, by the rever-ence with which he spoke of his favorite authors, by the happy smile on his face when I'd come across him reading in the library. I could tell he liked my close readings of poems. When one or the other of us made a comment in class, we locked eyes across the seminar table; there was a palpable sense of mutual respect and approbation between us. I had always nurtured a fantasy of falling in love with someone in an English class, and this tall, laconic, mysterious guy quickly became a romantic figure to me.

He kept his distance from the rest of us; he never lingered after class to chat or head to the local coffee houses with fellow students. He didn't attend most of the social gatherings and parties the grad-uate students organized. I'd frequently see him loping across the campus or zipping by on his bike; he'd nod a perfunctory hello and continue on his way. "What is the deal with Richard . . . ?" people asked. Many people thought Richard was aloof or cold, but I felt that they misunderstood and misinterpreted him. He wasn't quick with banter, or clever with his rejoinders. He was "shy, and un-practised in the strife of phrase" (Wordsworth, *Prelude*). He spoke slowly and deliberately, and couldn't quite keep up in casual or jocular group conversation. I loved it that unlike so many of the New York City boys I'd dated, Richard wasn't slick, savvy, or mate-rialistic. He appealed to me precisely because he wasn't a schmoozer or a self-promoter.

His lack of vanity extended to his physical appearance. He wore mismatched socks, faded flannel shirts, frayed shorts, and unstylish glasses; his hair was always falling in his eyes and looked in need of a comb. He was utterly unaware of his attractiveness, which attracted me to him all the more.

And penetrating Richard's reserve became an exciting challenge for me. I have always had a special tenderness for outsiders, for shy or awkward souls, and a talent for making them feel comfortable and drawing them out of their shells. In the early days of graduate school, I ran into him on a long line at the Yale Co-op bookstore; he was standing tall and austere, unsmiling, pulled into himself. "Hi Richard!" I exclaimed in my ebullient way. When he caught sight of me, his forbidding intensity dissipated entirely and his whole face lit up. He instantly took the heavy books I was juggling and put them on top of his own until we got to the front of the line. He did it in-stinctively. At one point, he took his glasses off to wipe them clean, and I was struck by his huge, startlingly blue eyes. As I chattered on, I could see that rather than intimidating him, my bubbliness actually relaxed him, my sunniness brightened him. I could feel him grate-fully at ease in my presence.

It was a few more weeks before I spoke with him again outside of class. One day, we were walking back from class with a fellow student, a handsome, charismatic, flirtatious guy named Ben. We were lamenting the unsuccessful tenure case of a popular female professor who'd had children, and Ben suddenly asked me: "If you could choose to have a happy family or a successful career, which would you choose?" I said, without any hesitancy, "A happy family." "Would you give up a chance at tenure to make sure you could have kids?" Ben asked, a bit incredulously. "Absolutely," I said. "What if you and your husband both got jobs, at top schools, but they were on opposite sides of the country?" Ben pressed me. "One of us would work as an adjunct or as a high school teacher," I said. Richard smiled a slow, affirming smile, and I knew right then that our values were shared.

I soon found out more about just what family meant to Richard. One day, I asked a mutual friend, who'd been in Richard's undergraduate class and knew more about his background, to tell me more about him. "Oh, he's had a very hard life," Jeff said sympathetically. "It's such a sad story." Richard's father had battled multiple sclerosis for much of Richard's life and had recently died; his mother had stage IV breast cancer; and Richard, the eldest son, had done a good deal of the caretaking of his father and of his mother. Hearing of the tragedies that had befallen this family, I was overwhelmed with sympathy and flooded with admiration for Richard. Despite all the suffering and loss, he wasn't hardened or cynical at all. And he put his family above all else. He skipped parties or colloquia flocked to by eager, on-the-make students, in order to take his mother to chemo or visit his dying grandfather in the hospital. His unwavering dedication to and fervent love for his family both impressed and deeply moved me.

A week later, at the one graduate student party he did attend, I saw him standing by himself in the kitchen, looking a bit lost. I went up to him, led him by the hand to a chair in the living room, and sat on the floor at his feet, smiling up at him. His warm, open smile;

the relief in his eyes when I reached out to him; his sweet, unself-conscious laugh were completely endearing. We spent an intense two hours hardly touching the plates of food on our laps and brushing off overtures from others as we basked in each other's attentive gaze and compassionate understanding. There were no attempts to impress or seduce; there was just open, honest, heartfelt conversation. We talked about everything from our senior essays (Melville for him, Wordsworth for me) to the Robert McCloskey's children's books *Make Way for Ducklings* and *Time of Wonder*, from our mutual passion for football and the Olympics to the much-loved dogs we'd had as children.

> We talked with open heart, and tongue
> Affectionate and true,
> A pair of friends.
> —Wordsworth, "The Fountain: A Conversation"

We began to spend more and more time together, over lunch and coffees and late-night chats at each other's apartments, and he began to really open up to me. Despite our almost diametrically opposed backgrounds—I had grown up in New York City with high-profile parents who'd divorced, he in the woods of Connecticut in a low-key family with parents deeply in love—we felt completely comfortable and at home with each other. We discovered that we'd both been raised by parents who limited television, fed us healthy food, and insulated us from popular culture, that we'd both had magical grandparents who'd influenced us profoundly in ways our own parents couldn't. We were both oldest children and had been the academic stars in our respective families. We'd both lost a vision of an intact family and we were both nostalgic for our early childhood when our parents were still strong, healthy, and reassuring figures for us. We commiserated on how hard it had been to watch our parents suffer, become frail, or express anguish. Richard listened patiently and sympathetically to the story of my parents' split—and those bewildering first three months in which I lost my dog, my Connecticut house, my father's daily presence, and, in a sense, my childhood. The next day, in my department mailbox I found a photocopy of a poem—Elizabeth Bishop's "One Art," a poem which begins "The art of losing isn't hard to master"—with a brief note: "For P—in solidarity—R." At our next coffee date, I shared with him the details about my father's near-death and arduous recovery from an unexpected heart attack the previous year. He understood.

Despite his rigorous, exacting mind and tall, impressive presence, Richard was a very gentle person. Like my father, he loved animals and babies, and they loved him; whenever we'd pass a dog or a baby on the street, he'd stop to lean down and pet the dog or smile at the baby. Another point of connection between us was that we'd both been camp counselors, and once, he described a trip he'd led in the White Mountains of New Hampshire, how he'd helped one boy who was frightened of the ascent, how he'd built a fire with the boys at night and woken them early to watch the sunrise. How lucky those boys had been, I thought. I would watch Richard's beautiful, strong hands holding a book in class or holding a coffee cup at one of our get-togethers and imagine them holding my hand or cradling a tiny baby's head or clutching a small child's hand as he walked that child across the street. I would listen to him read poems aloud in class and imagine that deep, soulful voice telling stories to a child.

The more time I spent with Richard, the deeper my feelings were becoming. One day I was rhapsodizing about him to a fellow student who'd quickly become my best friend in the program. She smiled an affectionate and knowing smile. "You are positively glowing. You're in love with him, Priscilla!" Sitting at a Formica-topped table in Yale's utterly unromantic Machine City (a windowless basement student hangout filled with vending machines, plastic tables and chairs, and a haze of cigarette smoke), I felt myself radiant, tremulous, expectant. Two nights later, I initiated a kiss. I knew from that first night we kissed that I would marry him.

Our courtship was conducted via poetry and lyricism: he wrote me poems, left photocopied poems with cryptic notes in my department mailbox, and made me mix tapes of Bob Dylan, Richie Havens, and Peter Gabriel songs (he claimed "Solsbury Hill" was a rewriting of a passage from Wordsworth's *Prelude*). We stayed up all night together writing analyses of John Donne's lyrics and Philip Sidney's sonnet sequence *Astrophil and Stella* for our seminar papers. We visited his childhood home and walked through the woods he had played in as a child. We met and felt remarkably comfortable with each other's families despite entirely opposite circumstances and settings: on Thanksgiving Day, my mother took the two of us, dressed up in our finest, to lunch at a New York City restaurant (since my parents' split, my sister and I had spent Thanksgivings with our father at a family friend's annual gathering, but that year my father was in Japan with his new wife), and an hour after the lunch, Mom called and left the following message on my voice mail: "Richard is a really fine person. I'm so happy to have met him." The next day Richard and I wore jeans and cozy sweaters to attend his uncle and aunt's belated potluck Thanksgiving celebration in rural Connecticut, where we walked around a frozen pond, gazed out onto vistas of trees, and played ping-pong in a nineteenth-century barn with his two younger brothers and many first cousins. I loved Richard's big, bustling family: his exuberant drama teacher mom, dressed in bright purple and turquoise, with a long silver braid down her back, lots of jangly silver jewelry, and a mischievous gleam in her eye; his handsome, open-faced, solid brothers; his eccentric and gracious aunts (one a social worker, the other a painter); his unpretentious and warm cousins—a photographer, a writer, another social worker, a geologist, a chef, an actor, and each one of them a lovely human being. I was instantly welcomed into this clan.

Wordsworth's "Tintern Abbey" laments the loss of childhood's "aching joys" and "dizzy raptures," but those first months of our love were certainly replete with both. Richard and I took a Wordsworth seminar our first semester in graduate school, taught by perhaps the most renowned living scholar of Wordsworth, and we spent many nights lying entwined on our beds or couches reading our Wordsworths together. We'd read lines out loud to each other and exclaim over their beauty and poignancy, we'd talk about how they evoked memories of our own childhoods. The green cover of the Wordsworth edition we used still evokes for me the sense of magical affinity we had in those days when poetry and love went hand in hand.

One night, we were sitting side by side on my blue-and-white striped couch, and Richard was at long last sharing, fully, the story of his family. His parents had met in college and fallen madly in love. Youngest children in their respective families, they had been the free spirits who superficially conformed but always longed for a more spiritually nourishing way of life. His mother had been an actress but ended up a drama teacher, his father had wanted to be an artist, but at his own father's insistence, majored in economics at Yale and became an architect. When Richard was eight, and his younger brothers six and four, his father resigned his position at a prestigious architectural firm in Richmond, Virginia; his parents sold their house, gave up their comfortable upper-middle-class life there, and moved back to the town of his childhood to build their own house in the woods. They were in retreat from what they saw as an acquisitive, materialistic, and competitive society—they ate macrobiotic food, built their own house powered by a wood stove and solar energy, had no TV, and made family togetherness their highest priority. But soon after moving to Connecticut, the vague symptoms—numbness in an arm, tingling fingers, weakness in a leg, a dragging foot—that had troubled his father since his late twenties became more pronounced. His mother, in a powerful gesture of denial, clung fiercely to the romantic dream of family insularity—she refused to acknowledge the severity of his father's illness and resisted getting sustained professional help for the longest time, because it felt like an invasion of their privacy, instead enlisting her three young sons to do much of the caretaking of their father, including diapering and catheterizing him. Eventually, however, the world had to invade the nest because of his father's illness; other family members felt compelled to intervene and insist that his father be administered every possible test, which resulted in a diagnosis of multiple sclerosis, and that the family come to terms with the necessity of relinquishing their privacy. When his father became unable to walk or bathe himself, they brought in home health aides; when he began to have some mental disorientation and difficulty speaking, they moved to a small apartment in an elevator building in a major town near a hospital; and when he became unable to communicate and started to have choking episodes, they put him in a nearby nursing home. This fifty-two-year-old man—vigorous, athletic, handsome as a movie star in all the photos from just a few years earlier—was now noncommunicative, emaciated, with withered legs, and no ability to use the delicate, agile hands that had once drafted plans for their house, hammered the nails for its walls, laid the planks of wood for its floors. Now, it had been exactly a year since his father had died, a fifty-four-year-old man in a nursing home, surrounded by his wife and three college-age sons.

As Richard spoke, in a halting voice, of the loss of a pristine, sacred space of woodland enchantment, of the invasion of a blissful innocence by the harsh glare of illness, suffering, and death, of the loss of his parents' intimacy and his family's privacy, I thought of Wordsworth's "Nutting," a poem we both especially loved. The poem tells the story of the boy Wordsworth's quest to gather nuts from a "dear nook / Unvisited," and his subsequent remorse and pain when confronted with the results of his "merciless ravage," a "shady nook / Of hazels" becomes a "mutilated bower," "deformed and sullied," exposed to "the intruding sky."

I touched Richard's forehead gently as I whispered the final three lines of the poem to him:

> Then, dearest Maiden, move along these shades
> In gentleness of heart; with gentle hand
> Touch—for there is a spirit in the woods.

Richard was a kind of "spirit in the woods"—this is what I saw in him, and wanted to nurture. I knew he needed a gentle heart and a gentle touch to bring him out into the world from his intense privacy. I felt so strongly that he deserved someone who would be patient and persistent with him, who would help him become more comfortable letting down his guard and getting in touch with his vulnerability and pain, who would allow him to relax into love. I wanted to save Richard from a fate of loneliness and isolation and not being appreciated or understood; I wanted to bring warmth and light, joy and abundance into his life. To be the light-giver was a very familiar, comfortable, and appealing role for me, and I'd never met someone so deserving of my attention.

I thought of Richard as a treasure house of riches that no one had properly acknowledged or appreciated. A fellow graduate student had once remarked, disparagingly, "Trying to have a conversation with Richard is like pulling teeth"; I felt a sense of indignation, even outrage at her comment. A professor of ours had once made a similar point but with a much more generous and positive spirit: he'd said that Richard's prose was incredibly difficult, so opaque, so finely wrought, that it took great patience and fortitude to figure out exactly what he was trying to say, although what was there was of the highest value and it was well worth the time and effort to get to the beautiful core. I felt about Richard's being as our professor had felt about his writing. There was so much in there that was of such value. Behind Richard's mess of hair and thick glasses and forbidding eyebrows lay his lovely eyes; behind the opacities and intricacies of his prose lay remarkable insight; behind the stiltedness of his social persona lay a kindhearted boy who had so much love to give.

Ever since my parents separated, I had wanted to create a family that would provide the children in it the emotional security that I'd lost when my parents split. To achieve that, I thought that I needed a husband who was, above all else, safe and trustworthy. But because I could never marry a simple, sweet boy in a baseball cap or a typical good-provider type, I was in a bit of a quandary. I wanted someone reliable and kind but also someone with an interesting mind, quirky, artsy sensibility, liberal politics. It was hard to find someone who fit both bills.

A "safe" choice seemed especially important at the time I met Richard, when I had just emerged from another grueling experience of a family destroyed, another idyll fractured. I had just ended my relationship with Mia Farrow's oldest son; I'd been a member of that family as they suffered through the revelation of and media maelstrom surrounding Woody Allen's affair with Mia's oldest daughter. This was a romantic and innocent family shattered by betrayal of the most adult kind—I was drawn to that family in many ways because it represented a kind of paradisal privileging of childhood above all else—and Woody Allen's relationship with my boyfriend's sister devastated me particularly because it was a betrayal not just of one specific family but of the ideal of family and childhood innocence. The whole situation reinforced my desire for a truly happy, uncomplicated family life.

I had grown up surrounded by a lot of brilliant, charming, fascinating men, but almost none of them had been family-oriented, trustworthy, sure to be faithful and not to sink into addiction of some kind. I shared with Richard the delight and charge of spirited and interesting conversations about literature, music, sports, and politics that I'd had with my father. But Richard was even-tempered, calm, not at all volatile or unstable, as my father had been. Richard had a complicated, subtle mind and was intellectually ambitious, but had none of the accompanying flaws. He'd had very few girlfriends. He had never smoked a cigarette or tried a single drug. He hardly touched alcohol. He lived an almost monastic existence in his spare apartment. Richard was someone I thought would never cheat, never betray, never mistreat, someone who would put family above all else, who would be gentle, reassuring, and present for me and for our children.

We got engaged late one night, three months after our first kiss, after having stayed up very late working on our Wordsworth papers. As we were falling into bed, exhausted and happy, Richard took my hand and with an unmistakable look on his face, said solemnly: "I want you to be the mother of my children." We were both ecstatic at having found each other. He took obvious pleasure in finding someone he could actually come out of his shell for without feeling threatened or judged. And he made me feel that two significant elements of my being—intellectual and family person—were both honored and understood. Most of all, we felt a return to the joy and freshness of our childhoods, and our childhood dreams, in the love and understanding we had for each other; we felt our "days . . . bound each to each." Together we would make our way through the minefield of academic politics and rise above the pettiness and help each other remember and honor what was most important: on the one hand, the beauty and truth of the literature and on the other the preciousness of family. In our marriage, these two realms—literature and real life—would intersect and mutually enrich each other. We absolutely and unconditionally adored each other. We felt ourselves "blest / With sudden happiness beyond all hope" ("Nutting").

Our engagement brought immense happiness to his extended family as well, who had worried a great deal about him and his two brothers and were thrilled to have a happy event to focus on instead of all the suffering, illness, and death that had consumed the family in recent years. At a celebratory lunch a few weeks after we'd become engaged, his mother laughingly presented me with a Paddington bear rattle (she said she'd wanted to give me the most open arms she could find), looked at me with misty eyes, and squeezed my hand hard. "I see little Ricko again," said his mother to me. "For the first time in so many years, he smiles like he did when he was a little boy." "You've brought dear Richard back to us and we can't thank you enough," his aunt told me at a family gathering a month later. "You've brought the light back into his eyes." It was his aunt and his mother who designed our rehearsal dinner invitation and chose to put on it two lines from Wordsworth's "She Dwelt Among the Untrodden Ways," a short lyric about a beautiful, innocent little girl the speaker dearly loved. Under a photo of the two of us was printed:

> —Fair as a star, when only one
> Is shining in the sky.

Our wedding weekend cast glances backward and forward, giving us a sense of rootedness in the past and exhilaration about the future. The rehearsal dinner space was covered in huge, poster-size photographs of Richard and me as young children, which our mothers had prepared as a surprise for us. My father gallantly walked Richard's mother—radiantly happy and bright in a vivid flowered dress and teal turban that covered her bald head—down the aisle (I came down alone to avoid upsetting either of my parents), and they happily danced together at the reception. Our wedding was filled with poems and references to the many children we looked forward to welcoming.

RICHARD AND I BEGAN our life together with buoyant hope, but stress and strain came quickly. The first signs of trouble had begun, in fact, almost immediately after I'd accepted Richard's marriage proposal. Our first set of graduate school papers was due a few weeks later, and he was unable to turn his in on time. But although I was a bit concerned, I also attributed his inability to complete things on deadline to his brilliance. That's how he put it to me—I can't be contained by these assignments and I want to do something larger and I need more time to do so—and I accepted his explanations. Besides, he eventually finished the papers, and they were spectacular. The summer after our engagement, we slept apart most nights—I in our big bed; he on the couch in his study, because he'd only get going on his writing after midnight and often stay up until the sun rose. I'd try to stay up with him, eating dark-chocolatey cookies or frozen yogurt to keep myself awake, but around two a.m. succumbing to sleep. We took only a two-day honeymoon at a local bed-and-breakfast, because Richard needed to return to New Haven to complete work on two long seminar papers he'd been unable to finish before our wedding.

Three weeks after our wedding, we were devastated to learn that the cancer had spread to Richard's mother's brain. We took a year's leave of absence from graduate school to spend as much time as possible with and help care for her. Sarah had quickly become a kind of alternative mother for me: she thought I should write children's books instead of dry, academic articles; she cuddled and snuggled with me on the couch; we laughed together over her students' antics, and danced together at family parties and weddings. Watching this vibrant, effervescent, supremely optimistic woman succumb to an illness she'd fought so valiantly for so many years, watching her anguish at leaving her children and their anguish at her suffering, and losing someone I'd quickly taken deep into my heart was extraordinarily painful for me.

Three weeks after Sarah died, at fifty-four, three years after his father's death at the same age, Richard and I began our most high-pressure year of graduate school: we were teaching for the first time while preparing for our oral examinations and then writing our dissertation prospectuses. And then, a few days after the school year was over, and about ten months after Richard's mother's death, we learned that my father had been diagnosed with metastatic lung cancer, and we were off to Japan (where he lived part of the time with Yasuko, my wonderful Japanese stepmother) to see him. All the while, we were in an intensely competitive PhD program, under enormous academic pressure, riddled with anxiety about finding job situations that would allow us to live together as a family. But the most important thing to us, always, was having a child; a year after my father's diagnosis and almost exactly three years after we'd married, we conceived our first son, whom we'd always planned to name Benjamin, a name we both especially loved.

We got pregnant instantly, the first month we tried, and the pregnancy itself was the most romantic time of our entire marriage. Since his mother's death, Richard had been more withdrawn, less emotionally expressive, but the pregnancy brought him out again. He was so thrilled and so supportive. Richard brought me toasted peanut butter sandwiches in bed every morning when I was too nauseous to get up, and made me pancakes with maple syrup every night for dessert. He'd sit on our bed and read to me, poems by Yeats and Whitman and Wordsworth—always Wordsworth—and children's books like *A Bear Called Paddington* and *Charlotte's Web*. We read all the parenting books and researched the baby gear and felt we were on our way to where we were always supposed to be. We actually enjoyed every single doctor's appointment and loved the labor/birth class we took together at Yale–New Haven hospital. Most nights we slept snuggled up to each other with at least one of his large hands on my expanding belly so he could feel every kick and flutter. The Christmas three months before my due date, all the presents we gave each other were related to the coming baby; presents under the tree were tagged "for Benjamin and his daddy" or "for Benjamin and his mother."

Everyone in our families was ecstatic at the news of my pregnancy. Benjamin was the baby Richard's mother had pleaded with us to conceive when she was dying, the first grandchild for my dying father, the child who would give Richard his own family, the new being who would make up for all the years of illness and pain and uncertainty, the arrival all our relatives welcomed as a new beginning for both families, representing hope, promise, and boundless possibility—the future.

Of course, in choosing to get pregnant while still in graduate school, without a completed dissertation or a job, I was taking a huge professional risk. Most of my professors and fellow graduate students greeted the news of my pregnancy with polite concern, surprise, even shock. I had just been awarded a prestigious dissertation fellowship, and that fellowship year was about to be consumed by fatigue, nausea, endless tests, bed rest, and sleepless nights. At the time I first became pregnant, only one other female graduate student in my department had had a baby (three children later, she left the profession), and almost all of the female professors had waited until securing tenure before trying to conceive. I was aware of the ominous studies and statistics showing that having children dramatically reduced a woman's chances of receiving tenure, but on some level I was deliberately embracing risk, because doing so would affirm my commitment to the life of relationships and feeling over and against the competitive, solitary, cerebral world of academia. The arrival of a baby would serve as a welcome reminder of the primacy of emotion over reason, family over career, love over argument. And doing it at an inopportune time—when I was supposed to be hard at work polishing my résumé for job applications the following year—was part of the point. Also, I wanted to prove that I could do both—indeed, at my dissertation advisers' urging, I went on the job market a year early, applied to two jobs in the area, did my interviews on campus (at seven months pregnant almost bursting out of my maternity suit), and ended up getting an offer from Yale. Most important, getting pregnant in my circumstances was an inherently romantic gesture, throwing caution and common sense to the winds, a defiance of convention. Children were going to be the antidote to the aridity of scholarship: they would put me in touch with deep feeling and essential values and restore me to myself.

But a month after Benj's delivery, I was feeling anything but restored. I had never been so exhausted, emotionally and physically, in my life. And when I opened the package containing the onesies from the professor who'd introduced me to Wordsworth, my reaction was one of simultaneous gratitude and bemusement; the contrast between my spit-up-covered, red-faced, smelly-diapered, caterwauling baby and the elevated language emblazoned across his new clothes was striking, to say the least. Having my own child had shown me just how idealized and dematerialized Wordsworth's picture of infancy was. But the true extent of the difference between conventional ideas of a romantic child and the reality of my own child would only be revealed in time. For it was more than the ordinary disillusionments many first-time mothers face, or the sheer unrelenting physicality of a newborn that had given me pause. There was something about Benj himself that seemed uniquely anti-romantic.

Our birth is but a sleep and a forgetting:
The Soul that rises with us, our life's Star,
    Hath had elsewhere its setting,
       And cometh from afar:
    Not in entire forgetfulness,
    And not in utter nakedness,
But trailing clouds of glory do we come
    From God, who is our home:
Heaven lies about us in our infancy!
    —"Intimations Ode"

BENJAMIN CERTAINLY HADN'T come out trailing clouds of glory. Instead, he made his entrance into the world after thirty-six hours of intensely painful back labor and four hours of pushing, covered in blood and thick green meconium, with a grossly misshapen and discolored head. He was blue and unresponsive and floppy. His initial score on the Apgar (a test that measures a newborn's functioning in five crucial areas) was dangerously low. He had a wizened face and long, incredibly skinny arms and legs. Richard wasn't able to cut the umbilical cord, because it was wrapped tightly around Benjamin's neck, and he was immediately whisked off to a team of pediatricians, who suctioned out his blocked airways. He didn't cry until he was fifteen minutes old and even then it was weak, whimpering, and muted. He wasn't given to me for at least half an hour.

His hospital photo, taken the second day of his life, shows him as a mini–mad scientist. He's still wearing the blue stocking cap with jaunty purple and green ribbons, which he was given at birth (the photographer began to take it off, but gasped when she saw his swollen, bruised scalp and quickly pulled it back on). His tiny hands are curled into loosely clenched fists and he is staring down at them with a serious, perplexed, intense look on his face. He looks aged and troubled, not simple, fresh, and young.

And there was nothing peaceful or heavenly about those first weeks with this strange child. He wasn't at all cuddly—in fact, he was so squirmy that the only time I held him was when I was nursing him. He was most peaceful and happy sitting alone in a bouncy seat, staring at the toys on the toy bar. He had an almost uncanny ability to focus on things that interested him. "Benjamin likes to look at the lights," my mother would cheerfully intone as she walked around her country house with baby Benj lying stiffly on his back across her outstretched arms, his head tilted all the way back to gaze high up at the recessed lights in the ceilings. Benj didn't turn his head regularly to a voice, but he seemed inordinately startled, even distressed, by loud sounds. His whole body would tremble when a door was slammed, and the sound of the blender or coffee grinder could induce a kind of panic in him. My soothing words and gentle snuggles seemed to have no effect on him. I mentioned my concerns to my mother and Richard, but they both said I was worrying about nothing.

Breast-feeding was agonizingly difficult. He wouldn't nuzzle his body into me, would hold himself very stiffly, and would never look at me or give me any indication that I was anything but a food-source for him. I persevered with the nursing, but feedings, despite what my parenting books said, were less bonding times than very tense attempts to settle him down so he could stay on the breast. He wouldn't stay in either of the typical nursing positions, so I had to use a complicated system involving a nursing pillow and rolled-up receiving blankets to get him positioned correctly, which made nursing outside the home very difficult.

My mother, who'd only nursed me for a few months and had given me formula all along, had no patience for what she called my "hippie mama" ways—"Just give him a bottle!" she'd say in exasperation. But I was adamantly committed to nursing Benj for at least the first year, the minimum recommended by the American Academy of Pediatrics and by my obstetrician. My only friend who'd had a baby, a fellow Yale graduate student (none of my high school or college friends was even married at the time I had Benj), was a passionate proponent of "attachment parenting" (wearing the baby in a sling, co-sleeping, nursing for an extended period of time) and urged me to follow suit. Although I drew the line at co-sleeping, attachment parenting's vision of maternal attentiveness and mother-child communion was very appealing to me.

In one of the most famous passages from the *Prelude*, Wordsworth presents the baby and mother's breast-feeding relationship as a blissful exchange of attentions and emotions and as the foundation for imagination and poetry and creativity:

> blest the Babe,
> Nursed in his Mother's arms, who sinks to sleep
> Rocked on his Mother's breast; who with his soul
> Drinks in the feelings of his Mother's eye!
> For him, in one dear Presence, there exists
> A virtue which irradiates and exalts
> Objects through widest intercourse of sense.
> No outcast he, bewildered and depressed:
> Along his infant veins are interfused
> The gravitation and the filial bond
> Of nature that connect him with the world.

. . . .

> —Such, verily, is the first
>   Poetic spirit of our human life,
> . . . .
>   From early days,
> Beginning not long after that first time
> In which, a Babe, by intercourse of touch
> I held mute dialogues with my Mother's heart,
> I have endeavoured to display the means
> Whereby this infant sensibility,
> Great birthright of our being, was in me
> Augmented and sustained.
>   —*Prelude*, II

This dialogue, intermingling, and easy exchange is the opposite of what Benj and I experienced. Breast-feeding was not a time of affection or interaction. Not only did Benj not "drink in the feelings of his mother's eye," he rarely looked me in the eye at all. There was nothing symbolic or spiritual about what we were doing. I felt again and again the crude physicality of it. He was a voracious breast-feeder but it wasn't a loving act of connection. It was a desperate physical need to suck something, anything; he sucked Richard's finger or the pacifier in exactly the same way. Whenever he was sated, I handed him off to Richard with immense relief. I remember after one especially difficult session pulling Benj off my breast forcibly and thrusting him into Richard's hands, saying "I just don't *get* him," and walking, or rather stalking, out of the room.

While the baby Wordsworth holds "mute dialogues with [his] . . . mother's heart," I felt a strange detachment from Benj, an inability to know what he was feeling or thinking or needing that baffled me. Benj's preternatural poise, his turning in, his inscrutability perplexed and puzzled me. I couldn't figure him out. I couldn't read his cries. "Is that a tired cry or a hungry cry?" I'd wonder. My friend and my parenting books told me I'd know instantly, but I never did, and that made me feel both inadequate and ashamed. I felt that both Benj and I were outcasts, he from the normal world, I from my child's private world. I never felt that I was the "one dear Presence" I had so longed to be. Wordsworth's baby is blest but also vulnerable, in need of a mother's love and guidance to make sense of the world and sanctify it for him. But Benj felt oddly independent from me, as if he didn't really need or want me. I was "bewildered and depressed." Did Benj feel any "filial bond," I wondered. Would he ever connect with me in a sustained and meaningful way?

Richard was an amazingly attentive, capable, and devoted father; his "instinctive tenderness" toward and "deep and reverential care" (Wordsworth, "Michael") of baby Benj were lovely to behold. Richard seemed to understand Benj's cries—much better than I did, at least—and he had a remarkable ability to calm Benj. He got up multiple times a night without complaint, and changed the diapers with pleasure. On the fifth day of Benj's life, while diapering him, Richard turned to me with tears in his eyes and said: "It feels so good to be doing this for someone who's supposed to be in diapers."

But Richard didn't think anything was odd or off about little Benj, which only made me feel worse. When I expressed concern about Benj, he either didn't respond at all or quickly dismissed me. But most of the time I kept my concerns to myself, because I really thought it was my deficiency, my failure to grasp this complex little being. So my alienation from my baby was intensified by witnessing the bond between the two of them. I watched them from the outside as if they shared a private universe I could never enter.

With Benj's first smile at five weeks, however, I began to feel somewhat more connected to him. The smiles were so genuine, so open, and they clearly came in response to us. And once Benj found his thumb at six weeks, he was able to soothe himself, began to sleep through the night, and seemed less frantic and odd. Richard would lean over the changing table or crib, gaze into the face of little Benj, and painstakingly form his lips into the shapes and sounds of *oooohhh* and *aaaahhh*. He called this the cooing game. Eventually he would get Benj to respond in kind. As long as I was singing and rhythmically bouncing Benj, he allowed me to hold him without incessant fidgeting or straining away from my body. He seemed to love my renditions of clever *Sesame Street* songs, and adored a particularly comic version I did of Dylan's "Lay Lady Lay"; he would chortle with glee. In general, he was a happy baby with a sunny temperament. He was still happiest on his own, in a bouncy seat or playpen, and seemed introspective and meditative in a way unusual for babies. But despite his self-sufficiency, what did reach him, always, was energetic rhythmic speech, especially if it involved rhymes or was put to music. If I spoke to him in a normal voice, he'd often act as if he hadn't heard a word. But if I turned the volume up or spoke in an especially animated voice (what my friends laughingly called my Muppet voice), accompanied by broad facial expressions and large gestures, or, best of all, sang my remarks to him, he gazed delightedly at me and at times laughed uproariously.

But aspects of Benj's development, especially his motor development, continued to concern me. He was unusually floppy (we jokingly called him Mr. Flopsy and Flopsydoodle). His head lolled around alarmingly. He had a great deal of difficulty raising himself on his arms when placed on his belly. When he was about three or four months old, I was convinced he had some muscle abnormality. When we'd put him down on his stomach, on a sheet or on top of our queen-size bed, he'd list to the side and make high-pitched, screeching sounds. Richard jokingly called him "Cap'n Benj"; "Right the ship!" he'd cry, "he's listing to the left!" I laughed, but I also worried. Particularly because of my difficult labor and his distress at birth, I feared Benj might have cerebral palsy, but my mother scoffed at this, and my pediatrician more gently dismissed my concerns.

Benj developed into a placid and good-tempered older baby. At home with us, and with familiar adults like his grandmother, aunt, and uncle, he was very responsive to friendly overtures; he giggled often and laughed a huge belly laugh. In group settings, he was quieter and more serious, but he almost never cried or even fussed; as soon as something began to make him feel anxious or upset, he would pop his finger into his mouth and soothe himself. Physically he remained aloof, but emotionally he seemed connected to us. And his independence actually made him quite easy; he was able to amuse himself and was very undemanding.

As a nine-month-old, he weathered a trip to Florida for Richard's grandmother's ninety-fifth birthday with what seemed to us like remarkable poise and good nature. He was alert, uncomplaining, even cheerful on the long plane rides and layovers. He slept well in his portable playpen. As both the only grandchild of Richard's late parents and the youngest person in attendance, he was the focus of much attention during the weekend's festivities, and he handled it with equanimity. He greeted each new person who came to our hotel room to meet him with the same calm, quiet smile. During large meals with twenty-five or thirty people gathered around a huge table, punctuated by loud singing, shrieks of laughter, and often raucous toasts, Benj had sat very straight and erect in his high chair, the cuffs of his white cable-knit sweater folded back neatly on his tiny wrists, and gazed around with big, serious eyes and a dignified demeanor. "He's like a little philosopher-king," one cousin exclaimed. "He's so *deep*!" One especially type-A aunt asked me rather disbelievingly, "He's not sitting independently yet? He's not crawling yet?" I told her my pediatrician had reassured me that he was well on the way to sitting, that "not all kids crawl," and it was nothing to worry about as long as he was walking by fifteen months. She didn't seem convinced. And then she commented on his aversion to tight hugs—"He's not very cuddly is he?" she asked when he pulled away from her arms. A cousin whispered to me: "I understand why Benj didn't want to be snuggled by her!"

Still, she'd touched a nerve in me. Benj did have trouble sitting alone and needed the support of toys or playpen walls around him. He never crawled. He walked late and unsteadily and fell often. But at every point when I'd begin to really worry, he'd hit the milestone, albeit a little late and a little uneasily. And my pediatrician always reassured me that there was "a wide range of normal," and as long as Benj was within that range we had nothing to fret about. Nonetheless, his physical unease and standoffishness—he hated to be held on our laps and fidgeted away from hugs and kisses—intermittently troubled me as they had Richard's aunt. But despite my misgivings, I wanted to resist thinking of my child in terms of how early or beautifully he hit his milestones or how much affection he showed me. He was developing at his own pace, he was a different kind of person than I was (he just wasn't a hugger!), and that was okay!

THE YALE ENGLISH DEPARTMENT hosted three festive gatherings a year, to which all professors and sometimes graduate students were invited and spouses, significant others, and children welcomed. Babies were novelties in the English Department, so each one became a minor celebrity. We'd taken baby Benj to both the fall party—a relatively casual outdoor gathering—and the holiday party, a more formal affair held in an oak-paneled room with a pricey seafood spread (we jokingly called it "the shrimp party"). At both events he'd sailed around the room borne aloft on our arms, calmly enduring the high-pitched squeals of female graduate students, meeting the interested glances of my colleagues with his own serene gaze. People had grabbed his feet and hands, patted his soft blond hair, run fingers across his plump cheeks, chattered to him, and he'd accepted it all. There was no fidgeting or whimpering, no restlessness or querulousness. So self-possessed was Benj, in fact, that he'd earned the moniker "Zen Baby" from an admiring colleague of mine.

It was a sunny late afternoon in May as Richard and I, carrying an almost fourteen-month-old Benj, dressed in his best, walked out into the courtyard outside the English Department building. Benj was getting heavy to hold for long periods of time—he was a large baby with a very large head—but I loved to hold him. Besides, he wasn't walking well yet, and I certainly didn't want to put him down on the hard and slippery slate flooring of the courtyard. I was looking forward to this event; I wanted to confer with some fellow members of the prize committee about essays we were judging and discuss possible questions for an exam I was putting together, and was excited to see and chat with my colleagues in a relaxed, informal setting. But most of all I looked forward to sharing Benj with my friends, colleagues, and mentors. These events were some of the times I felt the greatest continuity between my personal and professional lives.

The courtyard seemed especially crowded and loud on this day; the voices sounded hollow and echoed off of the slate ground. I could feel Benj's body stiffen, and his fingers went into his mouth. The cacophony of voices grew louder as we ventured further into the party. Our arrival was noted with excitement: people waved, smiled, and put their hands over their heart or mouthed "so cute" as they pointed to Benj. Benj, however, was becoming increasingly uncomfortable. He began to shake in my arms, and when I turned his head toward me I saw that tears were forming in his eyes. I stroked his head and cheek and held him tighter. I murmured what I thought were consoling words, but Benj didn't relax at all.

A very famous and very eccentric older professor saw that Benj was looking a bit fragile, and came up to offer comfort. He leaned toward us, waved his fingers playfully in front of Benj's face, and uttered some funny rhyming nonsense. Benj was so startled that his tears stopped, momentarily. He stared hard at this august personage and blinked a few times. His lips began to quiver. Then, as Richard and I watched, horrified, he screwed up his face and began to bawl. The professor, to his credit, didn't take this personally at all and backed away with a sympathetic smile. "Oh sweetheart, it's okay, Benji," I whispered to him, "I'm right here." I encouraged Benj to put his fingers back in his mouth. I hugged him tight and kissed his head. We moved further out of the direct sunlight and into a quieter spot, but to no avail. I handed Benj to Richard, but the crying didn't abate so I took him back. He was heaving with sobs. There was nothing, absolutely nothing we could do to calm him.

Heads spun around. People moved farther away from us so they could continue their conversations unbothered by a squalling baby. Friends sent me looks of commiseration and mouthed: "Poor baby!" A few people came up and attempted to comfort Benj, but that just made him cry harder. I was getting a lot of very annoyed looks, and the pitying looks were almost as difficult to bear. I decided to beat a hasty retreat inside and get us out of the glare, both figurative and literal. I told Richard he could stay and that maybe I'd be able to bring Benj out again after I'd calmed him down.

Once Benj and I got inside the English Department building, I sat down on a long wooden bench by the door, a bench I'd sat on many times as a student waiting for a friend or catching up on reading before class. I tried to put Benj's head on my shoulder but he stubbornly held it away from my body and continued to wail. I had never, never, not even when he was a tiny newborn baby, seen him so upset. "What's wrong, sweetheart?" I asked as I stroked his head and kissed him again and again. He looked at me plaintively, as if to say, "You know why I'm upset," but I didn't. After a few minutes of sitting down inside, alone, out of the sun, the wind, the noise, his sobs began to slow and to subside in volume, but they didn't stop entirely. One of my close friends, a junior faculty colleague, came to check up on us. "What happened to Mr. Mellow?" Chris asked in a sweet, concerned way. "I don't know," I said truthfully, "it's so strange because he's always been so calm at previous events, but today he just lost it." "Hey I might cry if Professor X made funny monkey faces at me!" Chris joked. But I knew Benj's discomfort had begun long before those funny faces.

I didn't think there was any chance Benj could venture outside again, so I sent Chris back out to get Richard, and when he joined us, together we walked to the garage to get our car and drive home. We'd planned to go on to a cocktail party at one of Yale's residential colleges, of which I was a Faculty Fellow and whose Master was a mentor of mine and Richard's, but it was obvious there was no way Benj would be able to make it to another event. "His sobs are so loud he'd probably drown out the jazz piano!" (a special feature of the party) I joked to Richard. Richard laughed, but then lapsed into silence. Benj continued crying in short bursts, interspersed with hiccups, until we got him into his car-seat, whereupon he promptly fell asleep.

Driving home, we speculated on the cause of Benj's crying. Maybe it was teething pain or lingering discomfort from the cold he'd had the previous week? Or perhaps it was something about the party itself: it had been too windy, the sun had been too bright, the space had been too noisy. But even as we ticked off a myriad of possible explanations, we didn't feel any of them could adequately account for the extremity of Benj's distress. I felt some embarrassment at having bothered others and not having been able to calm him, some frustration at not being able to chat with my colleagues and friends or have them see and appreciate the Benj I so adored. But most of all I felt as if I'd witnessed something very strange and disturbing.

I got home to find an e-mail from the professor who'd given us the onesies to celebrate Benj's birth. It began: "It was so good to catch sight of Benjamin. He is a thing of beauty and it must be hard not to just melt when you see a tear on his cheek!" This professor's reference to John Keats's romantic lyric poem "Endymion"—"a thing of beauty is a joy for ever"—only served to remind me of how unromantic, abrasive, uncomfortable the situation had been. Melting, a tear—these were euphemisms at best. I had been shaken to my core by Benj's torrent of tears. It had been wrenching to see him so upset, even more so because his were not mild expressions of unease or grouchiness. He hadn't gotten fussy. He'd been distraught. Terrified. Panicked.

Moreover, he'd been inconsolable, and he hadn't made any of the conventional comfort-seeking gestures toward his mother one would expect in a crying baby. He hadn't leaned into me, clung to me tightly, or buried his head in my shoulder; he hadn't cried "mama" when another person tried to engage him. He hadn't responded to any of my attempts to soothe his discomfort. I hadn't been able to make it okay for him. He'd been completely unreachable, in a mystifying way. The next day I wrote to a friend: "Benj had an unprecedented and shocking breakdown at the department party. Richard and I were deeply shaken by the experience. It was as if our calm, happy, easygoing baby had been replaced by an alien!"

Just a day later, however, I revalued the episode and made it a sign of his normalcy. In an e-mail to the professor who'd hosted the Fellows cocktail party, I wrote: "Benj had his first real attack of party/crowd/stranger anxiety and dissolved in hysterical tears. This anxiety is typical for his age, but we're sorry that its emergence meant we couldn't see you." Despite my seeming nonchalance, so spooked were Richard and I by this experience that we never took Benj to another English Department gathering. At my sister's wedding weekend a few weeks later, we kept him back at the apartment where we were staying, with a babysitter, instead of risking another episode.

But it was around this time as well that an extraordinary precocity in Benj began to emerge. One day when Benj was about a year old, Richard called me into the living room, pointed toward our television, and asked little Benj, "What letters do you see?" Benj cried: "S—O—N—Y!" He recognized all the letters by about fourteen months (he loved to find the *a, b, c, d* on a J. Crew or Pottery Barn catalog page), recited the alphabet with ease at sixteen months, read single words at twenty-two months, and began to read entire books fluently just after turning two. As an older baby and toddler, he'd methodically pull every book off the bookcase, then delightedly take his seat in the midst of them, surrounded by them, turning pages silently, looking up at us from time to time with an expression of sheer delight. As long as he had books, he was blissfully content. *The Snowy Day* was the first book he read through aloud from start to finish, to the astonishment of his parents. We thought perhaps he'd memorized it, but he turned the pages at exactly the right time. Soon he was doing the same with *The Runaway Bunny, Goodnight Moon*, and his personal favorite, *No Fighting, No Biting*. With that one, he memorized which page each story began on, and as he took it off the bookshelf, he'd announce the title and page number of the story he wanted to read before he'd even opened the book. At two and a half, he could take a page of my dissertation and read it aloud with fluency and perfect intonation.

Numbers were similarly fascinating to him. He could count from one to twenty by about fourteen months, and from one to one hundred shortly thereafter. He was able to tell time on our VCR counter by eighteen months. He learned how to tell time digitally, and if we said "What time is it?" he would run up to the VCR, look at it, and proudly say, "Time is two fifteen," or "three thirty," or whatever. He would often grab startled strangers' watches in the supermarket and greet visitors to our house with a friendly swipe at their watch.

His precocity extended to other areas as well. My art curator sister had given him sophisticated architecture and art books for children, and by studying them, Benj was able to recognize all shapes (not just triangle, circle, square, but also hexagon, star, rhombus, and octagon) and colors (including orange, gray, and purple) at a little under two years old. His facility with shapes helped him master geography, and at two and a half, he could identify any state in the United States by sight and knew the capital of each one. "Looks like Texas!" he'd cry excitedly, holding up a piece of his cereal bar. "Capital of Arkansas!" he'd exclaim when he'd see my aunt, who lived in Little Rock.

When he encountered a new person, he'd read the writing on their T-shirt, or call out the time on their watch, or find a letter or number in the shape of their jewelry. When he'd see his grandmother, instead of saying "Hi!" or "Hi Grams!" he'd walk up to her, excitedly grab her wrist, and cry, "The letter O!" (she had a bracelet with a large circular charm on it) or "Saxophone!" (the metal clasp on another bracelet looked like a saxophone). As a two-year-old, he wanted to spend most of his time reading, counting, or making long alphabet and number chains and spelling out words with his letter/number blocks. He'd cover the floor of our small apartment with these blocks, arranged in perfectly straight lines, with A or 1 at the front and Z or 20 at the end. He was ingenious in his construction of these chains. If he ran out of a certain letter or number, he'd use a pen as a 1 or a piece of string shaped into a circle as an O. Alternatively, he'd use the blocks to spell such words as *delicious*, *zipper*, *entertainment*, *fantastic*, and *celebration*.

From about age two on, his obsession with letters and numbers dominated all of our outings. When we'd be driving, every road sign, every store sign, every billboard had to be read out loud, and every license plate number proclaimed loudly and triumphantly. The nice manager in our local Stop and Shop supermarket called him her little counting buddy, because he'd exuberantly announce the aisle numbers as we made our way through the store. "Aisle nineteen!" "Aisle twenty!" He also memorized what type of food or product was stocked in which aisle. I'd say to Richard, "We need bread," and Benj would cry, "Bread—aisle ten!" The girl behind the checkout counter in the health-food store was amazed by him. "What color is Fernanda's shirt?" she'd ask two-year-old Benj.

"Mauve," he'd reply. Not purple, not red, but mauve. And he was right.

She'd take him into the aisles and point to the labels on the cartons of substitute milk. "What does that say?" she'd ask.

"Rice Dream Rice Dream Rice Dream Rice Dream Rice Dream Rice Dream WestSoy Lite Soy Milk WestSoy Chocolate Soy Milk," he'd reply. Her jaw would drop.

With an English professor and an English PhD candidate for parents, and an extended family that was exceedingly artsy, Benjamin's attraction to books, his reciting of poems, seemed only natural, if a bit extreme in its precocity and intensity. I had grown up in a family where literature was paramount. My father had won a speed-reading award as a teenager; both my parents read constantly; and I myself had begun to read a little before I turned three. As young children, my sister and I were voracious readers; instead of watching Saturday morning cartoons, as our friends and classmates did, we would grab huge stacks of books from our bookshelves and pile them high on one of our beds. Then we'd get into a single bed together and silently read side by side until well into the afternoon, only stopping to fetch snacks and drinks. Watching Benj luxuriating in a pile of books, I well remembered the heady deliciousness of this activity. Benj's extraordinary memory and what appeared to be his flair for the dramatic both did and didn't amaze us; I had acted as a child and teenager, and my incredible memory ("at the third seventh-grade dance you wore the purple sweatshirt with the cutoff neck") was legendary among my friends. Most of all, we simply accepted that we had an odd, unconventional, and possibly brilliant little boy on our hands.

> . . . books, we know,
> Are a substantial world, both pure and good:
> Round these, with tendrils strong as flesh and blood,
> Our pastime and our happiness will grow.
> —Wordsworth, "Personal Talk," 33–36

IN THE WINTER of 2000–2001, I bought Benj Robert Louis Stevenson's *A Child's Garden of Verses*, several children's poetry anthologies, and a DVD and book called *Baby Shakespeare*. A few weeks later, I wrote to a friend: "All Benj wants to do now is recite (along with Richard) Wordsworth's 'To a Butterfly,' Housman's 'Loveliest of Trees,' and Frost's 'Fire and Ice.' I think we may have a literary fellow on our hands!" Literary excerpts became the soundtrack to his life, appearing at the most seemingly improbable but surprisingly appropriate moments. Walking around the apartment, Benj would mutter in his throaty voice: "One day through the primeval wood / A calf walked home, as good calves should" ("The Calf Path," Sam Walter Foss). When we took him out of the car seat into a dark night, he'd look up at the moon and exclaim: "The moon spun round like a top!" (W. B. Yeats, "The Cat and the Moon"). When we brushed his teeth, he'd try to recite, through a mouthful of toothpaste, an Ogden Nash poem about a dragon's big teeth. When we gave him his food or put him down for a nap, we'd sometimes hear him mumbling Wordsworth's "To a Butterfly": "And, little Butterfly! Indeed / I know not if you sleep or feed." Toddling through the grassy flat fields that surrounded his grandmother's house, he'd stop in front of a tree and cry: "Loveliest of trees, the cherry now, is hung with bloom along the bough" (A. E. Housman). He always put a great emphasis on the last word of each line.

One day, a friend was over for supper, and we were bemoaning our graduate school travails and the vagaries and stresses of the academic job market. One of us mentioned a brilliant friend who'd failed to get a job after three tries on the market; the friend's dissertation was on Shakespeare. Benj suddenly declaimed: "I know a bank where the wild thyme blows." He recited six lines of Oberon's speech from *A Midsummer Night's Dream* perfectly as my friend's jaw dropped. When he was finished, we all burst out laughing.

The winter of 2000–2001 was a roller coaster for me and Richard, professionally. Because Yale had no tenure track, all assistant professors had to leave sooner rather than later (my colleagues and I joked that Yale was a Miltonic paradise from which we all had to exit), and we were encouraged to try for each appealing position in our field as the chances for a good job were better at a beginning assistant professor level, since many fewer positions opened up at more advanced levels. I had hoped to be able to commit to my Yale job for a few years, but felt a strong need to try for every possible job that might enhance the chances of finding something with long-term potential and that would also accommodate Richard's career. So just one year into my Yale job, and with my dissertation still incomplete, I applied for other positions, coordinating with Richard to maximize our chances of ending up at the same or geographically close locations. Richard applied for a position at Yale, made it through several stages of the process, only to be abruptly turned down (I heard later from a friend on the committee that although they'd considered his writing sample brilliant, they'd worried that he wasn't far enough along on his dissertation). We both applied for jobs at Boston University and Bard; Boston University interviewed him but didn't pursue me, and I was offered a tenure-track job at Bard, which dangled the possibility of hiring Richard as well only to hire someone else at the very last minute. We had spent countless hours writing job letters, gathering recommendations, traveling to interviews, putting together job talks, and the end result? We were staying put and had to do the whole thing over again the following year.

Academia was, it turned out, a place of vicious cutthroat competition: a thousand applicants for each job, only six to eight jobs a year in the entire country in my field (late eighteenth–early nineteenth century British literature), and only a few more in Richard's (nineteenth-century American literature). Many of our friends were in despair after either coming tantalizingly close to good positions only to be shut out or not getting anything after years of trying. Many were quitting the profession. We were worried and exhausted.

But even with all the anxiety, the wild ups and downs of the job market, the tumult swirling around us, our life with Benj felt like "a primeval wood," "a bank where the wild thyme blows," "days of sunshine and of song" (Wordsworth, "To a Butterfly"). Romantic lines and passages about promise, beauty, magic, joy reminded us of why we were pursuing careers as literary scholars in the first place. We needed these reminders and the nourishment they gave us.

BUT DESPITE THE ROMANTIC lines and songs that came from him, as Benj grew, his differences from me as a child—and from most children—became more apparent. He never seemed interested in or engaged by all the toys that came most highly recommended by friends or the parenting Web sites and books we consulted. Certain toys—a talking *Sesame Street* train, a squeaky mouse—seemed to terrify him, and he hid them far under his crib.

He had absolutely no interest in stuffed animals or conventional children's toys, and he had no desire to play imaginatively with me. Every time I made a stuffed animal talk to him or tried to engage him in a pretend situation, he either completely ignored me or irritatedly pushed the animal back at me. This was perplexing and disappointing to me. But Richard said he had never much cared for stuffed animals, and besides Benj seemed to have more important things on his mind.

Beginning when he was around one and a half, every night after he and his father read a story together, I would sing to Benj for a good half hour to forty-five minutes. I'd turn the lights off and hold him sprawled across my lap in the same glider rocking chair I'd nursed him in. His head rested on one of my arms, his feet stretched way beyond my other arm. I had a large repertoire of songs, in a wide range of styles and moods. There were show tunes from my favorite musicals, Beatles' songs, classic American songs that my father had sung to me at night in his cracked, quavery tenor, especially poignant ones from camp, most about childhood and growing up and losing things ("Leavin' on a Jet Plane," "The Circle Game," "Cat's in the Cradle"). I sang and sang—from "Somewhere Over the Rainbow" (*The Wizard of Oz* was a movie I'd always watched with my father and he'd been ecstatic when I'd gotten the role of Dorothy in my camp's production) to "Embraceable You" (Richard's and my first-dance song at our wedding), "Down in the Valley" (my father's favorite to sing to me) to "Somewhere" and "Tonight" from *West Side Story* (my favorite Broadway show and movie), until Benj finally dropped off to sleep. Richard would listen at the door and when the singing had stopped for more than a few minutes he'd come in, lift Benj off my lap (he was too heavy for me to carry), and gently lay him down into the crib.

Taken together, the songs represented a kind of overview of my life experience and I sang them with this intention:

> his childhood shall grow up
> Familiar with these songs, that with the night
> He may associate joy.
> —Samuel Taylor Coleridge, "The Nightingale,"
> about his baby son

On the one hand, during these singing sessions, Benj was captivated, rapt, exquisitely attentive; he hung on my every word and
note. Benj had continued to be aloof as he got older; he never reached
up his arms to be held or snuggled into us; he never hugged us, never
kissed us, and indeed turned his face away from our kisses. But when
he was in this drowsy state, he would let me stroke his head and
kiss him and I would do so again and again. I felt so grateful for the
chance to feel physically connected to him; I luxuriated in the warm
weight of his body, his soft cheeks, his delicious-smelling hair. Sitting in the darkened room, singing the familiar songs, holding Benj
in my arms, I felt a sense of coziness, peace, and continuity. I felt my
father near us.

But this peace was provisional and easily disturbed. When I'd
ask Benj, "What do you want me to sing?" he'd often repeat the
question. If I asked again, he'd grow indignant. "What do you want
me to sing!" he'd retort. If I narrowed it down and gave him two
choices—"Hey Jude" or "Surrey with the Fringe on Top"?—he
might repeat one. But sometimes he wouldn't answer, I'd start to
sing a song, and he'd scream out the name of another one. Moreover,
Benj had an amazing memory for the words, order, and phrasing of
songs, and would get upset if I was even slightly off. I'd think he was
dozing off, and then I'd skip a verse or fudge a line or sing the wrong
word or even use a plural rather than a singular, an "I" rather than a
"you," and his little head would pop up and he'd howl in protest. If I
changed a lyric to personalize it—sing "Sweet Baby Benj" for "Sweet
Baby James" or "Bless Benji forever" for "Bless my homeland forever"

("Edelweiss")—he'd scream "James! James!" or "My homeland! My homeland!" Just starting from the offending line wasn't enough. I'd have to start again from the beginning of the song before he'd relax.

"Why does he care so much?" I'd think. "Why does it bother him so intensely? This is supposed to be about mother-child bonding, about mommy's voice, about soothing, calming, and snuggling, about emotions expressed and ideas conveyed, not about perfection and precision and getting things just right!"

Benj had an intense need for things to be just right. The blocks in a row, the words of a song, the order of events: everything always had to be in perfect sequence. He had an obsession with arranging his toys in perfectly straight lines, and distress and agitation were the result when the slightest deviation occurred. As a two-year-old, when he ate his meals, he wouldn't begin until he had a *Cook's Illustrated* magazine to read. "*Cook's Illustrated* #52," he'd request. Flipping through the pages, he'd read the recipe titles out with excitement: "Bittersweet chocolate sauce!" "Breaded pork cutlet with apple compote!" Meanwhile, all he would eat was baby food. He insisted on a certain cup, a certain slant of his high chair's footrest, a paper towel right there to catch any spills.

Benj's fastidiousness could be amusing, but when it tipped over into compulsion it was deeply concerning to me. The shrieks, the howls, the look of sheer panic that flitted across Benj's face when something went awry—the line of blocks got crooked, I skipped a phrase when singing to him, he was given the wrong cup—made my heart tighten. It was the closest thing to the distress I'd witnessed in a more extreme form at that English Department party, and it so unsettled me. What troubles would he face in the future when things didn't work out the way he wanted them to or a situation wasn't just to his liking? As our babysitter straightened out his blocks or handed him his magazine, she always laughed and said: "He's just like his Daddy." Richard saw nothing unusual in Benj's perfectionism or his need for ritual; in fact, he found them both humorous and impressive, signs of Benj's brilliance and high standards. He often lamented the fact that he couldn't joke with his mother about how similar Benj was to him. We all assumed that Richard had been like this as a child, but had no one to ask, since his parents and grandparents were all gone (his grandmother had died a few months after the ninety-fifth birthday celebration we'd attended with Benj).

Although thinking this way usually reassured me, I occasionally wondered if it was something to take comfort in. Richard's rigidity and perfectionism often got in the way of his productivity and made him, at times, a difficult person to live with. He was continuing to have trouble completing his work; he could always think of something else he wanted to add, something more he needed to read. The writing could always be better, he said; he would tinker endlessly with what, to me, seemed like perfectly good sentences and stay up until five a.m. editing. Richard had elaborate rituals he followed in making his coffee, preparing food, prepping the car, getting himself settled for work. His procrastination (I was increasingly learning to see it as that) and odd habits put a strain on our life together, but I tried my hardest to accept them as part and parcel of who he was. Most likely, I told myself, Richard and Benj's shared eccentricities went hand in hand with their brilliance and originality. These were not ordinary people, I continually reminded myself. They were strange, sometimes baffling and frustrating, but wonderful and wondrous. I rebuked myself for wanting more or something different from either Richard or Benj; I needed to accept them for who they were and not try to change them or fit them into a box.

As a child of parents who'd had very clear and rigorous expectations of me, and as the product of traditional and demanding schools, I was very invested in the idea of allowing Benjamin to be himself, not forcing him to conform to anyone else's timetable or expectations. My own parents had projected their own fears and dreams onto me in a way that had both inspired and burdened, motivated and constrained me. So when I'd wonder why Benj was so compulsive or didn't like to play imaginatively, when I'd long for a hug or a response to my overtures, I'd quickly chide myself. "He's not you!" I'd tell myself, "and it doesn't mean that there's anything wrong with him!"

But despite my embrace of Benj in all his eccentricities and quirks, at times, I worried. I had a reputation in the family as a hypochondriac; I'd been very afraid of flying in my early twenties, and I'd had a number of health scares that turned out to be nothing serious. Perhaps this was one of the reasons my mother was so quick to dismiss my concerns, and with such peremptory force. When I puzzled over why Benj never seemed interested in crayons or markers, "I *never* wanted to draw when I was a child," she'd exclaim, "I totally understand how he feels!" "Have you noticed how much banging he's doing?" I'd ask her. "He's just a boy and boys bang," she'd briskly retort. "It's odd that he doesn't respond when we say his name," I'd worry. "He's in his own world, just like his father," she'd reply. "He doesn't like to play the way Claire and I did. It's weird that he doesn't like any stuffed animals," I'd sigh. "Oh, I never liked stuffed animals or dolls. I could never understand why you and Claire were so attached to them." She made me feel like a typical "fondly-anxious mother" (Wordsworth, "White Doe of Rylstone").

My mother was Benj's only attendant grandparent, and from the minute he was born, she was utterly devoted to him. For a woman with an extremely demanding career and an equally demanding social life, she spent a great deal of time with him. We'd visit her one weekend a month at her Connecticut house or New York City apartment, and she would come visit us for an afternoon every few weeks on her way to and from the city, always with lots of delicious food for the entire family, always with lots of enthusiasm and loving attention for Benjamin. When he was a colicky newborn, she sang to him—

usually improbable show tunes like "Someone to Watch Over Me" and "Don't Cry for Me, Argentina"—and rocked him in her arms for hours on end. She invented little rhythmic songs and chants to calm and amuse him. "Benjamin Bunny is his name, Benjamin Bunny is his fame," she'd sing while she jogged him up and down, and he'd stare at her with inquisitive eyes.

As he grew older, their bond only deepened. Although we could never get him to say "Mommy" or "Daddy," my mother taught Benj to say her name by teaching him to spell it. "G—R—A—M—S GRAMS!" he would crow. No one could bring a beaming smile to his face like Grams could.

My mother had always been the pragmatist of our family, a kind of foil to my father and grandmother when I was a child. She had absolutely no interest in imaginative play or my imaginative life. My father and maternal grandmother were the ones who read to us, who played with us, who embraced our insatiable desire for pretend and magic. My mother was the one who worked hard to make the money to support this wonderful childhood. As a result, she wasn't around a lot—our nanny and father did most of the caretaking—but she provided the bedrock and structure on which our fantasy life could flourish. My father, in a classic backhanded compliment, once described my mother in print as "an extremely rational person and a greatly competent businesswoman." She also had a very unromantic view of her own childhood: she always said she couldn't wait to grow up and get out of what she saw as a boring, conservative childhood in a small town in the Midwest. She didn't like to play imaginatively as a child and she wanted to be grown-up and sophisticated.

And it was my mother's very pragmatism and impatience with fantasy that made her especially appreciative of and patient with predictable little Benjamin. They had their routines and rituals, their very language of communication down pat; they both knew what was expected. As soon as my usually glamorous mom arrived at our apartment dressed down in jeans and a flannel Eddie Bauer shirt, with her hair casually clipped back, Benj would run down the hallway toward her, hand her a ball, and cry: "Get it!" This was a signal that their special ball game would begin. She'd literally roll up her sleeves and kick off her shoes, sit cross-legged on the floor, and jump right into the ball game they'd made up together. The game involved throwing or kicking the ball back and forth to each other while exclaiming a few set phrases—"get it!," "kick/throw the ball!," "what a good throw/kick!"—my mom had come up with and Benj had adopted as his own. I couldn't imagine how she could have the stamina to play this game endlessly with him, but it seemed that the repetitive motion and lack of emotional demands were pleasant and soothing to both of them.

After an hour of ball, it was time for reading. My mother had studied acting and majored in the Oral Interpretation of Literature in college, and all her skills were on fine display. She read with wonderful inflection and charisma, and captured Benj's undivided attention and interest. When she was done with one book, he'd instantly toddle over to the bookcase and get another, then drop it in her lap. She would read to him for hours, but she would never make up stories or enact pretend scenarios with him as our grandmother, her mother, had done with us.

Grammy Peg, effervescent, dramatic, emotional (a wonderful children's book like Rumer Godden's *The Doll's House* could make her weep), a little scatterbrained and nutty, was in many ways the figure my mother had defined herself against. Grammy was a Fairy Godmother, Mary Poppins, Mother Goose, Auntie Mame–like figure in our lives and in the lives of all children who were fortunate enough to know her. She was legendary in her small Illinois town for her house's elaborate decorations on holidays and for her generosity. Neighborhood children came over almost every day for treats—her homemade hot fudge sauce, custard, and Chex Mix; games, books—

her bookshelves were overflowing with beautiful illustrated editions of classic children's books like *The Tale of Peter Rabbit* and *The Tale of Benjamin Bunny*, *Raggedy Ann* and *Raggedy Andy*, *The Wind in the Willows*, and *The Secret Garden*; or simply to bask in her warm attentiveness.

All day, every day, she was with us, she threw herself into our imaginative life with total conviction. She'd dress us up as princesses in her diaphanous nightgowns and robes (Claire liked this much more than I did, as I was always most comfortable in my T-shirt and shorts or corduroy bellbottoms), cut out paper dolls with us, serve us "royal beverages" (frozen orange juice in wine glasses), help us arrange tiny furniture in our doll's house. She'd preside over candy hunts (she'd hide red hots, chocolate Kisses, and jelly beans around the house and call out "cold colder warmer hot!" as we made our way to them), sneak into our room at night while we slept to leave presents under our pillow, and play a role in every show or play I staged. Claire was always the female lead in one of my mother's old prom dresses, and I the prince/consort/male suitor in my grandfather's bowler hat or my dad's tie—this was the only way I could convince Claire to participate—and Grammy took whatever part remained— the fairy godmother, the witch, the dog, the baby—but would usually mess it up by laughing. When we were with Grammy, there were daily games of Seal School, a game she invented and named after two stuffed black seals she'd given us. The seals, Claire, and I were the students, Grammy the teacher, Miss Samantha. She sat at the bottom of the stairs and we on the steps above her as she led us through lessons about flowers (which she'd pluck in the backyard and bring in to show us) and fairies and the difference between simile and metaphor ("Priscilla's eyes are as blue as the sea" versus "her eyes are the ocean"). We'd take long walks with her in Central Park, Connecticut, Illinois, or the South of France the two summers my parents rented a house there, and on these jaunts we'd often play

Tom Sawyer—I was Tom, Claire Becky, Grammy Huck or Aunt Polly struggling to catch me as I scrambled over rocks, skipped stones across ponds, and collected shells and leaves.

Perhaps most exciting were the Getting Lost Drives, where she would let us decide what path to take in the car. "Go left, Grammy," Claire would excitedly command her. "Let's go down this teeny side road, Grammy!" I'd cry. It was a strange and purposeful letting go that epitomized the excitement and expansive sense of possibility that we experienced with Grammy. The idea of a Getting Lost drive would have bored or baffled my mother; she wouldn't have seen the point. "I don't know how Grammy did it with you two," she'd say. "Benj is so much easier. Throw a ball or read a book to him, and he's perfectly content!"

But while my mother's visits to our apartment provided us with much-needed respite and much-appreciated support, visits to her turf were quite the opposite. She vehemently refused to in any way childproof her large house in Connecticut or make any accommodations there, and being there with Benj was very stressful; we had to be constantly vigilant. Breakable knickknacks set on low tables, huge stone hearths with sharp corners, exposed outlets set into floors, rugs without rug pads and frayed edges for tripping, steep spiral staircases—the house was filled with hazard and risk for awkward, clumsy, uncoordinated little Benj. He seemed so unsteady on his feet. "So he falls, he falls," my mother would say in exasperation. "He'll learn not to next time." But Benj didn't seem to learn the way other children did. And he fell so frequently and with such force; he was always covered with ugly bruises. He'd taken two really bad falls after which we ended up in the emergency room with a huge bump on his head and a tooth nearly severed at the root. "Just let go of his hand and let him go down the stairs himself," my mother would exclaim. "We *can't*," I'd reply. I knew, just by looking at him standing there, bewildered, on the edge of the stair, that he'd fall headlong. So we set up makeshift oversize playpens or shadowed him around the house, our arms hovering right behind him, ready to catch him as he teetered, slid, or fell.

At her own house, my mother felt more at liberty to fret about Benj's development and to express her strong opinions about what she saw as our indulgent parenting. Meals at Grams's house were tense affairs as my mother watched Benj, and us, like a hawk, and scoffed at the tiny pieces we cut his food into, the way we lifted the spoon carefully to his mouth, his outright refusal of foods that were tough or crunchy. "He's so picky! When is he going to feed himself?" she'd ask impatiently. But whenever we left him to his own devices, he'd gag, cough alarmingly, and begin to choke. He didn't seem to want, or to know how to chew yet, but we told ourselves it would come in time and didn't want to rush him. "He's got to learn to do it himself. It's just that you don't push him. You cater to him," my mother would say. She herself was determined to push him. "I'm going to make him a hot dog/peanut butter sandwich," she'd say, brushing off our claim that the American Academy of Pediatrics said these foods should not be fed to children under four because of choking and allergy risk. "It's time he was toiled-trained," she'd insist when he was barely two and a half.

Richard supported and agreed with me in private, but with my mother he was silent. He'd leave me to do all the protesting and insisting—"Please don't leave him alone on the stairs, Mom!," "Please don't give him that grape, Mom!," "You have to hold his hand/put a diaper on him, Mom"—and I felt betrayed. She'd cite his silence as evidence of support for her position. "Richard just indulges you," she'd say, "he absolutely agrees with me; he's just too afraid to say it." He would never tell her that, in the privacy of our home, it was he more than I who cradled Benj especially protectively, painstakingly cut the food into tiny bites, and invented elaborate rituals to win Benj's compliance: counting to twenty in German while brushing his teeth, encouraging his eating by recording each bite he took on a dry-erase board—"Benjamin has taken 2/3/4 bites of apple sweet potato"—or clapping and cheering each time Benj would venture to feed himself. When I pressed him on it, he said my mother made him nervous, she intimidated him. He had an aversion to conflict and confrontation and had learned to survive tense times in his own family by keeping quiet. But his silence, his passivity, his refusal to stand up for Benj frustrated and infuriated me. What Benj and I needed was an advocate. Spending time with my mother drove a wedge between me and Richard, and it was always a relief when we came home to our little apartment and it was just the three of us.

Paradoxically, my mother was both laissez-faire and (to me) overly concerned with how quickly Benj was moving along. But for her, any problems surrounding Benj had to do with our parenting of him, not anything inherent in him. Whenever I voiced a concern to her, she'd reply, without equivocation, "Don't be ridiculous, there is absolutely nothing wrong with him." I alternated between worrying myself and feeling the need to vigorously defend Benj against what I took to be her excessively normative view of children.

> Why should we be in such desperate haste to succeed and in such desperate enterprises? If a man does not keep pace with his companions, perhaps it is because he hears a different drummer. Let him step to the music which he hears, however measured or far away. It is not important that he should mature as soon as an apple tree or an oak. Shall he turn his spring into summer?
>
> —Thoreau, *Walden*

EVERY TIME I'D RAISED a concern about Benj with my pediatrician, he dismissed my worries in the most reassuring way. Perhaps this was because he was so taken with Benjamin, who was precocious in ways that are particularly endearing to pediatricians in university medical practices. At one appointment, when Benj was about two and a half, I tentatively raised two concerns: Benj's obsession with letters and numbers and his difficulty chewing and feeding himself with a spoon (he was still eating baby food from jars).

"First things first, of course he'll chew," our pediatrician reassured us. "He'll chew when he's ready. Have you ever seen an eighteen-year-old who didn't chew?" "No," I smiled sheepishly. Benj was sitting on the examining table, his increasingly long and skinny legs dangling over the edge. As Dr. B poked and prodded him, Benj leaned around the doctor's shoulders to see all the signs on the walls, his eyes darting excitedly around the room. "Firearms are dangerous, keep guns away from your child!" he declared. "Exit," "hazardous," "vaccines save lives," "Dr. B, Pediatrics," he cried. The pediatrician watched him, fascinated. He grabbed a couple of Dr. Seuss books out of the toy basket in the corner and handed them to Benj. "Can you read to me, Ben?" he asked. Benj pushed the familiar books back at him and continued to scan the room for more new signs and words to read. "As you see, he's obsessed with reading," I said. "Is that okay?" Dr. B smiled the most beneficent smile. "Half the Yale faculty was like this at his age, my dear! In any case, he does have other interests, right?" "Well, he absolutely loves music," I replied. "He drum-beats on everything, he recognizes instruments." Dr. B tuned the radio to a jazz station. Benj, wearing only his diaper, unsteadily leaped to his feet and began to beat out the rhythm with a tongue depressor on the examining table. "Clarinet!" he cried, "key of A major!" Dr. B stared at him and then at us, amazed. "This kid marches to the beat of his own drummer," he said, shaking his head in astonished and delighted disbelief. "Don't let other people tell you what he should or shouldn't be doing. He's on his own timetable." Richard, a socially reticent Thoreau scholar, nodded happily, and we left the appointment feeling how lucky we were to have an understanding, wise, profound man as our doctor. He cherished Benj's quirkiness. He wasn't going to force our odd little son to march to anyone else's drum. He understood and appreciated our attempts to recognize and accept Benj for who he was. I resolved to stop worrying.

> I was detached
> Internally from academic cares,
> From every hope of prowess and reward,
> And wished to be a lodger in that house
> Of letters, and no more—and should have been
> Even such, but for some personal concerns
> That hung about me in my own despite
> Perpetually, no heavy weight, but still
> A baffling and a hindrance, a controul
> Which made the thought of planning for myself
> A course of independent study seem
> An act of disobedience towards them
> Who loved me, proud rebellion and unkind.
> —*Prelude*, VI

The "proud rebellion and unkind" refers to Wordsworth's decision not to read for Honors, an indirect way of refusing the fellowship that his family had wanted him to pursue.

IN THE LATE SUMMER OF 2001, I made the difficult decision to resign my position at Yale and take a job as a literary agent at my mother's agency in New York City. I had never felt fully comfortable in the world of academia, although I deeply loved Yale, whose English Department largely stood above the fray, and I was given such fantastic support and nurturing by my professors that I'd been able to keep going despite increasing unhappiness and nagging doubts. My father had trained me exceedingly well to be an eager and responsive student, to do what others wanted of me, and fulfill their expectations of me. My high school teachers and my college professors assumed that I would be a scholar of some kind. "Your mind is too good to waste," one said in an admonishing voice when I raised the possibility of not continuing on to graduate school, as if a decision to not get an advanced degree would be a betrayal of her and of myself. My professors became like mini–parent figures; the idea of letting them, or my parents, or my husband down filled me with horror. At one point during our second year of graduate school, I expressed interest in applying to MFA programs and studying creative writing, but Richard told me my real talent was in scholarship and urged me to stay in. And being a professor was bound up with my life with Richard; it was part of our dream together. Getting engaged and then married to Richard had given my studies a human connection and dimension that sustained me; our marriage was a kind of bulwark against the unromantic world of academia. We would both be literature teachers and spend our life reading, analyzing poems, editing each other's work.

So I'd suppressed my doubts and kept going, but I was increasingly unhappy, even more so after becoming a professor. Academia was filled with a lot of very bad writing, infected with trendiness and political correctness of the worst kinds. I didn't like having to engage in the contemporary critical debates, which I found largely irrelevant or irritating, and I didn't like the relentless pressure to publish publish publish on the "hot" topics.

Just as important as my disillusionment with the profession was the realization that my remaining in academia threatened the integrity and happiness of our family. The previous year's truly agonizing job search had brought home to us the fundamental insecurity and perilousness of academic life, at least until tenure. Despite the fact that we presented ourselves as a couple, we had absolutely no luck in finding joint positions. With jobs so scarce and two jobs at the same place or within commuting distance of each other even scarcer, the chances of ending up in a geographically and intellectually desirable situation seemed extremely slim, and the utter randomness of the process meant that there was no way to count on things working out in a favorable way for us. We'd heard story after story from other graduate students and junior faculty about couples who only saw each other once every few weeks or even every few months, fathers living apart from their children, children being moved from state to state and having their schooling disrupted. And so we decided that we couldn't risk the security and happiness of the family over the long term in the hopes of the "perfect situation" turning up eventually. If we hadn't yet had children, we might have been able to live apart for a few years or jump from position to position. But we already had Benjamin and hoped to have more children very soon, and neither of us was willing to live apart from them. We were even more constrained because we put limits on what we were willing to accept geographically; perhaps because of all the loss in Richard's life, being near our family and friends in the Northeast was of paramount importance to us. We hoped that this decision to move to New York would settle the family and also give Richard the geographical flexibility and financial security to maximize his chances of finding the tenure-track position he so passionately wanted and that I felt he so richly deserved.

I was excited about my new career—I'd get to read and work on behalf of a broad range of writing and use many of the skills I'd developed as a Yale grad student and professor: guiding and advising writers, mentoring talented people, serving as an advocate for people whose work I believed in—but sad about leaving teaching and very apprehensive about letting people down with my decision. My mother, who had so wanted me to get the PhD, now understood that life as an academic was nothing like she'd imagined, and fully supported me in my desire to leave. I built up my courage to break the news to my professors and to my father. I was most afraid of my father's reaction; I feared he would take the decision as a rejection of intellectualism, and even worse, as my choosing my mother over him. But I needed to put Richard's and my family first.

On the evening of September 10, 2001, I spent hours painstakingly crafting a series of e-mails to my professors, friends and family, and my father, announcing and explaining my decision to leave academia and our family's decision to move to New York. I woke the next morning to the horrific news that my city was under attack. Plans had been underway to give Benj a version of the New York City childhood I'd had: we'd hoped to live in the unpretentious family neighborhood where I grew up, send him to the low-key and joyous preschool my sister and I had attended, bring him up surrounded by our extended families. New York City was my place of comfort and familiarity. But now it felt so vulnerable, exposed, fraught with danger and darkness. The innocence of my attachment to my home, my faith in the essential goodness and stability of the world had been taken from me. The news out of my beloved city was so heartbreaking, I'd frequently escape upstairs to cry.

And others' reactions to the news of our plans were disconcerting at best. My stepmother in Japan wrote to say she hadn't shared my e-mail with my father because in the wake of 9/11 she didn't think he could "take another dreadful shock." Although some of my Yale mentors and colleagues were wonderfully supportive, others expressed dismay and even a sense of personal betrayal that I was leaving academia. I received e-mail after e-mail from friends and family members questioning our decision to move to New York City, assuming that we would not move now, expressing fear for our well-being once we did. We'd made the decision largely out of a desire to preserve the family unit, and being made to feel that we were instead putting our family in danger was very difficult. Richard was especially shaken; it had taken a lot to convince him that city living would be good for our children at all, and now that city seemed like a terrifying place, from which families should retreat. But in a year we'd be without jobs and without a clear future.

What we have loved,
Others will love, and we will teach them how.
—Wordsworth, *Prelude*, XIV

DURING THIS MOST DIFFICULT period, two things sustained me: books and Benj. Literature had always been my way to succor myself, and to be an English teacher in the days and weeks after 9/11 was to gain a new appreciation for the surprising and profound ways that literature could console, challenge, uplift. Grief and anxiety pervaded Yale's campus, and I spent a good deal of time both in and outside of class helping my students to cope with their feelings and fears. The implicit theme of my Introduction to Literary Study class was "Romance and Realism," and it had never been more apt. Shakespeare's sonnets on the fragility and ephemerality of youth and beauty, the loss of children and parents in *The Tempest*, or Cathy's desperate search for Heathcliff on the moors in *Wuthering Heights* took on new poignancy and resonance in light of recent events. Wordsworth's "A Slumber Did My Spirit Seal" encapsulated the students' sense of shock, disillusionment, and vulnerability:

A slumber did my spirit seal;
  I had no human fears:
She seemed a thing that could not feel
  The touch of earthly years.

No motion has she now, no force;
  She neither hears nor sees;
Rolled round in earth's diurnal course,
  With rocks, and stones, and trees.

When we read Auden's "In Memory of W. B. Yeats," a lament for the death of a great poet at a time of political crisis, students teared up, launched into passionate debates about the value of art, explored the vexed relationship between literature and life, grappled with perennial and timeless questions in a newly intense way. We discussed the inefficacy of poetry to halt tragedy—"Poetry makes nothing happen," says Auden in one part of his poem about Yeats—and the power of literature to both explain and affect real life. "Poetry survives, . . . a way of happening, a mouth," he claims in another. These substantive and charged conversations, the vibrant human connection I felt with my students, the power of the literature to comfort and nourish and make sense of experience went some way toward restoring my faith in academia. I thought with great sadness of giving up the sustenance that reading and writing about great literature and engaging with wonderful young people provided me, and began to reconsider my decision to leave the profession. I'd resigned my Yale job and there was no getting it back, but at the last minute I applied for a few choice college teaching jobs at other schools in the Northeast. I wanted to keep my options open. And increasingly unsure of whether we were going to follow through on our plan to move to New York City, Richard and I applied to nursery schools in both Manhattan and New Haven for Benj.

With so much up in the air—our jobs, where we would live, the future of my hometown—Richard and I entered a new phase of bonding with Benj and renewed commitment to and appreciation of our family. We conceived a second child just a week after 9/11, as a deliberate gesture of hope, a defiance of caution, an embrace of the future. And Benj was our "daily joy"; we "loved . . . [him] with increasing love" (Wordsworth, "Michael"). Benj knew nothing of the outside world and its horrors. We felt the pathos of his innocence all the more keenly. He seemed hopeful and optimistic. He seemed to know what really mattered. I would come home after a long day of classes and office hours and department meetings, ready to collapse after forging ahead all day through the first-trimester exhaustion and nausea, and Benj would walk up with a big smile on his face and sing to me or recite to me. He threw himself into his activities with total commitment. He was so funny; he made us laugh so hard. He had no guile at all. He was just so wonderfully himself, so strong in his passions, so forthright in his desires, so determined and so appreciative and so so happy. He really seemed to us to be blooming emotionally. It was clear now in a way that it had never been before that Richard and I were his partners; he was much much happier reciting *with* us, singing *with* us, dancing *with* us, reading *with* us. Although he still brushed off our kisses and hugs, although he still didn't call us Mommy or Daddy, we knew now, with absolute certainty, that he needed us, loved us, wanted us.

Moreover, Benj seemed to be becoming ever more passionately interested and invested in the music and literature we had loved as children and as always this provided a wonderful way to feel connected to him. With him I read, over and over again at his insistence, my favorite children's books—*The Little Bear* series by Minarik and Sendak, *Our Animal Friends at Maple Hill Farm*, *Frog and Toad are Friends*, *Little Fur Family*—books that celebrated family, friendship, the simple pleasures of daily life. He was reciting more and more poetry (from illustrated children's editions of Yeats, Wordsworth, and Frost I'd bought for him) and he always did so with charming appropriateness. "I will arise and go now!" he'd cry when I said "It's time for me to go now, sweetie"; "Some say in ice!" he'd proclaim when I put ice in a glass. The same Pete Seeger and Beatles' albums Richard and I had listened to as children became the soundtrack to Benj's days, and he and I danced around to them and sang the songs with each other. And he developed a special attachment to *Really Rosie* by Maurice Sendak and Carole King. As a child, I'd adored Sendak's *Little Nutshell Library*—Pierre, One Was Johnny, Chicken Soup with Rice, Alligators All Around— on which *Really Rosie* was based, and my sister had given me the set for Christmas a few years before Benj was born. With themes of numbers/counting, the alphabet, and the seasons, with clever rhymes, irresistible rhythms, and catchy melodies, the books and CD were tailor-made for Benj. We spent many hours singing the songs and reading the books together, and his zest and gaiety and most of all his ecstatic pleasure in the words and songs cheered me in many a dark moment. I felt I was imparting my history to him. What a joy it was to rediscover these gems and celebrate them again with Benj, who so exuberantly seized on them and made them his own.

One of Benjamin's favorite books at this point was a collection of Robert Frost poems for children, called *A Swinger of Birches*. He'd read this book endlessly, and memorized many of the poems in it. He loved to recite them to us and play a game in which he'd say all but the last word of each line and look laughingly at us until we filled in the blank or reverse the positions:

> Nature's first green is gold,
> Her hardest hue to hold.
> Her early leaf's a flower;
> But only so an hour.
> Then leaf subsides to leaf.
> So Eden sank to grief,
> So dawn goes down to day.
> Nothing gold can stay.

...

THE GRIM AND DISQUIETING news reports we listened to and read after 9/11 were counterbalanced by swaths of poetry, strains of music, a child who lived in his own strange and marvelous universe and shared the pleasures he found there with us. In the aftermath of the attack on New York City, and with me tired from the pregnancy, we traveled to the city less and spent more time holed up in our small apartment, just the three of us. The cookie-cutter modern rental apartment in a suburb of New Haven felt to us like a burrow, a haven, a nest, "a cloistral place / Of refuge . . . [a] safe covert . . . a tranquil spot" (Wordsworth, "When to the Attractions of the Busy World"). It was snug, cozy, and reassuring in its familiarity—yet also mysterious and enchanted by virtue of the strange little person who presided over it and infused it with his quirky spirit.

Even leaving the nest and venturing into the sometimes difficult terrain of my mother's house didn't have the same sting that it had previously had. Dr. B's reassurances had somewhat mollified my mother, and she was much less judgmental of our parenting. She was also increasingly dazzled by and immensely proud of Benj's amazing abilities, and loved to see others respond to his antics. On Thanksgiving weekend, she invited Richard's uncle and aunt over for lunch, and we all sat in the living room and watched and listened to Benj, who had no consciousness of the fact that he was "on display," so to speak. First, he and his father recited a Frost poem back and forth; one would do the bulk of the line and the other chime in on the last word. This poem, "Looking for a Sunset Bird in Winter," about the search for beauty and renewal in a barren landscape of ice and snow—was the first piece of literature I'd ever taught, in the first section I led as a teaching assistant for Yale's Modern Poetry lecture a few years earlier. Hearing it shared by Benj's young voice and Richard's deep one was deeply moving and reassuring. On that cold, gray, rather gloomy late-November day, Benj's enthusiasm and high spirits lit up the room.

Then I put on *Really Rosie*, and as soon as the first rousing drumbeat sounded, little Benj began to march with fervor, when the piano came in, he began to sway to the music, and when Carole King began to sing, he sang with her, in perfect unison: "Bel-ieeeeeeve me!" His dancing was rollicking, uninhibited, and filled with unself-conscious abandon. His singing was lusty and full-throated. He quivered with conviction and pleasure from top to toe:

> . . . as a faggot sparkles on the hearth,
> Not less if unattended and alone
> Than when both young and old sit gathered round
> And take delight in its activity;
> Even so this happy Creature of herself
> Is all-sufficient; solitude to her
> Is blithe society, who fills the air
> With gladness and involuntary songs.
> —Wordsworth, "Characteristics of a Child Three Years Old"

Richard's aunt was a little teary. "Oh, Sarah would have just eaten him up," she sighed. We, too, missed Richard's mother terribly, and wished so much that she could have seen her grandson's theatrical flair and hear him "fill the air / With gladness and involuntary songs."

Early December brought some bleak news on my own father's health; he had to have two major surgeries, and it seemed that he might not live much longer. He was in Japan, and both because I was pregnant (with no health insurance coverage if I traveled outside the country) and because I wasn't comfortable leaving Benj for that long, I couldn't travel there to see him. My stepmother confided in his children—my brother (my father's son from his first marriage, twelve years older than I), my sister, and me—that because she was now certain that Daddy would never be able to travel back to New York, she had made arrangements to sell his New York City apartment to their neighbors. She hadn't told my father—"It might kill him if he knew," she said—and swore us to secrecy. She urged us to think about what we would want to take from his apartment, and we began the process of sorting through precious things from our childhoods that he had taken from the country house when it was sold, or had saved over the years.

That year, with so much uncertainty and sorrow in our lives, I threw myself into the holiday season with even more fervor than usual; I strove to create a Christmas cocoon for all of us. I decorated our small apartment and, as Grammy Peg had, I made a Christmas Box: a large red-and-green-striped box in which I put all the Christmas CDs, videos, and books we owned; each day Benj could pick a book to read, a CD to listen to, and a video to watch. I sat to watch Rudolph and Frosty and *A Charlie Brown Christmas* and *The Little Drummer Boy* with Benj. He couldn't seem to follow the stories (especially the sophisticated verbal humor of *Charlie Brown*) but perked up whenever musical numbers came on. His favorite CD was *The Christmas Revels*, which had been the soundtrack of Richard's childhood Christmases and which we'd taken his mother to see the last Christmas she was alive. I called him my "jolly wassailer" and my "brave gallant," after lines from *The Christmas Revels*. Benj seemed so jolly, so filled with holiday spirit.

For as long as I could remember, my aunt had always sent my sister and me a holiday-season package in early December; this year, for the first time, she sent the package addressed to Master Benjamin———. It contained a musical advent calendar and a Little Golden Book of *The Twelve Days of Christmas*, and Benj appreciated both gifts mightily. He loved to find the numbered windows (although he usually needed help folding them back) and identifying the picture beneath. "Candle!" "Santa!" "Reindeer!" he'd blurt out. After I read/

sang *The Twelve Days of Christmas* once to him, he'd memorized it, and we'd sing the song together multiple times a day. "On the," I'd say, "Twelfth!" he'd shout; "My true love gave to me," I'd sing, "A partridge!" he'd reply.

We had a wonderful Christmas at my mother's house. I was out of the first trimester and my energy was returning. As the only young child in our extended family, Benj was the center of attention and he ate it up. He was physically more steady and capable, and Richard and I could relax a bit and enjoy the holiday. The Christmas gifts we gave him—a framed print from Dr. Seuss' *The Lorax*, D'Aulaire's *Book of Greek Myths*, a Richard Scarry Busytown train set—were all familiar and well-loved favorites from our own childhoods. We took Benj to church and he heartily joined in the carol singing. He was luminous with joy.

The day after Christmas, Richard left for the MLA convention—he had two job interviews at first-rate schools. This was the first time either one of us had flown since 9/11, and it was right after the incident with the shoe bomber. I was almost four months pregnant and my mother came to stay with us to help me lift and care for Benj. Richard returned on New Year's Eve, and that night we sat down as a family to watch *Emmet Otter's Jugband Christmas*, a classic Jim Henson video that my sister and I had given each other for Christmas (something we often did, inadvertently). I was so happy that Benj would sit somewhat near me on the sofa and let me occasionally pat him on the head and that he seemed even somewhat interested; he tuned in during the songs. "Maybe he's starting to be a real kid," I thought.

> My spirit was up, my thoughts were full of hope.
> —Wordsworth, *Prelude*, III, on his way to begin his
> studies at Cambridge

EARLY JANUARY WAS FILLED with good news. After an abnormal test result raised suspicions of spina bifida, a level-two ultrasound confirmed that we were having a healthy baby boy. We were both finalists for tenure-track positions at top liberal arts colleges in the Northeast: Richard at Williams and I at Vassar.

And in the second week of January, we were scheduled to take Benjamin on a visit to a New Haven preschool, one that was legendary in the Yale community. A few weeks before Christmas, Richard had taken Benj to visit a preschool in New York City (overcome by morning sickness, I'd stayed in New Haven) and reported that he'd done great. I was glad I was now feeling well enough to accompany Benj to his next "interview" and to see a school I'd long heard wonderful things about. Run out of a converted firehouse in the prettiest part of New Haven, within walking distance of the Victorian houses inhabited by Yale faculty and the prewar apartment buildings filled with Yale grad students, it was the school of choice for all the Yale English Department kids. I'd been hearing it praised effusively, by the people I most trusted, for years. It was supposed to be developmentally sensitive, laid-back, diverse and warm, with an emphasis on parent involvement, a sliding-scale tuition to allow a range of families to attend, and a throwback to the seventies sensibility. As we parked in the lot outside, I felt excited to see this place and excited at the prospect of Benj's being ready to go to school—a place I assumed he would thrive, given his love of learning and his intellectual gifts.

With Benj holding one of our big hands in each of his small ones, the three of us walked through the front door and into a huge open space that housed the kindergarten. The room was loud and bustling with high ceilings that made the children's cries and shouts echo, and Benj instantly clapped his hands to his ears. We gave our names to the receptionist, the assistant director came to greet us and take our coats, and finally the school's longtime director came out of her small office. A tall, gaunt, imposing woman, she showed us to a spiral staircase that led to the lower level where the younger children's class-rooms were. Benj froze at the top of the stairs, and Richard scooped him up in his arms and carried him down the stairs; I went ahead with the director, partially to distract her from our need to carry Benj rather than let him navigate the steps alone.

There were no children downstairs when we arrived—"They're out at the playground," the director confided, "so we have the whole place to ourselves." The classroom was warm and welcoming, com-fortable and homey, with lots of books, well-worn rugs, and simple wooden chairs and tables. The director proudly showed us around, pointing out the pretend play area, an inviting block area, easels and chalkboards for painting and drawing. Benj paid no attention to her comments and questions—"Ben, do you like firemen?" when we passed a dress-up area; "Do you want to look at the fish, Ben?" when we came to the fish tank. He was too busy confidently and curiously exploring the room on his own, turning to look at us with a big smile when he discovered something he especially liked—a copy of *Bread and Jam for Frances* on a book stand, a xylophone, some dice. We came to the art center—bins filled with beads, string, glue sticks, crayons, paints—and the director pointed to the walls, covered in colorful and, to me, surprisingly complex and sophisticated artwork. "We place a strong emphasis on imaginative expression through art." I looked at the drawings of houses and rainbows, dragons and princes, and couldn't imagine Benj being able to do art at that level. She handed him a marker and said: "Ben, do you want to draw?" Without indicating that he'd heard her at all, he turned the pen over and happily read the color off the label; it was some kind of taupe brown. The director smiled at us. "Wow, he's reading already!" "Oh yes," Richard chuckled. "He just picked it up on his own." The direc-tor added: "We don't formally teach math or reading and we don't do worksheets. We believe that children learn through play."

At that point, I heard the sound of children's voices and soon a large group of them began to trickle in, bundled up in parkas, snow pants, hats and mittens and boots. Many were wiping runny noses, coughing loudly, shouting animatedly, peering at us—the interlopers—with curiosity, shyness, enthusiasm, excitement. Benj didn't seem especially interested in them—he was more concerned with the books on the shelves and the signs on the walls—but I watched them with great interest, as they were the first large group of kids close to Benj's age that I'd seen since giving birth to him. I hadn't seen many children around Benj's age, period, since none of my close high school or college friends had children yet, and only a very few graduate students and junior faculty did, so playdates were few and far between. Moreover, the other faculty kids had parents who were already tenured and with whom I felt a little uncomfortable casually socializing or getting to know via our children, and the few kids we did know were either much younger or much older.

These children were three years old, between six and twelve months older than Benj, but to me they seemed both much older and much younger than he did. Although teachers helped some of them, many seemed surprisingly independent as they hung up their coats, wiggled out of their boots, and headed over to the rug where they were supposed to gather for music time. One teacher stood at a remove from the group to lead the song, and another snuggled up on a window seat with little children all around her. As the teacher began to sing, Benj perked up and riveted his eyes on her. All the kids' eyes, however, were on him as he delightedly beat out the rhythm of the song they were singing and joined in perfectly on the chorus despite having never heard the song before. Kids whispered to each other, some pointed at Benj. Everyone was watching him and he didn't notice at all.

The song ended and Benj—alone—clapped vigorously. Suddenly he strode forward purposefully toward the group. He walked right up to the group of kids, then pushed past a child on his way to what

I could see was the object of his interest—a huge hoop earring dangling from the ear of the teacher. Fascinated, he reached out to grab the earring and cried, "The letter *O!*" She brushed his hands away, and he reached out again, and I cried: "No Benj, you could hurt her." Richard sprung forward to retrieve him, but before he did the teacher had neatly extricated herself. She took Benj's hand firmly in hers, smiled at him, and said, "Yes, the letter *O.*" He smiled back at her. The other children looked at him as if he were a kind of curiosity. I gathered him up and we said our good-byes.

Driving home, sitting next to Benj as he napped in his car seat, I reflected on what I had seen and wondered why I felt so incredibly shaky. Benj had seemed so different, special, vulnerable. I kept thinking, "Something is fundamentally different about him."

This was the first time I'd seen Benj in a group child-care setting, and it had unsettled me. The other kids seemed so much more robust, sturdy, and resilient than Benj. At the same time, they seemed much less verbal and much less intellectually advanced. I couldn't imagine any of them being able to spell "dinosaur" or identify "ochre" or sing *The Christmas Revels* from start to finish with every word and note perfect.

Benj hadn't been shy or disconcerted at all. He'd been enthusiastic, radiant, ebullient. So why did I feel such a sense of uneasiness and sadness? I thought: he beams but he doesn't converse, he laughs but he doesn't giggle and bump and shove and whisper. He was in the group but not part of the group, as if he existed in his own little universe. There was Benj and then there were the others. Of course they were a preexisting school group but still he seemed entirely *other* to them, like a member of a different species. I was struck by how "different" he'd seemed in a conventional school setting, how much he stuck out. I teared up and said to Richard: "It's sad that he has to join the world."

It is not now as it hath been of yore;—
　　Turn wheresoe'er I may,
　　　　By night or day,
The things which I have seen I now can see no more.
　—"Intimations Ode"

A FEW DAYS LATER, I received a message on my answering machine asking me to call the admissions director of the preschool in Manhattan that Benj and Richard had visited before the holidays. It was, in fact, the same nursery school my sister and I and Richard's cousins had attended as children. The school was a classic Upper West Side institution, progressive in its methods, diverse, known for welcoming a wide range of kids, with different learning styles and personalities, from different socioeconomic, racial, and ethnic backgrounds. I didn't care that this school wasn't as top-tier as some others. In fact, I'd chosen to avoid the whole ridiculously competitive preschool application process by doing a legacy application to this school. Despite the cutthroat nature of admissions to preschools in New York, we'd assumed Benj would be accepted and welcomed there.

From the minute I got the admissions director on the phone, however, a woman who had been bubbly, warm, and effusive in our earlier conversations was now serious, restrained, and rather terse. After a quick hello, she got right to business. "We have some concerns about how Benjamin did at his visit," she said.

"Really?" I replied. "We thought he did well. He had a good time."

She paused. "No. He didn't do well. But because you're an alumna, we'd like to see him again and give him another chance."

"What was the problem?" I asked.

After some pausing and sighing, she finally came out with: "He seemed fixated on the magnetic letters and numbers. He didn't answer the teachers' questions appropriately or respond to the other children. We think he might do better in another school setting."

I was polite while the conversation lasted, but I hung up the phone dismayed and a bit angry. How could that woman, that school—one that prided itself on a joyful, progressive approach to learning—not see Benj for the amazing, original, bright little boy he was? According to Richard, who'd watched from against the classroom wall, two-and-a-half-year-old Benj had, in fact, taken the magnetic letters and spelled out "Benjamin," "flapjack," and "Friday," the day of the screening. He'd then arranged the numbers in sequence from 1 to 10, calling out each one in an excited voice while beaming up into the teacher's face. So what if he didn't say "Hello" or respond to the teacher's offer of crayons? Sharing his enthusiasm about the alphabet and numbers was his way of being friendly. And if he hadn't been as responsive to the other children as he could have been, there were plenty of good explanations for that. He'd just gotten out of the car after a two-hour ride into Manhattan. He hadn't eaten lunch or had a drink since he left home. He'd never been in a room filled with strange children before. How dare those teachers demand sunny normalcy from him? He wasn't a normal child. He was Benj, and if they didn't want him, then I certainly didn't want them.

But I wasn't only angry. I was also deeply worried. So after a day or so of lamenting the nursery school's inability to accept my son for who he really was, I began to realize that the concerns the admissions director described had resonated with me. I shut myself in my "study," a windowless walk-in closet off the small loft that overlooked our living room. I typed some phrases about early reading and trouble answering questions into Google, and the first thing that my search brought up was the American Hyperlexia Association's Web site. I read breathlessly about a syndrome I had never heard of:

HYPERLEXIA IS A SYNDROME OBSERVED IN CHILDREN WHO HAVE THE FOLLOWING CHARACTERISTICS:

- A precocious ability to read words, far above what would be expected at their chronological age or an intense fascination with letters or numbers
- Significant difficulty in understanding verbal language
- Abnormal social skills, difficulty in socializing and interacting appropriately with people

IN ADDITION, SOME CHILDREN WHO ARE HYPERLEXIC MAY EXHIBIT THE FOLLOWING CHARACTERISTICS:

- Learn expressive language in a peculiar way, echo or memorize the sentence structure without understanding the meaning (echolalia), reverse pronouns
- Rarely initiates conversations
- An intense need to keep routines, difficulty with transitions, ritualistic behavior
- Auditory, olfactory and/or tactile sensitivity
- Self-stimulatory behavior
- Specific, unusual fears
- Normal development until 18–24 months, then regression
- Strong auditory and visual memory
- Difficulty answering "wh—" questions, such as "what," "where," "who," and "why"

- Think in concrete and literal terms, difficulty with abstract concepts
- Listen selectively, appear to be deaf

I was thunderstruck.

The Web site had a message board and a listserv, which I immediately joined. The major issue at stake seemed to be whether or not hyperlexia could be a stand-alone diagnosis. Although many mothers on the list argued vociferously that it could and should, the consensus in the medical profession seemed to be that kids with hyperlexia comprised an extremely small subset of kids with high-functioning autism, Asperger's syndrome, or PDD (pervasive developmental disorder). I'd thought of autistic kids as kids who flapped their hands, spun in circles, banged their heads against walls, and never spoke or smiled. Benj had made eye contact, he was very smiley and happy and responsive, he'd laughed at us frequently and chattered gaily throughout the day. Why would we ever have suspected this?

The parents' guide to hyperlexia was called *Reading Too Soon*, something that seemed impossible to a lover of literature like myself. To us, Benjamin's hyper-literacy had been precocious but not abnormal, surprising but not disturbing. His love of reading and his abilities had seemed relatively "normal" in our family. And because he was so verbal—he talked all the time in an animated and expressive way and had a huge vocabulary—we hadn't worried much about his speech or his ability to communicate. There had always been an explanation for the lack of expressive or social exchange. A rationalization. An excuse. "We never wave at him, so how could he learn?" "He's not interested in small talk; he wants to cut to the chase." "He's just like his father: he'd rather read than chitchat." "How would he know how to play tea party if we've never shown him?" But the documents and postings on the hyperlexia Web site made it apparent that reading at an extremely young age could both be a red flag for developmental disorders and interfere with normal development. "Gesturing is a critical aspect of communication," I read, and realized that Benj had never used gestures to express his desires and feelings: no waving, no pointing, no shaking his head no or nodding yes. I ran through all of Benj's language in my head. He'd developed single words precociously, at a little under a year, started speaking in many two-word phrases at age two, right on schedule, and now was speaking in longer sentences, just as the parenting books had said he should.

But the more I read, the more I realized that most of Benj's spoken language was actually echolalia (repeating or echoing other people's language rather than creating spontaneous sentences). When he woke up in the morning or from a nap and we went in to him, he'd say, "Did you have a good sleep"? or "Are we getting up?" When he was ready for a meal, he'd announce, "It's time for supper/lunch/yogurt for you/Benj!" instead of "I'm hungry" or "I want yogurt"; when he was done eating and/or wanted out of his high chair, he'd say, "Are you done?" or "Do you want to get down?" When he was upset, he'd say, "What's wrong?" or "What's the matter?" or if he fell down or bumped himself, he'd say, "Are you okay?" or "No problem." It had seemed that he was almost giving us a prompt to ask or say these things to him, and we'd found it endearing. A lot of his phrases were very sophisticated and had sounded so funny and sweet in his little voice. When he drank his juice, he'd sing a little song—"Cup of juice, cup of juice, cup of juice!"—that I made up with him, and often say a phrase we taught him: "Cup of juice is not only tasty but also delicious!" When he was tired, he'd say, "Jack-in-the-box is tired" (from a television skit). When we went outside at night, he'd often say, with charming solemnity, "The moon is high in the sky and the stars shine bright," something Richard had said to him a long time ago. When he wanted to count something, he'd say, "Let's count and see," and after the counting, "Good counting, everybody!" (lines from *Sesame Street*). All of these phrases, I now learned, were "context-appropriate delayed echolalia."

I remembered twice he had greeted a loving adult's "Hi, sweetheart!" with his own "Hi, sweetheart!" The Stop and Shop cashier and my sister had found this adorable. But what had once seemed charming and funny now seemed alarming. His joyfulness, sociability, and engagement with us and with other adults mitigated against an autistic-spectrum diagnosis (he was never distant, blank, or flat in an obvious way), but so many other things matched up that I became really worried. Panicked, in fact.

I have no memory of how I initially broke the news of my discoveries to Richard. My memory begins with us in my tiny office, him standing somewhat reluctantly behind me as I opened the hyperlexia Web site and pointed to the screen. His initial reaction was skepticism and disbelief, but as I read through the symptoms one by one, I could see his face turn ashen and the realization dawning in his eyes. Later that night, after we'd put Benj down, Richard began to weep heavily. In the eight years we'd been together, I'd only seen him cry three times before: when a few months after we got engaged, we learned that despite aggressive chemotherapy, his mother's cancer had returned; during our wedding ceremony as he spoke his vows in a choked-up voice; and at his mother's memorial service. "Oh honey," I cried, "he's going to be okay. We're going to do everything possible to make sure of that. I promise you he'll be all right!" Richard lay down on the floor and wrapped his arms around himself and sobbed. I got down on the floor right next to him and put my arms around him, I rested my head on his back or his shoulder, but he was totally pulled into himself. It was like he didn't even feel or notice my touch. He didn't need, or want, or know how to make use of, reassurance and comfort from me. Listening to him sob in such a heartbreaking way and be completely unable to assuage the grief was almost unbearable to me.

That night, I sent the link to my mother, sister, and brother-in-law, and one by one they responded that they were certain Benj was hyperlexic. My mother called a few minutes after sending me an e-mail, and her calm, strong voice was very comforting. She apologized for having doubted me in the past, and confessed to me that both my sister and my aunt had raised concerns about Benj's conversational skills to her, and she had brushed them off. "I just thought he's a boy and we never had any boys in our family. And that he was brilliant and odd and a mini-Richard," she said. "I know, Mommy," I said, "we all did."

The next morning I slept late and emerged from the bedroom to find Benj clutching a note card, trotting from room to room with Richard following behind. I took the note cards from Benj. They read:

Where is your room?
Where is the living room?
Go to the living room.
Go to the green sofa.

Put the pillow on the white sofa.
Put the blanket on the white sofa.
Put the blanket next to the white sofa.
Put the pillow on the green sofa.

Put the cup under the table.
Put the cup on the table.
Put the cup next to the table.
Put the cup beside the table.
Put the cup between the chairs.
Put the cup in front of the chairs.
Put the cup behind the chairs.
Put the cup alongside the chairs.

"I'm testing his comprehension," Richard said, "and he's doing great." "But that's what hyperlexia *is*," I replied. "That doesn't mean he's okay. Can he understand if we just ask him? With no visual, nothing to read?" Richard didn't reply.

It was Martin Luther King day, and I had agreed to come to campus to meet with students even though there were no classes. Benj and Richard drove me to school, Benj shouting out the names of local realtors—"Beazley," "Century 21"—as we drove.

It was a gray, overcast, cold day and the English Department building was eerily quiet. I had meetings with about twelve students lined up over a three-hour period. Some were advisees I knew well and had taught several times before, others were students from the previous semester who wanted to go over papers I'd returned to them, and some were new students this term, looking to get acquainted with me.

Since having my own child, I'd found that I had renewed appreciation for the vulnerability and individuality of my students. A professor friend of mine continually warned other academic parents-to-be that after she had a child, she was no longer as committed to or excited about her teaching. Her line was: "I look at my students and think, 'These kids are not my baby.'" Being a parent had affected my teaching in precisely the opposite way. I would often look at my students and think: "Each of these kids is someone's baby." And on this day, when my own baby's situation seemed so precarious and my situation as his mother so uncertain, I saw the students even more clearly as the children of parents, as dearly beloveds, as the apples of eyes and the focus of dreams, as the most precious thing in the world to parents I did not know but could now understand and identify with all the more powerfully.

Many of the students I saw were there to talk about grades. "What does it take to get into the A range?" a new student, an earnest, hardworking boy in a baseball cap and a Dave Matthews T-shirt, asked.

A student I'd had the previous semester strenuously tried to convince me that he deserved an A rather than the B+ I'd given him, a B+ he felt would sink his chances of admission to top-tier law schools. Although grade-grubbing had always repelled me, I felt more impatient than usual.

But at the same time that the audacious requests to have grades changed disgusted me, I did feel a certain degree of kinship with the students, all of them, even the most aggressive and grade-conscious. For although I'd never contested a grade or asked a professor what it would take to get an A, I had been a student who wanted good grades and my professor's approval, and had felt a good deal of pressure to succeed and perform at a top level. But now the stakes that had seemed so high seemed so relatively low. As students complained about a less-than-perfect grade or fretted over med-school admissions, I kept wanting to reassure them, to cry out to them: you, we, have so much to be grateful for! There are so many much more fundamental and important things that we have and take for granted—the ability to converse, to joke, to decipher body language, to advocate for ourselves. The ability to go to college at all, let alone Yale University. The ability to have a meaningful exchange with another person. We are so lucky!

I talked with the students about classes they'd taken or planned to take, papers they'd already written or ideas for future papers, job and graduate school applications. They told me about movies they'd seen over Christmas break, gifts they'd given or received from their parents, family times, their romantic entanglements. And as the students rattled on fluently and fluidly and easily about their writing and ideas, their lives and experiences, I had to clench my fists under the desk to keep the tears from welling into my eyes. I wondered whether real conversation would ever be second nature for Benj, whether he'd ever be able to think and reason abstractly, make off-the-cuff jokes, engage in sophisticated back-and-forth exchange. Would Benj ever be independent enough to choose his own classes? Would he even be able to attend college, let alone graduate school? Would Benj ever debate the merits of a movie? Would he ever have a romantic partner? Would he ever buy me a gift, or receive one from me with genuine understanding and appreciation?

And even as I comforted, encouraged, and advised my students, even as I empathized, laughed, and commiserated with these many wonderful kids, I wondered: will I ever be able to have these kinds of conversations, this kind of connection with my own child? Will he ever come to me for guidance and support? Will I be able to impart wisdom and values to him? Will we ever be able to share our feelings, our experiences, our ideas, our inner lives?

Learning that I was a mother almost always intrigued and delighted my students. When I taught the "Intimations Ode," I would always tell my students about my professor's gift of the onesies and the messy, boisterous baby who wore them (but only occasionally, lest he ruin them). Former students often referred to Benj as "seer blest"; they loved to hear anecdotes about Benj's activities, oohed and aahed over the photos in my office, and walked me to my car so they could see the baby strapped in the car seat waiting for me with Richard. I had joyfully confided the news of my second pregnancy to them just before the winter break, and they'd thrown me a little party on the last day of class. Now, with me visibly pregnant before them and photos of Benj all around us, they asked many thoughtful and sweet questions about my children. "What did you give seer blest for Christmas?" "How are you feeling?" "You must be so excited!" "Do you know what the sex is?" I answered with as much cheer as I could muster, and never hinted that anything was wrong.

Just a month before, I had been their ebullient and poised Professor Gilman and Benj my "seer blest." And now everything had changed, but they didn't know and I couldn't tell them. I felt I had to be strong and authoritative, competent and solid, cheerful and optimistic, a wise, reassuring mentor and role model to them. And meanwhile my heart was breaking and my whole world was falling away.

DURING THE MOST UNCERTAIN time after 9/11, Richard and I would continually say, "At least we have Benj," or "Good old Benj." Benj was the sure thing, the bedrock, the fulcrum of our lives, the meaning of our lives, really. And then, just a few months later, as the evaluations began, the child I thought I knew was gone. Benj had been our refuge from the storm, our unadulterated, uncomplicated, simple joy. And then suddenly he *was* the storm, he was complicated and confusing and terrifyingly at risk.

One of the most painful things about those first days was that I was being made to feel that all the things that I'd considered unique and special about Benj were instead uncontrollable manifestations of a disorder. He was not unusual; he was typical, ordinary, a classic case. He didn't have an interesting mind; he had faulty wiring. He didn't have a distinctive personality; he had a syndrome. His jubilant recitations of Robert Frost's "Fire and Ice" and "Nothing Gold Can Stay" and word- and note-perfect renditions of many of the songs from *The Sound of Music*, *West Side Story*, and *Oklahoma!* were not the result of a love or appreciation for poetry or music but rather a mindless parroting. His animated recitation of scripts from *Between the Lions* and *Sesame Street* was not a dazzling display of his powers of memory as much as it was "perseveration," "echolalia," "video talk," and was to be discouraged. His ability to line up his letter blocks in alphabetical order and to make number chains from 1 to 20 was a compulsion, not a pleasure. His seeing letters everywhere—in the shape of his food (a string of spaghetti was an *S*) or the curve and lines of a piece of jewelry (little earrings of mine were *T*s, a linked bracelet I had was seven *O*s)—wasn't perceptive or imaginative— these were ominous signs of obsession. His not responding to questions or not turning his head in response to a voice wasn't a sign of single-minded focus on an engrossing activity so much as it was an inability to engage with the outside world. His early reading wasn't "just like his mom"; his perfectionism wasn't "just like his father," or at least not in any reassuring way. Both were symptoms, items on a checklist, pathologies. In my darkest moments, that is to say, I saw Benjamin as a textbook case, an embodiment of a syndrome rather than a distinctive individual. In those first days of questioning who my son was and what he would or could be, I had trouble finding strength because I wasn't sure what remained behind.

I read the same books to him, sang the same songs to him at night, but now tears flowed and I had to turn my head away so he wouldn't see me crying. While we danced around to "Here Comes the Sun" or "Skip to My Lou," Benj as buoyant as ever, I'd clench my nails into my arm or bite the inside of my cheeks hard to keep from breaking down, and would run to the bathroom afterward to sob, kneeling on the floor and running the water so he wouldn't hear me.

These precautions may have been unnecessary, as Benj seemed, as always, unusually insulated from my emotional state. Benj's obliviousness to the larger situation, his living in his own world, which had once served as a balm and a solace, now enhanced the pathos of the situation. He seemed to have no understanding or awareness of the radical change in his parents' consciousness about him, and showed few indications that he sensed that anything at all had changed. They say children always know when something is up, but I really don't think he did. And that his unruffled indifference was, in fact, a symptom of the disorder only heightened its poignancy for me.

Benj's reading and reciting were melodious, inflected, and they'd seemed sensitive and poetic, far from mechanical or rote. He spoke with beautiful expressivity and intonation. He'd seemed to understand exactly what everything meant—or else how could he emphasize just the right word and pause at just the right moment? But now we wondered—how much had he understood, of any of it? Were the lyrics of a Beatles song, the words of a Wordsworth poem, the lines of a witty and wonderful Ernie and Bert skit just pleasant but meaningless sounds to him? Had our word games with him, our singing to and reading with him, not been significant exchanges but instead just another perseverative activity? Were these books, these songs, these games merely tools in his "self-stimulatory behavior," the loci of his troubling obsessions? Benj was the same as he had always been. But what had he been??

Part of what made my dawning realizations about Benj so disconcerting and devastating was that I had thought I knew him so well. After the initial sense of alienation and despite my continued sense of a fundamental difference or distance between us, Benj, with all his quirks, had become utterly familiar to me. There had been no one more familiar to me than my son. I had considered myself totally tuned in to his needs and had accepted him on his own terms. In fact, I had embraced him for what he was, because I still wanted to be the devoted mother of the romantic child I'd imagined; even if (or especially because) the child didn't match the ideal, my love for him would. But now I wondered: was this acceptance instead based on a "fond illusion of my heart" (Wordsworth, "Peele Castle")? Was it a kind of denial, a refusal to help or even accurately perceive him? To question your grasp of your child is to suffer a great loss.

During those early days, I often found my thoughts turning to Wordsworth's descriptions of infancy and childhood and his poetry of nostalgia and longing. Wordsworth's writings on the loss of childhood innocence and of children themselves were newly meaningful and poignant to me in the aftermath of my discoveries about Benj. Before my experience with Benj, I had never really put Wordsworth's writing in the context of real children. Now, however, with a real three-year-old in my care and a sense of loss, anxiety, and grief pervading my days, poems I had always thought about (and written about, and taught) in the abstract, with an academic detachment, were suddenly relevant to my life in a way I could never have anticipated. My personal and professional life began to interact in such a way as to change both completely.

At the time that Benj's issues came to light, I was reading, rereading, and writing about two Wordsworth poems that had featured prominently in my courtship with Richard—"Nutting" and "She Dwelt Among the Untrodden Ways":

> She dwelt among the untrodden ways
>   Beside the springs of Dove,
> A Maid whom there were none to praise
>   And very few to love:
>
> A violet by a mossy stone
>   Half hidden from the eye!
> —Fair as a star, when only one
>   Is shining in the sky.
>
> She lived unknown, and few could know
>   When Lucy ceased to be;
> But she is in her grave, and, oh,
>   The difference to me!

"She Dwelt" is one of Wordsworth's enigmatic "Lucy" poems, about the speaker's love and loss of a mysterious, apparently invulnerable, young child. And it is quintessential Wordsworth: about something that was and is no more. The "Lucy" poems are poems of anxiety, fear, bereavement, disillusionment, disenchantment, about one condition suddenly being replaced by another. Moreover, they are about the loss of someone or something precious—inspiration, childhood, creative light—though perhaps only perceived as such by the poet. To lose Lucy is to lose something pure, innocent, unworldly, insouciant, and unself-conscious.

Both "Nutting" and "She Dwelt" depict the loss of a protected and sacred space of privacy and the threat of beauty and purity being violated when "the world" intrudes. They seemed to relate directly to my apprehensions about Benj's "becoming public" when he went to school, my concerns that he seemed odder outside the protected space of our nuclear family, my wistfulness about him having to leave the nest where he was understood, accepted, and cherished and become part of a larger world that might not appreciate him sufficiently or protect him in all his vulnerability. And now that the Benj I thought I'd known was gone, the elegiac nature of these poems had new force for me. Like Wordsworth's Lucy, Benj had led a rather isolated life before the evaluation process began. After Benj's inconsolable crying jag at the English Department party, we'd stopped taking him to big, noisy gatherings and parties. Friends of ours saw him when they came over for dinner or to spend the night on their way in and out of New Haven, but his exposure to other people had been limited. Now, with the outside world's judgments and prescriptions infecting our family, with the knowledge that we would have to have him formally evaluated in clinical settings, our peaceful happy private life, a life in which we—not teachers or doctors or therapists—defined his value and his identity, was gone. Benj was still his same sweet self, but my entire sense of him, of our family, of his and our future had changed.

Two lines of "She Dwelt"—"Fair as a star, when only one / Is shining in the sky"—had been used on our rehearsal dinner invitation to celebrate Richard's and my shining devotion to each other, but now, many years later, they took on an entirely new meaning. They exemplified what I had thought Benj was. It's what all parents believe their children to be: fair, bright, irreplaceable, the only one. And now my Benj appeared no longer unique but instead a type.

Just as "few could know when Lucy ceased to be," so very few people knew of what was happening with Benj. This was in part due to the fact that I have always had a tendency to protect people I love, especially my sensitive and vulnerable father, from unpleasant, sad, or disturbing news. A few days after the phone call from the nursery school, I sent the following e-mail to my father and stepmother in Japan:

> Dearest Daddy and Yasuko,
> Hope everything is well with you. We miss you! Your newest grandson is beginning to move around inside me and your first grandson is reading up a storm! He is also becoming a big fan of Pete Seeger.
>
> XXOO
> Priscilla

I continued to cast Benj's voracious reading as good news and to describe him as a fan of Pete Seeger even as I was being made to feel—by the Web sites I was consulting, the listservs I'd subscribed to, the books I was reading—that both his reading and his obsession with music were signs of a disorder rather than an enthusiasm or predilection. But I couldn't imagine telling my father what was really going on. Since my parents' separation, I had rarely shared worries with him, despite the fact that as a young child, I'd gone to him first, always. The rule was that Daddy was never to be disturbed when he was hard at work in his study, but to this rule there was one exception: we could always knock on his study door with a worry. He often addressed these worries in the persona of his *Sesame Street* alter ego Super Grover: "Do not worry, little girl, I will solve the problem." That was my father: zany, filled with energy and pluck, and never defeated for long, but despite or perhaps because of his lighthearted approach, I never felt that he would belittle me for my worries, no matter how inconsequential they might have been. Now, however, I had a profound worry, an unshakeable one, and he couldn't solve the problem and I didn't even want him to know about it. He'd survived the two surgeries a month earlier, and was doing better than expected, but he was still extremely fragile, and had lost his will to live repeatedly after his diagnosis. I honestly thought it might have killed him to hear of my child's challenges, that I was suffering, that our family was in crisis and know that he couldn't be there for me. And I felt that, as always, my role was to bring happiness and good news to him, not complication and worry.

But it wasn't just my gravely ill father and my beleaguered stepmother from whom I kept news of our situation with Benj. I told no one but my mother, my sister, and my brother-in-law. There were professional reasons for my silence. I felt that I couldn't let Vassar know or they might not hire me; my being a young mother and pregnant with a second child were already huge strikes against me. And a child with a severe disability? Moreover, I was less than two months away from Yale's dissertation deadline and thought that if Yale folks and my friends knew, the flood of concern, sympathy, and advice would be distracting and overwhelming. So I told my junior faculty colleagues, my students, my dissertation advisers nothing of what was going on with Benj; I pushed ahead, completing and turning in my dissertation six weeks after the call from the nursery school in New York. Richard told no one at all. I urged him to share some of what was happening with his two brothers, his aunts and uncles, his cousins, but he didn't until they heard hints via my mother almost a year later. And he urged me to tell as few people as possible, and out of respect for his wishes, I didn't tell even my dearest friends. On the one hand, his reluctance to share was due to his natural diffidence, his tendency to shun confidences and emotional intimacy. But on the other, his desire to keep things quiet stemmed from his uncertainty, an uncertainty I shared, about what there was *to* tell, a belief that there was no easy way to sum up Benj and our situation with him, that labels and capsule descriptions would lead to a reductive sense of who Benj was and a constriction of the possibilities for his life. We didn't want pity, we didn't want panic, we didn't want oversimplified explanations or unhelpful advice. We didn't want Benj exposed to "the intruding sky."

The genetics of developmental disorders had struck a blow to the heart of our mutual vision for our family. We'd wanted three or four children, but now we wondered not only whether we should have more children but also at how great a risk the baby already growing inside me was for his own problems. The happy news that we were having another boy—"It's nice to have brothers three years apart so they can be best friends and share a room, and then maybe we'll get a girl next time!" I'd written to my mother after the ultrasound in early January—now took on an ominous cast, as we learned that hyperlexia and developmental disorders were vastly more common in boys.

Richard and I shared this worry about future children, but we also experienced the discovery of Benj's condition differently, in ways that separated us. Most obviously, Richard had never felt the lack, the disorientation that I had. He had never felt anything was really amiss in his bond with Benj. So now he was looking at that bond, and questioning it, and questioning his own sense of who Benj was and who he was. That Richard had brushed off my concerns by explaining Benj's oddities in relation to himself must have only intensified the horror for him when he realized there was actually something wrong. That every book, every Web site, every questionnaire emphasized that there was an inheritable quality to the disorder must have been acutely painful for Richard, although he never explicitly spoke of it.

And learning about the genetics simultaneously reassured me, about both Benj and Richard, and increased my anxiety. On the one hand, the similarities between Richard and Benj were comforting— Richard had been successful in good schools, had friends, gotten married, had children. In addition, they explained aspects of Richard's behavior and helped me gain even more compassion for him. His brain worked a different way, and he had done amazingly well with his life considering. But I also wondered: was Richard, too, fundamentally incapable of sustained intimacy and emotional exchange, of the kind of partnership I wanted in a marriage? Is that what I had been feeling all these years but not quite acknowledging? Would he never "get over" his perfectionism, his reticence, because they were innate character traits? For so long, I'd chalked up Richard's difficulties completing work and his emotional withdrawal to grief over his parents' illnesses and deaths. I'd been overwhelmed with sympathy for him and a desire to give him the happy family life he had tragically lost. I'd believed that with my love and support, Richard would eventually complete his grieving for his parents and come more into the world. But perhaps grief had little to do with it?

At the same time, I yearned to comfort this man I loved so very much and I felt powerless to do so. I knew Richard was afraid, angry, mournful, but he wouldn't let me know the contours of his fear, anger, grief. I couldn't get him to open up to me. I had always been able to reach him, always. But now I felt completely helpless. I'd always felt a powerful desire to make things right for the people dear to me, and I didn't know how to make it better for Richard; that was very hard for me. I, too, needed support and a chance to share my feelings and fears, but I didn't want to overwhelm him with my own grief when he was so obviously suffering. So we never mourned the loss of our dream together. We never held each other and wept.

In "Michael," a poem about a father's loss of his only son, which Richard and I had always especially loved, Wordsworth writes that

> . . . a child, more than all other gifts
> That earth can offer to declining man,
> Brings hope with it, and forward-looking thoughts.

It was the loss of hope that so devastated me in those early days. "Am I even allowed to have dreams and hopes and anticipation for his life?" I wondered. When did hope become fantasy or denial? And what risk was I taking if I allowed myself to hope and then those hopes weren't realized? I didn't want to set my son up to fail. I didn't want to make my goals for his progress too lofty or my dreams for his future impossible for him to fulfill. I didn't want to expect too much of him or ask him to give me what he never could.

These lines from Wordsworth's paean to childhood bliss, the "Intimations Ode," kept running through my head:

> Whither is fled the visionary gleam?
> Where is it now, the glory and the dream?

My dream of Benj's happy life had disappeared.

> Questions, directions, warnings and advice,
> Flowed in upon me from all sides.
> —*Prelude*, III

THERE IS NOTHING LESS romantic, literary, or lyrical than the language of pathology, diagnosis, symptom checklists. As I read through these checklists over and over again, I was struck by the harshness, the crudeness of the terminology. And once the evaluation process began, more and more distinctly unpoetic terms were added to the list, as the problems quickly grew in scope and seriousness.

Although I was in the last stages of completing my dissertation, pregnant with my second baby, teaching at Yale, and preparing to give a job talk at Vassar, I spent my days and nights scouring the Internet for information on hyperlexia, autism, PDD, speech delays, placing phone call after phone call to psychologists and therapists, and initiating therapy with Benjamin myself. Even as I was making unremitting efforts to learn more, Richard retreated into himself, became more closed off, more fiercely private. I had many e-mail exchanges with therapists, I printed out articles, checklists, therapeutic suggestions, and ordered books, which I gave Richard to read but was never sure whether he actually did. As she always is in a crisis, my mother was supremely solid and reassuring. She was my staunch ally, and her determination and her energy were now wholly focused on supporting me in my quest to get Benj the help he needed; she called every friend or acquaintance she could think of who might know something or be able to help.

Benj's first evaluation was done by a top Manhattan developmental psychologist and speech therapist, whom my mother had found for us and we visited a few weeks after being contacted by the nursery school. Based on an hour-long "play session" with Benj and the information we gave her, her assessment was that he was "definitely not autistic" but he had a "severe expressive and receptive language delay." "But if the delay is this serious, how could our pediatrician have not seen a problem?" Richard asked, somewhat incredulously. "It's all too typical that he missed it," Dr. G responded. "He sees the child twice a year, the child is very high-functioning and gifted in many areas so that probably blinded him to the weak areas, and most pediatricians aren't trained to evaluate for these kinds of issues." She urged us to get Benj into three-times-a-week speech therapy as soon as possible. "You want to do as much as you can before he turns five," she admonished us. The sense of urgency was palpable, as was our despair at the time already lost, already wasted.

Every time we thought we had a handle on Benj's problems, we found out that another problem existed. Initially we thought speech therapy would be sufficient, but because of his "peculiar gait," the New Haven–area speech therapist who visited our apartment to evaluate Benj recommended an occupational therapy evaluation, which revealed severe gross-motor delays, moderate fine-motor delays, and a host of sensory issues. A small comfort to us was that because of the severity of his deficits, Benj would qualify for twice-weekly speech, occupational, and physical therapy sessions paid for by the state of Connecticut. The occupational therapist told us that Benjamin had abnormalities or deficits in his tactile (sense of touch), vestibular (sense of movement), and proprioceptive (sense of position) processing systems. He had a speech disorder, sensory integration dysfunction, motor delays. He was both underreactive and overreactive to sensory stimuli. He needed OT (occupational therapy), PT (physical therapy), SLT (speech and language therapy), SIT (sensory integration therapy). These harsh, ugly words and bland, cold acronyms soon became as familiar to us as the brush, comb, and mush from *Goodnight Moon* in our discourse about Benj.

> To me alone there came a thought of grief:
> A timely utterance gave that thought relief,
>   And I again am strong.
> —"Intimations Ode"

WE NEEDED TO SEE our pediatrician in order to get a referral to the Yale Child Study Center, which, by all accounts, provided the most definitive and comprehensive evaluations of children with issues like Benj's. Even though we'd already gotten him occupational and speech evaluations, we wanted a thorough developmental evaluation. We were very fortunate to even have this possibility open to us. Without that referral, we'd go on the two-year waiting list for an evaluation and have to pay out of pocket; with it, we'd get in within a few months and have the costs completely covered. I went into this pediatrician appointment with a complicated mix of emotions. On the one hand, I was determined to stand my ground and not let Dr. B talk me out of my concerns and give me false reassurance yet again. On the other, I felt a strong protectiveness toward and concern for

Dr. B and a good deal of anguish about the possibility of losing a treasured bond with him.

We deeply loved this man, and had cherished his role in our parenting and our lives. He had come to us with the highest recommendations from others with children in the Yale community. He was famous for his dynamic personality, his ability to calm even the most high-strung parent and soothe even the fussiest baby, and most of all for the way he approached each child in his care as a distinct and precious individual and got a genuine kick out of his patients. And on the first visit we'd had with him, when I was about six months pregnant, he'd won our hearts completely. He possessed a remarkable combination of intense vitality and deep calm. He answered all our about-to-be-new-parent questions with thoroughness, patience, compassion, and humor. He spoke glowingly of his wife of many years and with immense affection for and delight in his own, now college-age children. With a gleam in his eyes but a seriousness in his voice, he told us we were about to enter not only the most important but also the most magical time of our entire lives. He was so excited for us and with us. For reading in that last stretch of the pregnancy, he recommended a book called *The Magic Years*, and this title perfectly encapsulated his attitude toward childhood and our own experience with him. He had fun with Benj every time he saw him, even when shots needed to be given or tests administered. He'd laughed when Benj pooped on his hands while he was being examined and lovingly talked him through every stage of every exam. He helped us to see things from baby Benj's perspective, and shared with us funny and poignant stories of his son and daughter's childhoods. He calmed Benj's fears of sticks down his throat and bright lights with clever approaches—giving him a tongue depressor to play with, letting him hold the otoscope before using it on him, counting to twenty as he checked each ear. He not only adored but also lovingly respected Benj. He hadn't just been a doctor; he'd been a kind of "tutelary spirit" of our life as parents. He'd been so in line with our ethics and philosophy and sensibility. He'd supported us in our embrace of Benj with all his quirks and eccentricities. We actually looked forward to our doctor's appointments, because at each one we felt part of a charmed circle of love and appreciation and care of Benj and celebration of the wonders of children and childhood.

But this appointment I was not looking forward to at all. I agonized over how I could be firm and aggressive while still being kind. How could I get what I—and Benj—needed without suggesting or implying that Dr. B had failed in some way in the past? I so feared going in there and seeing him and having the magic of all of our appointments and our bond with him taken away and our relationship severed. He would become "the one who missed it"—and I never wanted that to happen. Moreover, I'd heard that his beloved wife was gravely ill with breast cancer, and I was so worried that I'd be hurting or burdening him with guilt or regret or sadness at this most difficult time in his life. I didn't want to seem as if I were accusing him of missing a diagnosis, and I also dreaded giving him the sure-to-be-distressing news that the Benj he loved dearly was not the healthy little boy he'd assumed him to be. But I needed him to believe me.

We hadn't seen Dr. B without Benj since my pregnancy, and it felt odd to be in that familiar room without the child we were there to discuss. As soon as we took our seats, I poured out the whole story: reminding him of concerns I'd already expressed to him, filling him in on the call from the New York City preschool, describing the hyperlexia Web site, telling him that the speech therapists and psychiatrists we'd spoken to had recommended that we get a full developmental evaluation at the Yale Child Study Center. He listened patiently and didn't interrupt once. He didn't seem rattled or surprised or defensive in any way. When I was finished, he nodded slowly. "Well, I do agree he needs the full developmental workup, not just a speech evaluation," he said. I was so grateful he was acknowledging the gravity of the situation that I let out a huge, audible sigh of relief.

"What do you think is most 'different' about Benj?" he asked. "Can you give me an example of what you think he should be able to do and can't?" I knew immediately how to respond. "Well, for instance, while we were sitting in the waiting room just now, a little girl said 'Hi Daddy!' when her father arrived. Benj would never do that. He just wouldn't." My voice quavered and tears stung my eyes. Dr. B nodded. He understood.

"We all know that Benjamin is a quirky little boy, an amazing, fascinating little person," he said. "And we also know that sometimes society is too quick to label someone who's different as 'disabled.' That doesn't mean that you shouldn't get him evaluated. Clearly you should. And you, and Benj, will be in good hands at the Child Study Center. They do great evaluations—beautiful eloquent reports, actually. They won't rush to label him." "That is such a relief to hear," interjected Richard, who had been silent up until this point. "Yes," Dr. B said. "It's going to be tough, but try to think of all this testing as a way to understand Benjamin even better than you already do, as an opportunity to learn about and appreciate even more your incredible little guy." Richard and I smiled tearily at each other.

"And some speech therapy will be wonderful for him," Dr. B went on. "He's so smart and he enjoys interacting so much; he's bound to make great progress. But while obviously we want to get these issues addressed, we also want to work on getting others to accept Benj the way you have accepted him."

Dr. B turned to me again. "What's your deepest, darkest fear about Benj?" he asked, in the kindest, most respectful voice imaginable. "That he's autistic," I replied. "Why does that scare you more than anything else?" he asked gently. Again I felt tears coming into my eyes and I gazed imploringly at him. "Because that would mean his brain was fundamentally askew, that he couldn't improve or get better or that if he could, his life would be essentially constricted and limited, and that he wouldn't have what I believe matters most in life: loving, intimate relationships with other people." Dr. B smiled. "This child has been given to you, Priscilla, for a reason," he said, gazing straight into my eyes with a look of steadfast belief and absolute confidence. I jumped up and hugged him for a very long time. His words felt like a benediction.

Dr. B could not have given me a greater gift than his intuitive belief that I would be able to help and make a difference in Benj's life, that simply to love Benj was thereby to "treat" him. He didn't scant the value of a clinical evaluation and he expressed his firm belief that therapies could help Benj live a more fulfilling life. But he also made it clear that the most important treatment for Benj was love. He set up the act of evaluation not as a cold clinical process or as an admission of failure or disorder on Benj's part but as still enchanted. All the questionnaires, the tests, the bubbles I'd filled or have to fill in or checklists I'd filled or have to fill out, were retrospectively and proleptically explained as ways to appreciate Benj, not to dissect him. This was so important. Evaluation and therapy and intervention were defined not as harsh and distanced and aggressive acts of interrogation and classification but rather as investments of love and energy, care and attention. Dr. B revived our romantic vision, but in a deeper way, in his office. This child is going to prosper from your caring, Priscilla, he told me. This is not about a label or a diagnosis. It's about both unfolding and preserving the mystery of his self.

THE FORMAL EVALUATION AT Yale Child Study Center was scheduled for two months later, but there was no time to waste. It had become clear that intervention would have to be pervasive, thorough, and not a quick fix. We were in this for the long haul. There would never be a time when we could afford to let up or relax our guard.

We secured regular therapy sessions with local therapists who came to our apartment to work with Benj. The therapists told us it was a good thing we hadn't forced him to chew or left him on his own on the stairs; he'd needed our protective gestures, our enveloping arms, our special accommodations. "You sensed, intuitively, that something was wrong, and you protected him," the occupational therapist said. "Of course, it would have been better if you'd gotten him help sooner, but it's not too late; there's still a great window of opportunity." His difficulties with chewing were attributed to low oral-motor muscle tone; he needed therapy—blowing bubbles, chewing on "chewy tubes"—to strengthen his muscles and essentially teach him how to chew. The first time the occupational therapist met him, she asked him to walk up stairs and he did so, laboriously, clinging to the banister with one hand and her with the other. But going down? He had no idea how to proceed. She stood a few stairs below him and asked him to "come to Nicole." He looked utterly baffled, then lurched forward and fell into her outstretched arms. His difficulty was due, she told us, to deficiencies in "motor planning" and "sequencing." He likely would have choked, fallen, hurt himself badly if we'd left him to his own devices, if we hadn't made the accommodations we had.

Some of this feeling of vindication Richard and I shared; we had been allies, if only in private, against my mother's insistence that if anything was wrong with Benj, there were only his parents to blame. I also felt vindicated vis-à-vis Richard. Both my mother and Richard had pooh-poohed the worries I'd periodically express about Benj, albeit for opposite reasons: Richard, a hopeful romantic, because he embraced eccentricity (and probably identified with Benj on some level), my mother, a no-nonsense pragmatist, because she thought our indulgent parenting was at fault. But I didn't want to waste any time on recriminations or second-guessing. We had so much to do. And finally, we were actually acknowledging and doing something about Benj's issues, and that brought some relief.

Richard and I began to do tons of "therapy" with Benjamin our-selves—hours and hours of speech games and physical exercises. The therapists gave us lists of recommended home activities for us to do with Benj and circled items in therapeutic product catalogues. I bought a small trampoline for him to practice jumping on every few hours, a big inflatable ball for bouncing on, kicking, and throwing to build muscle strength, endless canisters of play dough and bottles of bubbles, a step stool to practice stepping down and up on, tongs and clothespins with which to pick up small objects, beanbags to squeeze and throw at or into targets. I made him a "sensory bucket"—a plastic Tupperware container filled with dried macaroni; fuzzy pompoms; felt, satin, and nubby squares of cloth; gooey rubber animals; coins; and poker chips; using it helped Benj build fine-motor skills of re-trieval and gave him sensory experiences of touching different fabrics and textures. Benj and Richard or I would sit for hours picking up tiny objects with plastic tongs, sticking pegs into a pegboard, blow-ing bubbles, sipping juice through a straw. To develop his language skills, we'd ask him to put things behind, next to, in front of, on, under the table or the chair. We'd model choice-making and turn-taking for him, "Daddy, do you want the red book or the blue book?" I'd ask. "The *red* one, Mommy," he'd reply, ostentatiously taking the red book from my outstretched hand. Every time we spoke, it felt like an act of intervention. I became hyper-aware of everything I said and did around Benj, trying to model for him the correct phrase or reac-tion, calling his attention to me so he could learn from my example. "The book fell!" I'd cry; "I'm hungry," I'd say, swinging the refrigera-tor door open with exaggerated force.

My mother was fully on board, and she got Benj to do things that no one else could. She had an amazing ability to coax him into try-ing new foods. She formulated rules—"call me Grams, Benj, use my name!," expressed them in simple succinct phrases, and was consis-tent with them. He responded with alacrity and followed them obligingly. My mother was a strong believer in the Protestant work ethic; "Anyone can do anything if they set their minds to it," she'd always say, and her "If at first you don't succeed try, try again," became one of Benj's most comforting and effective mantras; he'd determinedly repeat it to himself as he attempted any difficult new task.

I began to keep a "speech journal" of every single thing Benj said and in what context; I typed the notes up weekly and sent them to his speech therapist and the Yale psychologist who was to evaluate him. I made an effort to understand every last thing he was saying when he muttered under his breath and to document it. All this painstaking attention to his (and my) every utterance and movement was exhausting, but the attentiveness and constant vigilance also kept me focused and comforted me.

Part of what I was learning from my research and from Benj's therapists was that because of his physical limitations (congenitally low muscle tone, weakness in his trunk and upper body, difficulty planning and executing complex movements) and his sensory sensitivities to noise and textures, Benj was not and would never be a lithe, graceful, carefree Wordsworthian child. Throughout his poetry, Wordsworth celebrates youthful energy, grace, and physical exuberance. Wordsworth's children are intrepid and heedless, adventurous and enterprising. The child Wordsworth "bound[s]" "like a roe / . . . o'er the mountains," "wheel[s] . . . about / proud and exulting, like an untired horse," and revels in his "glad animal movements." Wordsworth's iconic young child Lucy is "sportive as the fawn / That wild with glee across the lawn, / or up the mountain springs;" " o'er rough and smooth" she "trips along" and "never looks behind." Wordsworth's gang makes a "din" and "loud uproar"; their "bursts of glee [make] . . . all the mountains ring." Benj could not have been a member of Wordsworth's boyhood gang; that "tumultuous throng," that "noisy crew," "boisterous" group would have been too fast, too loud, too daring, too reckless for my son. One of the reasons he walked so unsteadily and tripped so frequently is that he walked on the tips of his toes, which I now discovered was a major red flag for autistic spectrum or other developmental disorders. Benj couldn't handle uneven terrain. And he certainly would look behind frequently to make sure someone was near to guide and help him. He couldn't jump, hop, or skip. Unlike Wordsworth and his buddies, who climb trees, skate across frozen ponds, and hurl themselves into the wind, three-year-old Benj had an intense fear of climbing, swinging, sliding.

And there was something else that held Benj back from impassioned involvement in life. The following paragraph, from Carol Stock Kranowitz's *The Out of Sync Child*, perfectly describes my anxious and avoidant son:

> Children with SI [sensory integration] dysfunction exhibit unusual responses to touch and movement experiences . . . If they are oversensitive to touch sensations (tactile defensiveness), they will avoid touching and being touched and will shy away from messy play, physical contact with others, pets, certain textures of fabric, many foods . . . If children are oversensitive or defensive to movement experiences, their feet will never leave the ground. They will shun playground equipment and object to riding in the car or elevator. They may refuse to be picked up . . . [this is] a problem with regulation, or modulation, of sensory stimuli. When children are hyperresponsive (overresponsive) to sensations, they will be "sensory defensive"—on alert and ever vigilant to protect themselves from real or imagined hazards in a scary and confusing world.

When his occupational therapist first gave us materials on sensory integration dysfunction, so much about Benj began to make sense. This was why he had never liked to be held or cuddled, and had always rebuffed physical overtures—he'd resist my kisses, stand a few feet away from me while I read him a story, and sit at a distance from me while we watched a video tape and calmly and methodically remove my arm from his body. This had hurt me deeply; I'd taken it personally. Now, however, I understood why he needed to do what he did.

Benj's sensory sensitivities, his need for cleanliness and order, his distaste for certain textures and for getting dirty, also explained his ongoing difficulties with food and his aversion to arts-and-crafts. He would cry out "Wipe wipe!" or "Paper towel!" whenever he spilled even the tiniest drop of food on himself and would not relax until he had been thoroughly cleaned. He shrank from anything art-related. "No draw!" he'd scream when I'd spread art supplies out on the table or floor. Many boxes of different-size crayons and markers, colored pencils, finger paints, and sheaves of brightly colored construction paper, all bought in attempts to entice Benj, sat on the shelves un-used. Therapy involved exposing him to various textures and sensory experiences—finger-painting, playing with shaving cream, or dig-ging around in sand or uncooked macaroni. He initially resisted, flinched, or recoiled, but we held our ground and coaxed him into trying. Essentially, we wanted to get him comfortable with being messy and dirty. Being, in other words, in the world.

In addition to his tactile defensiveness, another obstacle to Ben-jamin's full and easy engagement with the world was his striking sensitivity to certain sounds, or hyperacusis. Desensitization activi-ties included exposing him to "talking toys" and toys that squeaked or buzzed (each time a new one was introduced, he'd immediately flee to the corner of the living room), playing for him tapes of vari-ous sounds (violin, motorcycle, car alarm), and teaching him how to cover his ears in preparation for elevator buzzes and honking horns.

Benj's sensory sensitivities made it difficult for him to interact with other young children, and his inability to play with his peers was one of the things that pained me most on his behalf. In his first organized group experience with other children, a music and movement class we'd signed him up for right around the time we discovered the hyperlexia Web site, every time another child came up to him, he stiffened and/or moved away. He was extremely apprehensive about the noises and physical activity of other kids. The children's sudden, unpredictable movements and unexpected, often unpleasant sounds were threatening to him.

Benj's difficulty with reciprocal interaction was one of his most strikingly "unromantic" qualities. Although he talked incessantly, when he was first evaluated, Benj was incapable of conversation at even the simplest level. One of the primary reasons for this was his inability to understand the difference between "I" and "you." He didn't use pronouns correctly or say "I" to refer to himself until he was over four years old (I learned from our speech therapist that most children begin using pronouns at two and fully master this skill by age three). When the therapist would come with a bag full of toys and games, Benj would say, "What's in my bag?" or "Open my bag." "Open your bag, Sharon," Sharon would model for him. "I, Sharon (pointing to herself) will open the bag for you, Benjamin, to look inside."

Before we learned about hyperlexia, Richard and I would never have said that Benj had "trouble answering questions." Benj could effortlessly answer questions like "What color is that?" or "What's that?" or "Where's the bird in this picture?" And he could answer a slew of questions that would have confounded, stumped, or baffled not only most three-year-olds but many grown-ups. If you asked him, "What period is Mozart/Bach/Tchaikovsky from?" he'd instantly answer, "Classical/Baroque/Romantic!" and in response to "What's the capital of Nevada?" he'd triumphantly declare, "Carson City!" He gleaned this knowledge from his books, encyclopedias, DVDs, and Leap Pad programs/interactive books and cartridges. But unless questions had a factual basis or tapped into his amazing store of often arcane knowledge ("The highest instrument in the orchestra is the piccolo!" "Pluto is the planet farthest from the sun!"), he would either completely ignore his interlocutor or repeat their question with a smile. More open-ended questions, such as "What did you do today?" were even harder, and "What do you want to do?" and "How do you feel?" impossible for him.

The conventional strategies for teaching language to hyperlexic children were inherently anti-romantic, and what we were advised to do with Benj went against everything I'd wanted for my child's education. Although or perhaps because I'd attended traditional schools, I'd been strongly leaning toward progressive education for my own children. But the *Hyperlexia Handbook* told me to "expect rote learning and make it acceptable," and that "the language of problem solving—asking and answering questions—must be taught specifically." Instead of encouraging Benj to speak spontaneously, we were instructed to "teach scripts to tell the child exactly what to say" (*Hyperlexia: Therapy That Works*). Some of the most important scripts involved simple requesting: "I need help," "all done," "look at," "I want," "want more," "more please." Benj's not answering basic questions had seemed to us like a lofty refusal to indulge in petty small talk; we'd always thought he just didn't want to answer—that he couldn't be bothered. But now we were realizing he actually didn't know how to answer. So we modeled frequently asked questions and taught him appropriate answers:

"What is your name?" *"My name is Benjamin."*
"How old are you?" *"I am three years old."*
"How are you?" *"I am fine."*
"When is your birthday?" *"My birthday is March 16th."*
"Are you a boy or a girl?" *"I am a boy."*

We wrote out the questions and answers on note cards that he carried around and read to himself. Because his memory was so extraordinary, he was able to pick these up very quickly. The problem was that he memorized both question and answer and memorized them as a series. It took a while for him to drop the question part!

I knew that this scripted approach would work with Benj, but it was still so difficult for me to accept that the easy free flow of conversation would never come naturally to him. So even as he was making great strides, memorizing the expected answers and beginning to answer questions appropriately, I often wondered to myself, yes, he is learning how to "function," but is he really learning how to connect deeply, flexibly, authentically with others? Or are we just helping him to "get by," to "pass" more easily? Will he ever experience genuine intimacy? Will he ever be real?

This concern was one of the reasons why at the same time that we used scripts and patterned language, we gravitated toward the approach of Stanley Greenspan, a psychiatrist who pioneered the notion of floor time (getting down on the floor with your child and following his or her lead) and play therapy as treatments for children with developmental disorders. I happily embraced Greenspan's principles: to focus on emotions, to help the child to express his feelings, to encourage imaginative exploration and creativity.

Benj's speech therapist, who'd recommended Greenspan to us, told us that he had deficits in imaginative play, or "impaired play skills." I hadn't thought of play as a skill, but as soon as she said this, I knew she was right. Most children dress up in their parents' clothes, pretend to talk on the telephone, cook, do housework, feed, hug, and put a stuffed animal or doll to sleep. Benj never engaged in imitative pretend play of this kind. At the time he began therapy, his favorite "games" were tapping on various surfaces—the washing machine, glasses, doorknobs—with a pen or a xylophone stick to elicit what was, to him, a fascinating assortment of sounds, reciting with perfect intonation and expression a ten-minute "sketch" from a *Sesame Street* video, and arranging his Legos and blocks in complicated numerical sequences. Ever since he could read, brand names were more important than the toy they described. "Fisher-Price!" "Playskool!" he'd shout as he brandished his little people. He treated them as objects, no different from blocks. He didn't make them engage in activities, talk, kiss, walk around. But I'd thought that was just because he didn't want to, not that his not doing it signaled a deficit or problem. And learning that his lack of interest in my playful overtures was not something he would outgrow was both reassuring—I would never again take it personally—and saddening. But much stronger than my sadness at losing the relationship to my child I'd envisioned was my sadness on his behalf. I felt so sad for him. How much he'd be missing! My sister's and my immersion in fictions and our imaginative play had been such a respite from and buffer against pain and loss. It had both fostered and sustained the deep bond between us. And it had been the realm where we felt most fully alive, happy, and free. What would Benj do without that joy and sustenance?

Initially, the idea of play therapy seemed ludicrous to me. Forced, unnatural, the very term was an oxymoron. But I soon discovered that imaginative play could happen for Benj only if it was modeled in a structured way. He had to be shown how to build with blocks or Legos, have a picnic, act out scenarios with little figures. Once he had a basic routine down, we'd try to encourage slight changes or expansions of it. For example, the picnic game involved handing out plates and cutlery to the assembled "guests," usually his stuffed Big Bird, Elmo, and Cookie Monster, asking what they wanted to eat and drink, serving them, and cleaning up. Modifications could be offering different foods or inviting different guests, and each one was resisted by Benj mightily. At other times, I would sit him down with a Fisher-Price play set: a zoo, a school bus, a farm. At first, it was agonizingly difficult to get him to do anything other than hum or line up the figures. Benj was stubbornly resistant to this kind of work, and I oscillated between feeling frustrated by his unresponsiveness—I'd approach him with such enthusiasm and animation and there was nothing, nothing in response—and wondering why Benj needed to do the very things he simply wasn't wired to do. But slowly he began to, at the very least, repeat scenarios I had modeled for him (like having the farmer put the animals down for the night or feed them hay), and occasionally there were little hints of creativity: a pig wakes up early! The farmer goes to sleep in his bed. Before long, these little hints started to feel like big strides.

Overall, things were looking up. The results of the Yale evaluation, conducted by a psychologist over a period of three weeks in April, were promising: Benjamin did not "meet the diagnostic criteria for an autistic spectrum disorder"—primarily because he was so "warm" and "related"—and the language disorder and major gross and fine-motor delays the evaluator identified had already improved significantly by the time the report was written. As of July 1, I'd be an assistant professor of eighteenth-century English literature at Vassar. Although a year earlier I had been on the verge of a new career and life in New York City, in the wake of 9/11 and my discoveries about Benjamin, I retreated from change and risk. When Vassar made our family an extremely tempting offer—a plum tenure-track job for me and a guaranteed half-time position for Richard, in a location one and a half hours from New York City but in a safe and affordable pastoral setting—I jumped. We used some of the little inheritance Richard had received from his parents to make a down payment on a lovely, large family home just a mile and a half from the Vassar campus. Because Richard and I would both be Vassar faculty, Benjamin was admitted to the top-notch Vassar laboratory preschool without having to visit or be interviewed there and his tuition was significantly discounted. We felt so fortunate and so relieved. But now a new, huge challenge loomed for Benj, and for our family: the impending arrival of his baby brother.

She's happy here, is happy there,
She is uneasy every where.
    —Wordsworth, "The Idiot Boy," of a mother

THE NORMAL ANXIETIES OF a mother as the birth of her second child approaches—how will the older one handle the new one? how will she be able to love the second as much as the first?—were augmented for me by the fact that my older one had just been identified as having special needs that would make a new baby especially tough for him to deal with. I knew that the chaos and upheaval that an infant brings would be anathema to orderly, routine-oriented Benj. How would Benj, with his sound sensitivities, handle the loud crying? How could I do the hours of therapeutic work with Benj when I was sleep-deprived and nursing round-the-clock? How could I continue to give Benj the time, the attention, the unqualified devotion that he would need to flourish when there was another child to care for as well? Once the baby arrived, Benj would no longer be the "only one . . . shining in the sky" of our family ("She Dwelt Among the Untrodden Ways"). And how could I give the new baby the focused regard and care he deserved, the respect for his individual needs, when I was so wrapped up in caring for Benjamin?

I tried to prepare Benj with books such as *I'm a Big Brother* and Mr. Rogers's *The New Baby*. I showed him the tiny clothes he had once worn and had him help me wash and dry and fold them. We brought him with us to buy a car seat and diapers. We took him to a "sibling class" at Yale–New Haven hospital. I couldn't tell how much, if any, of it was really registering with Benj.

And then, in the last trimester of my pregnancy, we received some terrifying news. An ultrasound showed an "enlarged fetal stomach," and we were told that the baby might well have an intestinal obstruction that would require surgery immediately after his birth. The doctors even mentioned the possibility that there could be other associated anomalies (heart or urinary), and there were also concerns about the baby's growth rate. I was to be monitored carefully throughout the rest of my pregnancy. In the eighth month, I was put on modified bed-rest when my blood pressure went up, and had Benj join me in bed for reading and therapy activities. My PhD diploma was mailed to me, since I was unable to walk in Yale's graduation. A few weeks before my due date, our babysitter was hospitalized with a blood clot near her heart, and from that point on, Benj had to accompany us to most of my thrice-weekly doctor's appointments. While I was being examined, Richard walked Benj around the doctor's offices and hospital, counting doors, reading signs, in an attempt to soothe him. Benj began waking up in the middle of the night (which he hadn't done since infancy) and the reciting from videos increased in frequency.

But a week before the due date, our support team returned: our babysitter was declared okay, and my mother was back from a long trip to Europe and on call to come as soon as I went into labor. And, to our huge relief, labor and delivery of James were relatively quick and easy, and he was born pink and healthy and crying lustily.

From the moment I heard his first cry, I felt bonded to him. After he was washed and bundled up in the hospital blankets, the nurse handed him to me, and he immediately nestled into me. When I stroked his cheek, he nursed vigorously. When I cuddled him, he stopped crying. He gazed at me with huge dark blue eyes, "drink[ing] in the feelings of his Mother's eye," holding "mute dialogues with

[his] Mother's heart" (Wordsworth, "Blest Babe"). The first half hour after nursing him was a tense time, as we, and the team of pediatricians on hand, waited to see whether or not he would vomit (this would support the theory of a possible intestinal obstruction and the need for CT scans). But when he kept down that first feeding, there was such a flood of gratitude and relief. And when he was taken away for his first bath, or at night to the nursery for a few hours so Richard and I could get some sleep, I missed him terribly, and I always knew when he was about to return; I would wake bolt upright from sleep when I heard his cry—instantly recognizable amid the cacophony of cries of a maternity ward as he was borne down the hall toward my room. This was the mother-child bonding I'd always imagined.

But as soon as we got home from the hospital, a more difficult side to James's need for me emerged. He was what politically correct pediatricians refer to as a "high-needs baby." James was a crier, and a loud one; his piercing shrieks were very difficult to endure. He craved touch and the human voice. He couldn't sleep in the crib, because there was too much space around him; he'd fidget and fuss, obviously searching for some bulwark against the emptiness. The only way we could get him to relax enough to fall asleep was to secure him tightly in his car seat and fill every inch of space between his body and the frame with rolled-up receiving blankets. I had to carry him everywhere. He needed to be tightly swaddled and stroked and kissed and cuddled virtually nonstop. We called him our "little woodland creature," because he so longed for dens, burrows, nests. His neediness, his snuggliness were endearing, especially so given Benj's detachment as an infant, but they were also exhausting. Three weeks after James's birth, I developed a severe breast infection and fought through a high fever, shakes, and chills.

Benj, however, astonished us with his resilient adjustment to this strange new being in our midst. After hearing my mother exclaim "He's so small!" when she first caught sight of tiny James, Benj would say, "He's so small," over and over again, often as a kind of mantra when James was being especially difficult. He would also recite lines from the New Baby books—"Babies cry a lot," "Mommies need time to take care of babies," "Babies cry to tell us something"—to get him through tough moments. And at the same time that James's volatility made Benj skittish, he was also truly fascinated by James. He would kneel down next to baby James in his car seat or stand close to me while I held him and study his brother with contemplative wonder. A simple yawn or chirp or stir would elicit a delighted response from Benj: "He yawned!" "He made a sound!" "He's moving!" I gave Benj tasks to feel helpful and connected to James: ferrying diapers and singing to James with me. When I told Benj that I'd named James partly after the song "Sweet Baby James," and that Benj could sing that song to him with me, he was thrilled to have a baby we could sing the right words to—he'd always resisted when I changed "James" to "Benj" while singing it to him. Every time we got to "sweet baby James," he put a smiling emphasis on the "James."

James always seemed to calm when Benjamin spoke. So, one afternoon, I took an especially fussy James into Benj's room, and sat with him on the rocking chair I'd nursed Benj in. I gave Benj, who had just woken up from his nap, a pile of books and asked: "Do you want to read to James?" Benj said, "Read to James," opened the first book, and began to read, glancing up every now and then to make sure James and I were listening. Almost as soon as Benj began to read, James quieted down. There was an exquisite stillness in the air as Benj read from the familiar books in his throaty lisp. If Benj paused for too long in between pages or books, James would start to whimper. "He loves your reading, Benji. I think he wants more," I'd gently say to Benj. "Wants more," Benj would reply, and continue reading. Richard quietly stood in the doorway, videotaping the scene. Looking at Benj through the bars of his crib, feeling the warm weight of James in my arms, I felt such a sense of peace and happiness:

Love, now a universal birth,
From heart to heart is stealing,
From earth to man, from man to earth:
—It is the hour of feeling.
　　—Wordsworth, "To My Sister"

WITHIN FOUR MONTHS OF starting professional therapies and six to eight hours a day of "therapy" with his parents, Benj was age-appropriate for fine-motor skills and almost age-appropriate for gross-motor skills, and he'd made huge advances with his speech. He was cutting with scissors and stringing beads and going up and down stairs unassisted. He'd mastered all of the requests—"I want" and "please help" were the most important—and had even begun to generate novel sentences (sentences that he created on his own rather than repeating). He was asking lots of "What's that?" questions and understood and was starting to use "because," "if . . . then," and "how." He was beginning to say "yes" rather than responding with echolalia to express his approval or consent, and the echolalia in general had dropped off dramatically. He'd become much more adept at turn-taking and making choices. Richard and I were overjoyed.

But late that summer, we moved to Poughkeepsie, where I'd start my new job at Vassar, and Benj had to adjust to a new home, begin working with new therapists, and go to school for the first time—all within the span of one week. I interviewed many potential therapists and agonized over the decision. We missed the old ones terribly and worried about Benj's losing these people, to whom he'd become strongly attached. We weren't sure our explanations to Benj about why we had to leave New Haven made sense to him. How confused and disoriented must he be feeling? Would he continue to make the same amazing progress without these two magnificent therapists who had connected deeply to him and who understood so well how to motivate and inspire him? What if all the progress of the past six months was to be undone? Or if he were to stall in his growth, no longer making the big strides he had been? Had I made the right decision in moving the family to Poughkeepsie rather than to New York City, where there was a much bigger pool of schools, doctors, and therapists to choose from?

We had a new pediatrician, Dr. P, who was far less congenial than Dr. B. This doctor, who'd come highly recommended by other Vassar professors and whose son had a diagnosis of Asperger's, warned us sternly against the Vassar nursery school we already had Benj enrolled in—"they'll never accept him or make you feel comfortable," she said—and subjected us to a barrage of rapid-fire questions whose answers she already seemed to know in her smug certainty: "Does he like trains?" "He hates sweets, right?" "Is he afraid of supermarkets?" She was right less than half the time. She also issued confident pronouncements about what "children like Benjamin" (a phrase that always sent a shiver up our spines) would do, fear, develop into. As quickly as we could, we switched to a different doctor in the practice.

We moved into our new house two days before Benj was to start school. James was two months old and hardly sleeping at night. In the days leading up to the move, I'd written Benj a little story about moving, and he read and referred to it frequently, repeating comforting phrases to himself: "We will bring all of our books and toys, our pictures and furniture to the new house"; "The new house will be a wonderful home for our family." On moving day itself, and in our first days in the new house, he surprised us with his chipper, upbeat attitude. He cheerfully read the movers' names off their tags and counted the boxes. Once we arrived, he showed lots of excitement and curiosity about his new environment. He loved the big new house with lots of rooms to explore and a thirty-foot kitchen-living-dining room to run up and down, and the fact that he and James each had a room of their own (in the apartment, James had slept in our room).

But as soon as school began, so did the troubles. I'd told the pre-school's director about Benj's developmental history, and given his teachers the Yale Child Study Center report and reports by his occupational and speech therapists. But even with this preparation, the first few weeks at the nursery school were torturous. Every day I heard reports of all the difficulty the staff was having with Benj, who was unable to make his feelings clear to them and who resisted many activities mightily or simply withdrew in silence. Benj would approach another child by reading the logo on his baseball cap or reciting a sequence of dialogue from a *Sesame Street* episode, and the child would just stare blankly at him. Benj, in turn, would stare blankly when a child greeted him with an enthusiastic "Hi!" or "What's your name?" "Do you want to play?" a child would ask, and when Benj ignored him or occasionally replied, "You want to play," the other child would look perplexed, ask again, "No, do YOU want to play?" and eventually walk away in confusion or frustration. The teachers, too, seemed to be perplexed by Benj; they didn't know how to reach or help him. Two weeks into the school year, we were summoned to a meeting with the teachers and the school's director and it seemed there was a real chance that he'd be asked to leave the school. Had Dr. P been right?

But through extensive discussions, daily conversations and e-mailing with the staff, and with the support of Benj's wonderful new occupational and speech therapists, who worked with him in school as well as at home, the teachers eventually figured out ingenious ways to reach Benj through his strengths and to use those strengths to address or overcome his weaknesses. One of his teachers got around Benj's resistance to wearing a smock during art time by making up a game that broke down putting on the smock into a fun series of rhythmic actions and musical rhymes. The teachers helped facilitate peer interactions by having Benjamin read stories to his classmates, hand out name tags, be the number counter in bingo games, and man the cash register in the pretend store. During a theme unit on the brain, the teachers had the kids form a long line with Benj at the end: the kids were each neurons and Benj was the brain. They handed the first child in line a note, and that child passed it to the next child, who passed it to the next child, and so on. When the note reached Benj, he was told to open and read it to the others.

Nonetheless, concerns remained; Benj was too reticent, he withdrew and wandered too frequently, he was unreachable at crucial moments. At my request, the Yale psychologist consulted with his nursery-school teachers, and in late October, she sent me the following report on her conversations with them:

> They have seen significant improvement in Benjamin since the beginning of the year, but they continue to be worried about his tendency to withdraw and his wandering when someone is not able to be with him . . . I told her I thought that Ben could learn to make choices of activities when he begins to wander . . . I also told her I did not think it was the worst thing in the world for Ben to wander at some points during the day. [They] asked me what goals they should have for Ben. I said to form relationships with his primary teachers, to continue to develop imaginative play skills, and to feel and express his feelings in ways that the teachers can understand him.

I was so grateful for her advocacy, and her words reminded me of one of Wordsworth's most famous poems:

> I wandered lonely as a cloud
> That floats on high o'er vales and hills,
> When all at once I saw a crowd,
> A host, of golden daffodils . . .

The poet's solitary wanderings are what enable him to be surprised by natural beauty, and his discovery sustains and inspires him in future moments of solitude:

> . . . oft, when on my couch I lie
> In vacant or in pensive mood,
> They flash upon that inward eye
> Which is the bliss of solitude;
> And then my heart with pleasure fills,
> And dances with the daffodils.

It was true that if Benj was by himself, left completely to his own devices, he was often lost in a bad way, and that he needed constant pulling back into meaningful interaction. He could happily spend all day by himself, engaged in seemingly "unproductive" activities— drumming on the furniture, reciting or humming to himself, rolling a ball or marble along the floor. But at the same time that I knew the teachers were right to coax him into the group, I also felt that sometimes Benj simply needed to be alone. And I sensed that many of his ostensibly perseverative activities were actually helpful coping mechanisms or exciting explorations for him. I had his occupational therapist observe him in the classroom at school, and she agreed with me that sometimes he just needed a little private time to "reorganize himself" and that what seemed like aimless wandering or pointless activity was actually useful for him. She wrote to his teachers: "At times, Benj appeared to become overstimulated in the classroom. He would leave an established play area and wander. These breaks are most likely a way for Benj to regroup and prepare himself to engage in the tasks at hand . . . These breaks away give Benj time to process the activity and prepare him for ongoing participation." Although the occupational therapist didn't say this, I could also tell that in his time away Benj was investigating, exploring really, the sounds things made, playing around with tempo, rhythm, and volume—that what looked to a teacher or parent's eye like goofing around or wasting time might actually have some deeper, satisfying meaning or purpose for him.

With the occupational therapist's advice and support, and my suggestions, the teachers figured out a good balance between trying to integrate Benj into the larger group and giving him the space he needed to be on his own:

> Not seldom from the uproar I retired
> Into a silent bay, or sportively
> Glanced sideway, leaving the tumultuous throng,
> To cut across the image of a star
> That gleamed upon the ice.
> —*Prelude*, I (Wordsworth about himself as a boy leaving his
>   group of friends)

Hearing stories about him from his teachers and therapists and watching him myself, I found myself often overcome with admiration for Benj. For his courage, his perseverance and determination, his openness to instruction. For, as his teachers put it in their November report, "the way he bravely accepts the little challenges he's given every day (putting his coat on a hook or getting a friend to help him remove his smock)." For the way he coped with all the novel challenges his therapists presented to him: a noise-making toy, a cup to drink from, a game whose rules he couldn't understand. For the way he painstakingly worked to master conversational language (his speech therapist told us that he was learning to speak in the way that a non-native speaker would—he was having to unscramble everything). When I thought about what was actually going on in Benj's brain and nervous system, it seemed incredible how well he was doing. How difficult must every single day be for him? So many demands to contend with, so many new situations to respond to. How amazing that he was as buoyant and optimistic as he was! He was always teachable and willing to try. And when he was happy, no one was more incandescent.

Thank goodness school was going better for Benj, because I was hanging on by a thin thread trying to manage all the details and meet all the demands of our new life. Richard and I had both started teaching just three days after the move, and those first weeks were filled with a seemingly endless train of meetings, parties, orientation sessions, get-to-know-you coffees or lunches with all my new colleagues. We were getting the hang not only of Vassar but also of Poughkeepsie: figuring out where to buy groceries, sneakers for Benj, office supplies, investigating new dentists and doctors, finding a dry cleaner, a bagel store, a pharmacy. We had no time to unpack anything but the essentials, and I was continually rummaging through boxes to find a book I needed for a class, stationery I needed to send a thank-you note, medical records for our new doctors. The house was a recently built one, and there were many kinks to work out: leaks, problems with the sewer, appliances and outlets that didn't work, a wasp infestation on the deck. Every night I'd look around at the many boxes still to unpack, the pictures still to hang, the empty spaces where new furniture was needed, and think: "It'll be at least a year until we're settled in here." There was no breathing room.

That late fall and winter seemed like one giant blur of overwhelming fatigue and illness. Richard and I were both teaching freshman English and had loads of papers to grade, and three of my five classes that year were ones I had never taught before so I was generating syllabi and lesson plans from scratch. Benj got strep throat and two bad colds within the first month of school, and the whole family came down with a flu (despite having dutifully gotten the flu shot) we were unable to shake for weeks. James was up at least three times every night, and Richard and I were exhausted. Wordsworth's vision of maternal bliss and infant joy had never seemed so idealized or inaccurate. I never saw my fussy little James as either a philosopher or a prophet. An angel, perhaps, but also, especially after the third waking of the night at three a.m., a little devil! I was so tired I would have delusions in the middle of the night, waking up from sleep to chastise Richard—"You left James on the bureau—you've got to get him before he falls off!" Every day was a struggle to keep all the details straight. I led class discussions bleary-eyed on two hours of sleep, pushing through blinding fatigue on days when the room of faces swam in front of my eyes, snuffling and sniffling and croaking my way through class as I contended with endless colds caught from the kids, rushing home in between classes to nurse. The students saw the spit-up on the lapels of my blazers, a nursing pad falling out of my blouse onto the seminar table, my wet hair because I had to take a second shower minutes before leaving for work after James spat up in my hair. And although they were usually very sweet and understanding, I felt harried and scrambling all the time.

One night in mid-November, I rushed home from class to nurse four-and-a-half-month-old James before heading out to an evening English Department event, a reading by a visiting author followed by dinner at a local restaurant. I was sitting in the glider, drinking cocoa—the only source of caffeine I allowed myself—and when James moved suddenly, I spilled some on his arm. He let out an ear-piercing shriek; his arm instantly turned blood-red and wrinkled up; skin hung off in sheets. Benj came running, and when he saw James's damaged skin, screamed, "Will James's arm fall off?" over and over again in anguish.

We rushed into the car to drive James to the pediatrician twenty minutes away. I was racked with guilt: how could I have been so clumsy or so stupid to hold a hot beverage while also holding tiny James? I had been trying to accomplish two things at once, and I had hurt James. I couldn't go to the department event; I called the organizer from my cell phone and left a message explaining what had happened. Fortunately, a soothing cream assuaged James's pain, and the burn left no noticeable scar. But my sense of guilt and overload continued.

Although sometimes it was unavoidable, in general we tried to keep Benj as sheltered as possible from James's cries and needs and ended up often with one adult per child in separate rooms. About six months after James was born, when we moved him into his own room, Richard and I stopped sleeping in the same room. James was up so many times a night—and when he awoke, he screamed at the top of his lungs until we picked him up—that I would either take James into bed with me while Richard got some much-needed sleep on the couch or Richard would sleep in a sleeping bag on the floor of James's room so he could quickly get up and pop the pacifier into James's mouth before his wails awoke Benjamin. Our major concern was Benj; we would do anything to make sure he got a good night's sleep. We were sick, run-down, exhausted, cranky. But in Benj's presence, we almost never betrayed any fatigue or strain. We were overwhelmed with relief that things were going more smoothly for him and absolutely determined to keep them on an even keel.

And things were undoubtedly going more smoothly. But as time went on, Richard and I were also becoming more aware of the pervasiveness and persistence of Benj's problems, and increasingly wondered about his "diagnosis" or "label." His reciting and echolalia had dropped off dramatically, but he still had significant trouble with pronoun reversal. His imaginative play was still very limited. The teachers at a special state-funded language preschool we were sending him to three afternoons a week described him as "Asperg-y."

As Benj's language became more functional, and subtle social and pragmatic deficits became more the issue, his speech therapist wrote up rules for conversation on a note card that he carried around with him. The note card read as follows:

Karyn's Rules for Conversation:

—stay in one place
—look the other person in the eye
—listen to what the other person is saying
—when the other person is done speaking, then you can speak
—reply to the question
—if you don't know the answer, say "I don't know" or "I don't understand"

Although internalizing these rules helped him to participate in conversations with more appropriateness, he would sometimes blurt out one of the rules in the middle of what was supposedly an easygoing chat, startling his interlocutor and reminding me of the programmatic nature of even his most seemingly offhand exchanges.

Moreover, with all the progress there also came more and more of a sense of the limits any progress would eventually bump up against, the intractable nature of his underlying brain chemistry. I was realizing that it was not that he was merely delayed and would "catch up" with therapies; it was becoming clearer and clearer that he was disordered and would need special help to master any new challenge. It was not, in other words, about checking items off on a list of activities he needed to master and then we were done; it was about accepting that everything that was a hurdle for any child would always be that much more of a hurdle for him, and for us.

And although, within a few months of beginning school, Benj was managing to "fit in" and had developed warm, caring relationships with his teachers, he still wasn't playing much, if at all, with the other children. He was happy to be with other kids, he commented on their play, and would interact with teacher facilitation/verbal scripts, but he rarely initiated play and couldn't sustain interactions for long.

While continually improving, his problems with social-pragmatic language (conversational exchange, literal versus figurative meaning, the expression of feelings, inference, abstraction, and idiom) were also coming more clearly into focus. He was beginning to seem even more "different" from other kids as their fantasy play developed and they were beginning to form real friendships.

I'd started keeping a little journal of Benj's activities and my feelings about them, and one night I wrote:

> Can Benj ever be a real kid? Will he ever have a friend? I can't imagine him acting in a little play or wanting ice cream or looking forward to Halloween. I can't imagine him having a sleepover or camping out under the stars or sharing a conspiratorial laugh with a buddy. I can't imagine him saying "I love you" in a spontaneous, heartfelt way.

At times I felt sad because I feared Benj didn't want or need to connect the way I and others wanted and needed to connect with him. But sometimes I felt sad because I felt so strongly Benj's desire to connect, to communicate, and thought about how many obstacles there were for him in being able to do that effectively. Because I truly believed that he wasn't essentially disconnected. His speech therapist and I agreed that we could vividly see and feel his ideas and thoughts in his facial expressions and actions, and tell how much he wanted others to grasp them. He just needed a little help organizing those thoughts and expressing them successfully in linguistic form. And he needed others to express their thoughts and feelings to him in a way that was accessible and comfortable for him.

Although as a two-year-old, Benj would sit rapt for hours as we read to him, as he grew, he didn't much like to be read to—if anything had a complicated narrative, he would start to zone out, hum, or read his own book. So now, I connected with him most easily and powerfully through music. Every day, I'd play songs for him on my computer: Elton John's "Rocket Man," the Go-Go's "We've Got the Beat," the Who's "You Better You Bet," and the Grateful Dead's "Franklin's Tower" were some of his favorites. We'd dance to them, thump out their beats with pencils on my desk or on large books Benj would pull off the shelves, or sing along to lyric sheets I'd find online.

That first fall in Poughkeepsie, I invented a daily ritual of "the Mommy and Benj sentences." I sat and typed them; he stood stock-still next to me and watched, mesmerized, and as the words magically materialized on the screen, he'd read them aloud. Each day I'd use a similar sentence structure with slight variations to help him learn syntax, and sometimes I'd start the sentence—"Today at school, Benjamin . . ."—and encourage him to finish it: "played at the water table," "built a tower with blocks," "learned about apples," "made pumpkin stew." Benj almost never volunteered personal information or answered questions about what he had done or wanted to do, but somehow this format helped draw out more details from him and give me a little more access to what he was feeling or thinking about.

After a certain number of sentences were done, it was "time to print the sentences." Benj waited for the page with great anticipation, and once it was printed and I gave it to him, clutched it hot out of my printer in his hand, read the sentences over and over to himself and later to his father or babysitter. He kept the sentences in a large stack on his bookshelf and often read and reread old ones. I eventually hole-punched them and put them in a notebook for him.

I intended the sentences to be a kind of language therapy for Benj, but I also hoped that they'd help him gain a sense of control over his experience and give his days, and his life, contour and shape, meaning and definition. Sometimes we recapped what Benj had done that day, sometimes we previewed especially challenging things (like a doctor's appointment, new bed, change of routine) on the horizon. At other times, I'd use the sentences to address emotional dynamics like sibling rivalry or to underscore for Benj the sanctity of our family:

Mommy and Benj Sentences

October 22

I love Benjamin very much.
Benjamin is my son.
He is three years old.
James is three months old.
He loves his brother Benjamin very much.
James is only a baby.
He can't answer questions.
He can't eat Cheerios.
He can't dance or sing.
Benjamin can answer questions, eat Cheerios, and dance and
     sing.
Daddy is a wonderful man.
We all love Daddy.
He is very tall and he has black hair and blue eyes.
He is a very nice and kind person.
He loves Benjamin and James very much.
We have a wonderful family!
Now it is time to print the sentences.

I also saw the sentences as perhaps the most powerful vehicle I had to express my love to Benj. When I told him I loved him, which I did many times a day, I was never sure he even heard me or that the words meant much, if anything, to him. One night I wrote in my journal: "Does he know how much I love him? Will he ever know??" I wondered if he would understand and internalize my love better if it was expressed in writing. So every week I'd write a version of the following:

Benj and Mommy Sentences

November 17

Hi Benjamin!
I love you very much!
You are my little boy.
You are my favorite three-year-old in all the world.
I love to spend time with you.
I love to play games with you.
I love to read books with you.
I love to sing songs with you.
I love to write sentences with you.
You are a wonderful person.
You are sweet, and kind, and loving.
I am very lucky to have you as my son.
I am your Mommy!
I will always be your Mommy and I will always love you.
I will always be here for you.
I love you, Benji!
Now it is time to print the sentences.

Writing sentences like these, I'd think of Wordsworth's hopes for his young sister as she grows up, his belief that his love for her would reassure and comfort her in future years:

> when thy mind
> Shall be a mansion for all lovely forms,

Thy memory be as a dwelling-place
For all sweet sounds and harmonies; oh! then,
If solitude, or fear, or pain, or grief,
Should be thy portion, with what healing thoughts
Of tender joy wilt thou remember me,
And these my exhortations!
  —"Tintern Abbey"

Would my exhortations heal and sustain Benj through solitude, fear, pain, and grief? If I was in the moment with him, I could help and support him, but did he remember what I said, did he internalize it, could he generalize from it? Would my lessons stay with him? When he wasn't with me, would I still be with him?

And we are put on earth a little space
That we may learn to bear the beams of love.
　　—William Blake, "Songs of Innocence"

IT WAS ALWAYS BENJ'S unresponsiveness to others that worried me most. Perhaps this partially explains why the news of Mr. Rogers's death in the late winter of 2003 hit me with such surprising force. As children, my sister and I had adored the gentle, compassionate Mr. Rogers and the whimsical, imaginative world he created. Watching him again with Benj, I'd newly appreciated how ahead of his time he was in his emphasis on emotional intelligence and his respect for the uniqueness of each individual child. Learning that he was seventy-four and that he died of cancer within a year of being diagnosed only intensified my grief—my own father had been diagnosed with stage IV lung cancer at seventy-four, although six years later, he was still holding on. As I sat at my computer, scrolling through the tributes and eulogies, tears streaming down my face, it somehow felt as if the death of my childhood, the inevitable death of my father, and the death of my romantic dream of parenting were hitting me all at once.

During the news hour, I retreated upstairs to my bedroom to watch the tributes on TV, and came across an excerpt from an interview Mr. Rogers had done with Charlie Rose. At one point, Mr. Rogers told Charlie, "The greatest gift you can give a person is to be a good receiver," and my heart sank. That's it, I thought. Benj is not a good receiver. He doesn't kiss or hug back. He doesn't understand gifts and presents—in fact, he always calmly handed presents back to the people who gave them to him ("No, Benj, that's for you to keep!" they'd say). He rarely says thank you, he doesn't respond appropriately to the friendly overtures of his classmates. I thought of how many times a perplexed or hurt child had asked me, "Why doesn't Benjamin listen to me?" or "How come Benjamin never answers me?" or "Why doesn't Benjamin want to play with me?" Over and over again, I would hear some variant of the refrain "We talk to him, but he doesn't talk back." Will people continue to give to him, I wondered, if he doesn't seem to acknowledge what, or that, they've given? At what point will the other kids give up on him? Can he receive all the love and nurturing and lessons we want to give and share with him? Is our giving to him in vain? Perhaps what was most unbearable was the thought that no matter how much love and affection and tenderness I showered on him, it would not stick, not make an impact, not support or uphold him.

A few weeks later, we celebrated Benjamin's fourth birthday at the Mid-Hudson Children's Museum in Poughkeepsie. This was the first party he'd had that involved other kids, and all the children from his nursery school class were invited. Because Benj already knew and loved this small, hands-on museum full of interesting gadgets, and because the party would be mostly unstructured—the kids would be allowed to roam freely through the exhibits, only gathering as a group at the end—I'd thought a party there wouldn't demand too much of Benj in terms of novelty or interaction. I thought it was our best bet for a successful event.

Benj was incredibly excited and happy as we drove up to the museum, and while he didn't take the gifts thrust at him by the arriving kids or respond much to their greetings, he smiled broadly and scampered off happily with his father and the other parents and kids to explore the exhibits. After an hour or so, which I spent alone downstairs in the party area, setting up the long table with plates, hats, napkins, cups, and paper blowouts, receiving the pizza delivery, and making the goody bags, the children trooped downstairs for the food and cake. Their happy shouts and excited faces indicated to me that they were having a good time. Relieved, I poured apple juice into their cups, asked whether they wanted plain or pepperoni pizza, passed bowls of popcorn and pretzels. As they began to eat, I looked up to see Benj sitting all alone at one end of the long dining table with all his classmates clustered at the other end. There he sat, perched on his birthday-boy "throne" (an oversize golden chair with a high back, to which festive balloons had been tied), the birthday crown on his head, with at least three feet of empty space and empty chairs on either side of him. The most unsettling thing was that he didn't even seem to notice. I felt a pang of guilt and chided myself for setting too many place settings. It wasn't necessarily that the kids had chosen to sit at a distance from him—they'd plopped themselves down in the first places available and his chair was at the far end of the table—but that didn't make it any less haunting. As the other kids chattered and laughed and poked each other and blew their blowouts into each other's faces, Benj sat alone with a distracted look on his face, tapping his blowout on the table, humming to himself. I immediately sat next to him and gestured Richard to the seat on the other side of him; the other parents followed suit and quickly took the remaining chairs, filling in the space between Benj and the other children. Benj was quite tractable in many ways: with some coaxing from me, he put on his Blues Clues party hat (the first time he'd ever been able to tolerate the string under his chin), with a little help from his father he blew out his candles. He even took a bite of cake, which he'd normally refuse. But I couldn't get that image of little Benj—high on his throne, resplendent in his birthday-boy specialness, but utterly and entirely alone—out of my head.

And then I was feverishly handing out goody bags, exchanging pleasantries with all the other parents and kids as they packed up to go. The last family left, and I let out an audible sigh of relief that we had survived with no major moment of anxiety or awkwardness. We gathered up the presents in bags, put them in a large shopping cart, and went outside onto the porch that wrapped around the building. Below us, the other children and their parents were piling into their cars, turning around to shout last thank-yous and good-byes and wave to us on our perch. Benj got to the ramp, down which I began to push the shopping cart full of presents, and froze. He began to whimper and moan, "No ramp, no ramp." I saw his face turning red and heard his volume rising. As I smiled broadly and nodded and waved cheerily to the departing cars, I gripped Benj's hand hard and whispered through clenched teeth: "It's okay honey, I'm going to hold your hand, you're not going to fall, please don't worry, you can do this, Benji." I prayed that his meltdown wasn't too noticeable to the kids and parents waving to us from the parking lot below or from their cars. As we drove home, I listened to Benj reciting the instructions from a board game he loved and thought to myself: "How much longer can Benj 'pass' or survive in the mainstream?"

Ever since we'd first realized that Benj had special needs, his schooling had been our primary concern, and the experience at his birthday party greatly intensified this anxiety. We'd been told again and again—by Benj's teachers, therapists, and doctors—that given his difficulties with noisy environments and large groups, and his oddities, no conventional public school classroom could work for him. We feared that, in public school, he might end up lost, overwhelmed, and bullied in a large mainstream classroom or isolated in a self-contained special-education classroom. Moreover, Richard had a strong aversion to public school; he'd attended them for much of his childhood and had always felt like the oddball or the geeky smart kid. "I was bored and I was misunderstood," he said. "Benj has to be somewhere where he isn't mocked for loving math, where he can find like-minded friends." But would any private school take a chance on him?

The more information-gathering I did that spring—I talked to or e-mailed with everyone I possibly could think of who might be able to help us sort out the school options for Benj—the more I realized that the school district our house was zoned for just wouldn't work for Benj: its elementary school was a little rough around the edges and its middle and high schools were too large. After living in a series of small, impersonal rental apartments since we began graduate school, we had been so happy to find our house, an unusual three-story Arts and Crafts–style house on two and a half wooded acres; it was a five-minute drive from the bustling Vassar campus but felt private and countryish. "A perfect compromise for P the city mouse and R the country mouse!" we'd told our friends and family when we'd found it. The idea of selling our new house and moving yet again was both sad and daunting, but I wanted to ensure that Benj would have an appropriate school. We never settled in or fully dedicated ourselves to our new house—never hung our paintings, never unpacked completely, never did the built-in bookshelves or cabinets we'd planned—because we just weren't sure that it could be our home in the long run. Once I identified the most promising district, I endlessly scrolled through real estate listings in search of a family home that we could commit to. A few weeks after Benj's birthday party, we went to look at the supposedly best public school in the area, but it felt cold and sterile, with too much of an emphasis on test scores and not enough on social-emotional development. The houses in that district were also more expensive than we could really afford, but in a moment of intense anxiety, we put down a deposit on a house, which we later forfeited when we realized we just didn't yet know whether that public school would be the right place for Benj.

THAT SPRING, AS I worried about Benj, I also worried intensely about his father, and the problems in our marriage grew more acute. Virtually our entire marriage had been consumed with caring for the dying or caring for the newborn and very young, with hardly any time where ordinary life just unfolded and we could be a (relatively) carefree couple. Then there were the rigors of life with a newborn and the maelstrom that ensued once Benjamin's issues were identified. And now Richard and I rarely spent any time together where we weren't either taking care of the kids or discussing the kids. We never went out together as a couple; we didn't feel that a babysitter could handle both children, and Benj especially needed one of us to manage his complicated nighttime routines. The limited alone time together we did have, we spent watching sports or movies on television, and even then Richard always had a book or his computer on his lap.

But the problems were much more grave than those of the typical young couple exhausted and harried by two young children, or even the strains on a marriage often caused by a special-needs child. After his mother's death and even more after the revelation of Benj's issues, Richard's perfectionism and tendency toward isolation and emotional withdrawal had worsened dramatically. Especially after we moved to Poughkeepsie, work on his dissertation slowed, as library books and note cards piled up and sentences and pages went unwritten. He'd sit at his desk all day, reading, taking notes, reading more, and never really putting his thoughts and ideas into sentences, paragraphs, pages, chapters. As he became less and less productive (one by one, all of our graduate school compatriots either left academia or turned in their dissertations and got academic jobs and he was the only one who had done neither), he withdrew even more from the world and from the people who loved him. He let phone calls and e-mails from his friends, brothers, his aunts and uncles, his dissertation advisers go unanswered, so I kept up ties with them on his behalf. Just as he had shunned social interaction and raced off after class in those early days of graduate school, now he would hurry back to his books or his computer screen as soon as his duties with the children were over or he had put them to sleep at night. He rarely smiled, unless he was with the children, who always brought out the warmth, the playfulness, the deep reserves of love in him.

I did everything I could possibly think of to help him and to protect him from the judgments and frustrations of others. I'd offer to brainstorm with him or edit pages or take notes, but he wouldn't ever take me up on my offers; he was reluctant to surrender any control over his work, to delegate, and perhaps to let me see how little was actually getting done. He had never been especially demonstrative, but he'd always responded to my affectionate gestures with warmth and receptiveness; now he barely seemed to register them. And I so missed our intellectual exchanges, our discussions about our work; he wouldn't talk about his work, or much of anything, anymore, to me or to anyone. I'd fend off queries from his family members, students, friends: "Where is he?" "Why hasn't he responded to me?" "Can you make sure he takes care of this, calls this person, sends this card?" I defended him vigorously against others who were hurt or baffled by his seeming inattentiveness. Even more after the discovery of Benj's issues, I saw Richard's lapses as stemming not from character flaws but from brain differences. I knew he loved me, his family, and his old friends. Nonetheless, I was terribly worried about him, but he continued to deny that there was anything amiss. His unruffled demeanor, his imperturbable insistence that he was fine, made me even more anxious.

I told no one, not even my mother and sister, about what was going on with Richard and in our marriage. I so feared exposing Richard to the "intruding sky," the unsparing, relentless light of the world's scrutiny and disapproval. I felt that allowing others to know the extent of his issues would be to betray him. My role, as I saw it, was to smooth things over for him and clear the path for him to succeed in the way I knew he could and deserved to. I never wanted to complain or in any way publicly acknowledge that Richard was anything less than a joy for me. None of his issues were his fault. He was a treasure, just as Benj was. And I was very attached to the idea and the promise of our happy marriage and our happy family, and to tell anyone that it wasn't happy would have been somehow to break or spoil it, taint it. I wanted to preserve it in its purity and beauty, not to sully it with negative words or doubts expressed to an outsider. And, of course, Benj's situation was still so precarious, and perhaps as he settled down and improved, and when we felt more secure about his future, Richard's isolation, procrastination, and withdrawal would at long last ease. I wanted to be patient and give him time. But I was so so worried and so very lonely.

As the school year drew to a close, however, wonderful developments with Benj distracted me, if only intermittently, from my concerns about his father. I began to hear of major breakthroughs in Benj's interactions with the other children and in his ability to communicate, each reported to me or Richard at drop-off or pick-up. Benj had begun wanting to sit on the potty at school, in imitation of his peers. He was zipping around the playground on a trike and calling out "This is great!" as he zoomed past. His teacher joyfully reported that Benj was beginning to tentatively join in some little girls' imaginative game on the playground. The game involved a family of dinosaurs gathering thorns for supper; he'd been watching the girls play it for a few days, memorized it, and one day announced, "Dino gets thorns," and brought some sticks to the girls, who received them with delighted smiles. Most gratifying, Benj had begun to regularly use "me," "my," and "I" to refer to himself! Richard and I could hardly believe it.

And a few weeks later, we were even more overjoyed when we received a glowing end-of-year report from his teachers:

Benjamin has made astonishing progress throughout the course of this school year. He has been able to achieve many of the goals we've set for him in remarkably short periods of time.

We continue to offer him new challenges and are delighted to see how far he's come. Long gone is the echolalia that was his means of verbal communication at the beginning of school. He not only answers questions, he comments on things that are happening around him and clearly makes his needs known. He has also become very comfortable with all of his classmates. He no longer appears frightened as another child approaches him, but enjoys an occasional hug and frequent interactions with his friends. We no longer see many of the behaviors that he once used to comfort himself (i.e., tapping). He occasionally falls back on old habits, forgetting that he's mastered a new skill (turning on and off faucets, for example). He sometimes becomes resistant when reminded that he can do it, but recovers quickly. It has been tremendously rewarding being Benjamin's teachers this year. We admire his remarkable determination and courage. These qualities will undoubtedly continue to serve him well in the future!

I immediately typed this report into an e-mail and sent it to my closest family members and friends, to all his doctors and therapists, current and past, to everyone who had worked with and loved Benj. The psychologist who'd evaluated him at Yale Child Study Center wrote back: "I have tears in my eyes; I am so proud." I had tears in my eyes every single day. Living with Benj was like experiencing an unfolding miracle.

Our gratitude for Benj's school experience and growth there was immeasurable. At the nursery school's end-of-the-year party, we presented his three teachers with three children's picture books—all special favorites of ours and Benj's—inscribed with notes of gratitude. In the first, *Louisa May and Mr. Thoreau's Flute*, we wrote: "To Amy, thank you for helping Benj discover his 'own inner music.'" In *Walking With Henry* and *Henry Builds a Cabin*, two books in a series about a bear named Henry Thoreau, which my aunt had given to Richard one Christmas, we wrote, "To Gwenn, thank you for walking next to Benj every step of the way," and "To Joanie, thank you for building Benj's confidence."

> Then did the boy his tongue unlock,
> And eased his mind with this reply . . .
>> —Wordsworth, "Anecdote for Fathers," a father
>> about his son

From this point on, every week brought a new breakthrough in Benj's ability to express his needs and feelings and in his emotional development. It was only a week or two before he started school the previous fall that he'd begun to be able to say "yes," and at that time he'd had hardly any spontaneous complete expressions. Benj was at last saying things like "My ear hurts," "I'm hungry," and "I like this"; these ostensibly simple statements had the force of revelation for us. He was requesting beautifully: instead of an urgent "Open! Open!" it was now "I need you to help me open the straw, Mommy"; instead of a vehement "Fix it!" it was now "Daddy, can you please straighten out my sheet?" Now when he neared tears because he thought he might not be able to do something, instead of totally breaking down, he'd say, "I'm worried," or ask in a shaky voice, "What if I can't do it?"

Learning or recalling a useful and comforting phrase or idiom made all the difference in containing his anxiety; having these at hand helped him cope with all sorts of situations and worries. One time, he was eating ravioli and he was getting a little frustrated that he couldn't get it on his fork. I looked over at him and said, "If at first you don't succeed . . ." and he immediately brightened up and his mouth was full and he was chewing and he was grinning and he couldn't wait to swallow and chime in with "Try, try again!" And he did try again, and he got that ravioli in his mouth. A few days later, his speech therapist reported in an e-mail: "Benj and I talked a bit about what to say when you forget something. At one point he couldn't remember what he had to drink at lunch and started to get upset (looked like he might cry). I said, 'It looks like you forgot. It's okay. Just say, "Oh, I forgot" or "I can't remember what I had!"' He looked so relieved and instantly returned to his happy, enthusiastic self."

It was wonderful for me and Richard to see the slow-motion un-folding of Benj's ability to put his thoughts into language. We could see him trying to think of the rule, the convention, the right word or phrase, the necessary information, and then he would remember, he would piece it together, and he would be so pleased when he conveyed what he was feeling or thinking. It made us, two English professors for whom language had always come almost effortlessly, newly ap-preciative of the wonders of language acquisition. We marveled at each little step forward together, we laughed over Benj's funny habits and ways, we strategized both short-term and long-term, and that kept us connected to each other.

Once Benj learned the conventions of social interaction, he actu-ally became extremely polite and gracious. He now never failed to say "hi," "good-bye," "excuse me," and "have a nice day," always with sunny deliberateness. He never forgot "please" or "thank you" and reminded us to say them when we forgot. He unfailingly praised oth-ers for their efforts. "Good throw, James!" he'd cry when baby James awkwardly heaved a ball toward him. We also helped Benj develop more effective ways to access and express the empathy we'd sensed he felt but hadn't been able to productively express. Benj had always been very sensitive when other children were upset. One of his teach-ers called this his "Howard Cosell" imitation as, like a sportscaster might, he narrated the scene [nearby] of the child who was upset: "Oh no! Hannah bumped herself! Hannah is crying!" Now he was learning how to channel that fellow-feeling into expressions of concern and offers of help and support. We told him that if someone cries or says they're hurt, you can ask, "Are you okay?" or hug the person or kiss the place they're hurt to make it better.

That June, as James's first birthday approached, I began to feel intensely vigilant of his development. Although he was walking and his motor development seemed right on track, he wasn't pointing or waving and he didn't seem to understand much of what I would say to him. One afternoon, I was on the phone with my mother, crying with worry about James, when Benj, who I'd thought was reading in the other room, suddenly appeared by my side. He asked, "Are you okay, Mommy? Don't cry Mommy," put his head on my shoulder, and then lay down on top of me on the sofa and put his arms around me. I began to cry even harder, but this time for joy. I explained to Benj the concept of "crying for happiness." Just a few days later, James said his first words—"cup" and "Bej (Benj)"—and his language development was smooth from that point on. Soon he was walking well, climbing everywhere, going up and down stairs.

And Benj continued to astound us with his progress. His work in occupational therapy had made him far more able to tolerate the loud noises and boisterous play of his peers, far more open to different foods and sensory experiences, far more able to participate in vigorous rough-and-tumble play with other children. At a classmate's birthday party, he gobbled up pizza, potato chips, cake, and chocolate with gusto, stood in the kiddie pool and calmly and good-humoredly endured horrendous shrieking and splashing from an especially vivacious little girl, batted balloons around with two or three kids. At one point, he ran up to a little boy who'd been absent from camp for the past week and said with excitement: "Lincoln, you came back!" and "Where were you, Lincoln?" As the *I*s and *you*s finally straightened out, spontaneous verbal interactions with peers were becoming possible.

By the time he began school that September, he was speaking

very fluidly and fluently, with complex sentence structures and logic, and no real errors except for mixing up "he" and "she" from time to time. He'd developed the ability to speak with relative ease about his and other people's emotions: "I don't want to go upstairs"; "Daddy looks puzzled"; "Mommy, you're bugging me!" (this thrilled me!); "James looks worried!" A witty playfulness about the conventions of language also began to emerge. Passing a sign that read CROSSWALK, Benj asked jokingly: "What is a cross-run?" He'd pick up his juice box and read, INSERT STRAW HERE, then ask, with a mischievous grin, "What does *outsert* mean?" One morning, when dropping him off at school, Richard said: "Okay, Benj, I'm going to take off now," and Benj asked, "What does *take off* mean?" "Leave," Richard replied. "Well," Benj said, smilingly, "then I'm going to take on!" He turned around and ran toward a group of his classmates.

Benj was beginning to take great pleasure in his own expressiveness, marshaling and deploying adjectives and idioms with self-conscious glee. One day in mid-September I asked Benj, "How was your day?" and he answered, "My day was *fun*!" This was so astonishingly ordinary that it was extraordinary for Benj. "Exciting" was a word he especially loved. That Halloween, he cried: "It's so exciting that I'm wearing a Giants football helmet!" I called my father in Japan and had my stepmother hold the phone up to his ear so he could hear Benj. A few weeks later, his occupational therapist brought a Lite-Brite toy, and as the Lite-Brite went on, Benj said with excitement: "This is so exciting!" "This is awesome!" "This is incredible!" After encountering it in a book, "jumping for joy" became one of Benj's favorite expressions. At Thanksgiving dinner, delighting in the festive atmosphere, Benj asked me: "Can I jump for joy and you jump for joy?" Jumping had always been a challenge for him; he couldn't stand having both feet off the floor. But that day we jumped together, holding hands.

Thanks to the human heart by which we live,
Thanks to its tenderness, its joys, and fears,
To me the meanest flower that blows can give
Thoughts that do often lie too deep for tears.
——"Intimations Ode," final stanza

Children put everything into perspective, they remind you of what's important, you see the world anew through their eyes—Benj was suddenly making all these sentimental truisms take on an ever deeper resonance. He'd say, "I'm happy," when I gave him a chocolate treat, or "It's pretty" when we picked a flower from beside our drive-way, or "I can't wait!" the night before his school's pajama day, and each tiny utterance meant so much. It was such a triumph that he was doing and saying these things at all; a year earlier, all this would have been unimaginable. In our life with Benj, the simplest things—a "yes," a hug, a shared gaze—and the most common actions—walking up stairs, sipping juice from an open cup, drawing a stick figure—had extraordinary significance. I felt often how Wordsworthian Benj was; he took great pleasure in the "simple produce of the common day" (Wordsworth, Prospectus to "The Recluse," 55). And hearing that he was happy, knowing that he was excited and joyful, meant so so much to me.

Benj also began to ask almost metaphysical questions about iden-tity, the passing of time, and the nature of the future, questions that would have been unfathomable coming from him just three months earlier. Eating a snack one afternoon, he asked: "Will I be the same person when I am a man?" One night, when I was putting him to bed, he suddenly asked me: "How many minutes does it take to get to first grade, Mommy?" We talked about the number of minutes in an hour and the number of hours in a day, the number of days in a year and how many more years it would be until he was a first-grader. He then asked: "What comes after first grade?" "Second," I

replied; "What comes after second grade?" he laughed; "Third," and
on and on we went until we got to high school and then college and
then . . . "What comes after college?" he asked. I paused for a moment and finally answered: "Life." "What comes after life, Mommy?
What comes after life?" I was speechless:

———A SIMPLE Child,
That lightly draws its breath,
And feels its life in every limb,
What should it know of death?
    —Wordsworth, "We Are Seven"

As Benj developed more sophisticated language, he became inter-
estingly defensive about his identity and existence. The fall he was
four, Benj began to be interested in playing a version of charades. We
called it the "pretend game." The scenarios were usually quite basic:
I would pretend to stir a pot and put it on the stove—"cook!"; his
father would cry and hold out his arms to be picked up—"James!"
He loved to guess who we were but he didn't quite understand the re-
quirements of pretending. When it was his turn to pretend, he'd run
up and down the length of his room and delightedly exclaim, "Run-
ner!" or hop around chortling, "Rabbit!" before we'd even had a
chance to guess. After the "pretender" had completed his or her feint
and a successful guess had been made, Benj would always say with a
sigh of happy relief, "Oh, now you've turned back into a Mommy" or
"now I've turned back into a Benji." When we pretended to be different characters, if I insisted too strongly that we were really something
other than ourselves, he'd say: "And now we turn back: I'm a kid and
you're a *mommy*." He was always careful to draw the boundaries, to
signal when he wanted the free-floating associations to end. Once,
when his father was pretending to eat him up, like a gorilla eating a
banana, he cried: "No, Daddy, I am still in the world!"

He also vehemently resisted any kind of jocular nicknaming: if Richard or I would say, "See you later, gator," he'd retort, "I'm not a gator!" If we or a teacher or someone in a store referred to him in good-natured raillery as "buster" or "sir," he'd cry: "Don't call me buster/sir!" This, of course, stemmed in part from his need for control and his insistence on the literal. But it also exemplified his ability to articulate what many children feel but don't express. As a child, I'd often inwardly recoiled or groaned at adults who called me "little lady" or "kiddo," but I always swallowed my chagrin and smiled politely at them. Benj's frankness, his lack of a filter or a censor, meant that he was expressing what kids often wish they could say to adults: "See me as an individual, not as a kiddo or a little lady or a buster or a mister." Benj put into words what kids often feel when adults use pat, canned, impersonal, generic phrases or locutions with them; he talked back to them and said "no." He did it bluntly, often tactlessly, but there was a bracing honesty to his attitude. "I'm Benj," he'd always say. "Benjamin."

> My former thoughts returned: the fear that kills;
> And hope that is unwilling to be fed . . .
> —Wordsworth, "Resolution and Independence"

DESPITE BENJ'S AMAZING GROWTH that fall, anxieties lingered and new problems emerged. We had some difficulties with his pre-K teachers at Vassar's lab nursery school, who, while perfectly amiable, were a little less educated about developmental and learning differences and a little more concerned about how easily and smoothly Benj could fit into the larger group than his first year teachers at the same school had been. At my November meeting with them, they expressed impatience with what they saw as Benj's "dawdling" in getting his coat and shoes on and off. "He delays the others," one said;

"He disrupts the routine," added the other. I looked them square in the eye and in a firm, clear voice, I said: "Do you know that a year ago he couldn't hold a pencil correctly? Feed himself with a fork or spoon? Drink from an open cup? Do you know how amazing it is that he can get his shoes on at all given his profound motor delays?" They replied, hurriedly: "No, we hadn't realized quite how severe his delays were; wow, he has made great progress then." I said quietly: "Any time you get frustrated or irritated with him, try to remember how far he's come rather than how far you still want or need him to go. It helps. It's helped us." They nodded.

They also had issues with the fact that Benj shied away from some art projects. "He'll just shut down and refuse to do them," one teacher said. "He can be so negative; if only he'd try harder," the other sighed. At the same time that I shared their belief that Benj could do more than he thought he could, I thought to myself: does he really need to do every last art project? How much should we "normalize" him? How much should we try to make him conform?

As a child, I'd been very outgoing and social, and I'd had a relatively easy time in school, but there were a few things I was terrible at. I remembered dreading gym at school when somersaults—which terrified me—were involved and being mocked by some of my classmates for my trepidation and given a big, hard push by my unsympathetic gym teacher. I think I completed the roll, but was that really a victory? I've never done one again and the idea of them still makes me shudder. I remembered in second grade having terrible trouble with arts and crafts, because I didn't have the dexterity required for some of the projects (I still can't thread a needle), and my teacher calling my mother to school for a special meeting to discuss my "bad attitude." "Priscilla is disobedient and lazy," she told my mother; "No, Mommy, I just can't do it!" I'd insisted when my mother reported the teacher's remarks to me. I thought about how I could really have used a little occupational therapy, and a little understanding that there were certain things I just wasn't good at and didn't enjoy. Kids are expected to be generalists, but grown-ups are allowed to specialize and not have to do every last kind of activity. It is so hard to be a kid!

In early January, we tried a "therapeutic listening program" Benj's occupational therapist had been urging us to do for months, with disastrous results. The program involved Benj's listening to specially calibrated and orchestrated music on a Walkman with headphones several times a day; the purpose was to knock out any remaining sound sensitivity, improve his focus, and diminish his sensory issues. But instead of helping, the program made things much, much worse. His sound sensitivity became acute to the point where he couldn't stand the whistle of the tea kettle, the ring of our cell phones, the high-pitched chatter of other children. He was more distractible at school, wouldn't stop humming loudly, was more tuned out, less reachable.

Even in the periods of his greatest progress, there had always been some bad moments, days, periods, when Benj would do more reciting and demonstrate more tics and anxiety, but this time the regression was much more dramatic and scary. The worst and most problematic of his early behaviors returned. He began to echo more of what we said. He was doing much more reciting—the message on his grandmother's answering machine, *PBS Kids*, lines from a favorite book or TV program, with a goofy smile on his face. At times he spoke in a robotic and monotone voice, a voice we'd never heard much and hadn't heard in months, and had always hated (Richard would admonish him "no computer talk!," "no TV talk!"). He didn't answer a lot of questions. He mixed up his *I*s and *you*s, which had completely straightened out, to our great relief and joy, six months earlier. He toe-walked much more obviously. He showed some anxiety about noise-making toys, which he hadn't demonstrated in a good nine months. It was a huge regression. It killed us to think that something we had done to help him could have set him back. We feared the extreme sound sensitivity and the compulsion to echo and recite would not go away, and that the language setback would be difficult to reverse.

But after we took him off the listening program, just a week later, the reciting had dropped off to almost nothing, the anxiety had greatly lessened, and an amazing development with Benj's reading, and his growth more generally, was beginning.

> May books and Nature be their early joy!
> —Wordsworth, *Prelude*, V, on children

As his fifth birthday approached, Benj started to integrate what he'd learned from books into his daily life in useful and wonderful ways. From the time he was two, he'd loved to identify the different states on a map and countries and continents on a globe, and now he was using this knowledge functionally. "Uncle Sam will swim in the Atlantic Ocean!" he'd cry when Richard's brother mentioned an upcoming trip to Maine; "Your daddy lives on the continent called Asia!" he'd tell me when I addressed a letter or package to my father in Japan. "Now I am walking west!" he'd excitedly announce as he pointed to the compass he often wore on a string around his neck. He was demonstrating a new understanding and appreciation of idiom, slang, and metaphor and using ones he'd encountered in books in appropriate real-life situations: he'd say, "How cool was that?" when a football player made an especially good run and "Cut to the chase!" when he wanted his father to answer his question.

Even more exciting, Benj began to refer to story characters and their adventures and actions to explain his own feelings and experiences. He'd always had a terror of fire drills, so we'd either hold him out of school until the fire drill was over or one of us would go to school and take him away while the fire drill was in progress. One day that winter, as Benj and Richard were standing in the parking lot of his nursery school listening to the fire alarm from a distance, Benj cried, "Daddy, I am not afraid! Just like Frog and Toad!"—a reference to a story called "Dragons and Giants," in which Frog and Toad face down some scary experiences by telling themselves that they "are not afraid." Another day in the car on the way home from school, Benj said: "Mommy, I did not have confidence that I could open the ice cream. That's why I told my teacher, 'I can't do it.' But I did it! So now I have confidence! Like George!" I'd recently been reading him the George and Martha books—stories of two hippopotami best friends—and a few nights earlier we'd read a story in which George was on a tightrope and did great when he felt confident, but when Martha undermined his confidence, he began to fall. Then he said: "Mommy, I do not have confidence with my fingers sometimes." I told him, "Kristen (his occupational therapist) helps you with your fingers so that they can get strong and you can have confidence in them," and he said, "The more practice I get the more confidence I can have!"

Benj was also developing a great appreciation for and sensitivity to nature and the natural world. Like the child Wordsworth, he was:

> A lover of the meadows and the woods,
> And mountains; and of all that we behold
> From this green earth . . .
>   —"Tintern Abbey"

Through the large windows of our living room, he watched the birds, groundhogs, and deer in our backyard with hushed attentiveness. He studied leaves with intensity, collected stones and twigs, and pored endlessly over his animal, bird, weather, rocks, and ocean encyclopedias. Like a romantic poet, Benj truly found "a world in a grain of sand" (Blake) and a life in "flower and tree, in every pebbly stone" (Wordsworth, *Excursion*, IX).

He diligently and enthusiastically kept track of the changing seasons, months, and weather patterns. When one day he cried, "March is an in-between month, in between winter and spring. In March, winter is waning and spring is nigh!" Richard and I just looked at each other in astonished delight—we had no idea where that quotation came from! He loved to identify the type of rain falling when we went outside—drizzle, sprinkle, shower, or downpour—and to specify the exact nature of a cold day: "I need to wear my hat and mittens and boots because today will be more than chilly, it will be *frigid*!"

Benj's intellectual curiosity was finding more and more outlets and avenues of expression, and he was pursuing his interests with focus and fervor. He might have sometimes exhibited his enthusiasms in idiosyncratic ways—rattling off the names of the seven continents and the countries that comprise them, elaborating on the difference between cirrus and cumulus clouds, or explaining difficult chess moves to startled but charmed parents on the playground—but the enthusiasm was enormous and endearing.

But it was also precisely his glorious passion, his intense enthusiasm for things others might ignore or scoff at that caused me anxiety on Benj's behalf. Partly because of his inability to pick up on subtle details and nuances of social situations, Benj seemed extremely innocent and vulnerable. He was oblivious to peer pressure. He didn't understand the concepts of lying, manipulating, being mean to another person. He was uninhibited in the way he expressed himself, and not at all self-censoring. He became deeply distressed if he thought he'd done something wrong, and didn't pick up on others teasing him. His teachers and therapists always remarked on how innocent and sweet Benj was; one wrote in a report: "Clichés like 'He doesn't have a mean bone in his body' and 'He has a heart of gold' truly describe Benj." I was terrified that Benj, like many quirky kids, would be especially susceptible to bullying. Wordsworth's "To H. C., Six Years Old," a poem he wrote for his friend and collaborator S. T.

Coleridge's son Hartley, frequently came to mind when I lay awake at night fearing the torments other children might inflict on my unknowing, open-hearted son:

> What hast thou to do with sorrow,
> Or the injuries of to-morrow?
> Thou art a dew-drop, which the morn brings forth,
> Ill fitted to sustain unkindly shocks,
> Or to be trailed along the soiling earth;
> A gem that glitters while it lives,
> And no forewarning gives;
> But, at the touch of wrong, without a strife
> Slips in a moment out of life.

But for the time being, Benj was in a safe place, a warm and loving school that treasured him and protected him from "unkindly shocks" and "the touch of wrong."

And in the spring of that year, just after he turned five, we were fortunate enough to have a wonderful choice before us: Benj had been admitted for kindergarten to both of the mainstream private schools in the Poughkeepsie area—a very loose, progressive school and a sweet traditional school. How far he had come! Benj came to be known as the Vassar preschool's triumph, proof that special-needs children can thrive in the mainstream, that amazing progress is possible with the right approach and attention. And one afternoon that spring, Benj came home after a long day at school tanned, filthy—dirt and sand and grass stains covering his clothes, paint not only on his fingers but on his forearms and elbows—with skinned knees and bruised shins, exhausted and incredibly happy. Maybe he wasn't climbing trees, skating with abandon across frozen ponds, or hurling himself into the wind, but he was sliding down the slide and finger-painting, he was becoming more comfortable getting messy and disheveled. And he was learning to express feelings and to connect to those who loved him most. "I had fun at school," he said, leaning his body against mine for a split second, "but I *missed* you, Mommy!"

> Our childhood sits,
> Our simple childhood, sits upon a throne
> That hath more power than all the elements.
> —*Prelude*, V

JUST A FEW DAYS AFTER the heartening news from schools, the Vassar preschool director and I gave the first of what became a series of joint presentations, talks called "Early Intervention: Perspectives from a Director-Parent Team" or "Parent-Caregiver Collaboration with a Special-Needs Child." This was a wonderful way of reaching out to others and sharing my experiences. At early-childhood conferences, on listservs, in daily interactions, I had many moving and enlightening encounters with educators, therapists, doctors, and other parents, and I felt such a sense of productive and vital work. I briefly considered going back to school in order to become a child psychologist. I dreamed of founding a school for gifted/learning-disabled kids, or a pre–K-12 school that would be open to kids with learning differences and emphasize the development of the whole person, not just the transcript or CV.

I felt both more comfortable and more alive in the nursery school or at early-childhood education conferences than in the English Department or at professional literary conferences. Moreover, the emphasis in the developmental psychological literature on the importance of play and emotional intelligence helped me to see how narrow the academic mind-set and traditional models of education could be. And, repeatedly, in my interactions with children, in my reading about children, or in my daily work on Benj's behalf, I thought of these lines from Wordsworth: "One moment now may give us more / Than years of toiling reason" ("To My Sister").

Vassar was a wonderful college, but my doubts, my dissatisfactions with academia remained. I would find myself warning my students against following my path; I couldn't in good conscience encourage them to go to graduate school when they said they wanted to read great books all the time and teach great students like I did. They were so idealistic; they had starry eyes and great hopes. I wished one of my professors had been more honest and blunt with me early on; I wished I'd known what I was getting into, that being an English major bore little or no relation to being an English professor. I was reading much less literature, especially world literature, now that I was a professor. I had to read endless scholarly articles, book reviews, and student papers. I had to immerse myself in the minor writers of my period. And, of course, there were virtually no jobs; my career was an aberration, not a model that could be easily replicated.

I had great colleagues—really smart, interesting, compassionate people—but many of them seemed unhappy and restless too, and often at odds with each other. For like so many English departments, Vassar's was fractured, contentious, and filled with tension. I would sit in interminable department or all-college faculty meetings where minutiae would be debated for hours, people got up in arms about the smallest matters, and both the bickering and the venom bore no relation to what was really at stake. The stakes, every single day, were so high with Benj—would he ever be able to manage his own self-care? would he be allowed to stay in school? would he ever have a conversation, a friend?—and that helped me to see just how low they were in academia. Whenever I'd bring up the possibility of quitting academia once and for all, the refrain was the same: but you'd be throwing away all those years of studying and hard work and sacrifice forging your career, you'd be divesting yourself of the prestige that so many people long for. But that didn't matter to me anymore, at all.

Moreover, I increasingly felt that I couldn't be on a tenure track—with the need to publish articles regularly and travel frequently to conferences and complete a book in six years—and be the mother I needed to be. The first few years after the discovery of Benj's issues coincided with my first three years on a tenure track. During that time, I gave everything I had professionally to my teaching and everything I had personally to Benj and baby James. Turning my dissertation into a book seemed like an enormous undertaking that would require a degree of single-minded focus, commitment, and time that I couldn't spare given the boys' enormous needs and my unshakeable commitment to my students.

Once I got to Vassar, I no longer had the anxiety about the unknown, but a new problem emerged; I realized that I had been so fixated on the elusive brass ring of a tenure-track job that I hadn't completely faced the fact that I just wasn't suited to scholarship. I had always dreaded the stage of academic writing where I had to do the footnotes; I hated parrying this and defending against that. And now, the idea of buffering my dissertation's claims and bolstering its arguments with more research and/or more theoretical apparatus (my Yale dissertation readers had complained about the dissertation's paucity of footnotes and the lack of a "consistent methodology") made me feel exhausted and a bit repulsed. I knew what I had to do to get tenure, but I couldn't bring myself to do it. And so:

> I lived henceforth
> More to myself, read more, reflected more,
> Felt more, and settled daily into habits
> More promising.
> . . . .
> Who knows what thus may have been gained, both then
> And at a later season, or preserved—
> What love of Nature, what original strength

Of contemplation, what intuitive truths,
The deepest and the best, and what research
Unbiassed, unbewildered, and unawed?
  —*Prelude*, VI, where Wordsworth is writing about himself
  as an eighteen- to twenty-year-old once he left the fast-track
  academic path

I didn't want to read or study anything dry or too far removed from real life, argue for the sake of argument, engage in intricate or showy analysis with little feeling or profound motivation behind it. I wanted practical help and yearned for penetrating insight, emotional resonance, and imaginative expansiveness. And so what I devoured—had an insatiable appetite for—were nonfiction books by pediatricians, developmental psychologists, neurologists, therapists (Stanley Greenspan, Howard Gardner, Oliver Sacks, Mel Levine, Antonio Damasio, T. Berry Brazelton, Pema Chodron, Jon Kabat-Zinn) and pure literature—not writing *about* literature. Yeats and Ishiguro, *Gilead* and *Great Expectations*, Shakespeare and Austen and Toni Morrison, Rilke and Nabokov and most of all Wordsworth got me through this most difficult period. I read while standing on lines at the bank or supermarket, sitting in the lobby of Benj's school, in the waiting rooms of doctors' and therapists' offices, while nursing (a ton while nursing), while on phone hold. I carried books with me everywhere and used every opportunity to read. It kept me going.

That literature has the power to comfort and sustain might seem obvious, but as a professional scholar of literature, I had been made to feel that literature was there to be analyzed, debated, or "worked on," not to be turned to for consolation, solace, or inspiration. In a section of his autobiography called "a crisis in my mental history," John Stuart Mill asserts that Wordsworth's poems "proved to be the precise thing for my mental wants at that particular juncture . . . a medicine for my state of mind." These remarks are often referred to disparagingly by academics as an example of "nineteenth-century" or "psychological" criticism, but I had always agreed with Mill, and never more so than now.

Through Wordsworth, I was teaching values and stances and ideas that were in opposition to those of my profession, and doing so helped me to clarify my problems with academia. One Wordsworth poem in particular, "The Tables Turned," which I taught in a class on later eighteenth-century literature called "Sense and Sensibility," exemplified my feelings:

> Up! Up! my Friend, and quit your books;
> Or surely you'll grow double:
> Up! up! my Friend, and clear your looks;
> Why all this toil and trouble?
> . . . .
> Books! 'tis a dull and endless strife:
> Come, hear the woodland linnet,
> How sweet his music! on my life,
> There's more of wisdom in it.
> . . . .
> Enough of Science and of Art;
> Close up those barren leaves;
> Come forth, and bring with you a heart
> That watches and receives.

Among other things, this poem reminded me of Mister Rogers's point about the importance of "being a good receiver." Being receptive in this way—empathically sensitive to others' feelings—was something Benj had special difficulty with, but it was also a mode that was particularly hard to sustain in the competitive academic arena, where it was all about projecting oneself, asserting one's ideas and theoretical stances, making interventions into the discourse. In my desire to leave the tenure track, I yearned to explicitly choose my "heart / that watches and receives" over all else.

Wordsworth, especially, was my constant companion during this period, and as he helped me cope with my situation, so my situation made me look anew at him, through different eyes, with deeper understanding. I read not only his poems (including many I'd never read before) but also his letters, including a beautiful collection of love letters between him and his wife, edited by one of my favorite Vassar colleagues, who'd become a Jungian analyst. It all meant so much more to me now. As I read up on Wordsworth's family situation, I realized that I'd never really considered him as a son and a father, never fully reflected on the horrific losses that he'd suffered. I thought frequently as I learned about Wordsworth's life—on my own—this had never happened in a class: How can it be that I wrote many undergraduate and graduate essays, my senior thesis, and a dissertation chapter on Wordsworth and never till now fully registered that he had lost both his parents at a very young age, two children (both of whom died in 1812), and his brother? Wordsworth became not just a poet but a person for me—he was humanized for me—and I wept reading "Surprised by Joy," about the death of his young daughter, and "Peele Castle," about the death of his brother in a shipwreck:

> So once it would have been,—'tis so no more;
> I have submitted to a new control:
> A power is gone, which nothing can restore;
> A deep distress hath humanised my Soul.
>
> Not for a moment could I now behold
> A smiling sea, and be what I have been:
> The feeling of my loss will ne'er be old;
> This, which I know, I speak with mind serene.

· ·

Farewell, farewell the heart that lives alone,
Housed in a dream, at distance from the Kind!
Such happiness, wherever it be known,
Is to be pitied; for 'tis surely blind.

But welcome fortitude, and patient cheer,
And frequent sights of what is to be borne!
Such sights, or worse, as are before me here.—
Not without hope we suffer and we mourn.
　　—Stanzas from "Peele Castle"

I had little time, energy, or inclination for scholarship or academic writing. But what I did write—starting almost as soon as
we discovered hyperlexia—were notes on what Benj was doing and
what I was feeling—these nightly jottings were absolutely necessary for my emotional survival. What I was doing with Benj was
the opposite of what I was doing as an academic. I was doing everything I could to take him on his own terms, to strip away the need
for labels, theories, jargon, to not care what the establishment said,
to develop my feelings and attitudes based on personal experience,
intuition, and what was present right in front of me. I longed to do
this with literature as well.

I had the tenure-track job at a top liberal arts college, but I still
felt restless and dissatisfied on good days, fraudulent and repelled on
bad ones. And I felt guilty for feeling this way, as my own husband
so passionately wanted what I had. Richard couldn't understand
my dissatisfaction. Sometimes when I'd express my frustration with
an arcane piece of scholarship, a drawn-out and unpleasant department meeting, the need to footnote everything, he'd sigh and say:
"It's still the best job anyone could have." He still wanted to be a
professor so much, but as the months and years passed and he failed

to complete his dissertation, it became increasingly clear that if he were to stay in academia, it would probably have to be on my coattails—as a "spousal hire." So while I longed to leave academia, I stayed in large part to enable him to stay. All this put a huge strain on the marriage.

And the knotted-up quality of Richard's emotional life was becoming increasingly arduous and exhausting to navigate. His statements and responses were often so convoluted and opaque that I couldn't understand what he was getting at. At other times, my efforts to communicate, to make any kind of contact with him, were met with no response at all. I tried to touch with a "gentle hand," but the woods were by now so thick and overgrown, I couldn't reach the spirit anymore. I had been the one person he came out for. But now he wouldn't come out, even for me. Or, to put it another way, I had been the one person able and willing to push through the "tangled thicket," to make my way through the undergrowth and "move along [the] . . . shades / In gentleness of heart" to find the spirit. But this time the brambles snapped back at me, the trees were too tall, too obdurate. The way was blocked. Frustrated and afraid, I tried to get his attention and reach him any way I could. Occasionally I lost my gentleness, and spoke to him histrionically or harshly, but that was just as ineffective.

During these difficult years, I don't think he ever once asked me, "How was your day?" "How are you feeling?" or "How can I help?" I don't think it occurred to him to ask, as it wouldn't have occurred to Benj. We hadn't been physically intimate—not even kissing—since we'd conceived James almost two and a half years earlier, and he seemed to have no interest in our ever being so again. But even when I told him I couldn't go on any longer like this, that the marriage was in serious jeopardy, he was silent, blank, completely unresponsive. I couldn't see any end in sight to this arid, empty, sterile life. I felt my spark, my dynamism, my optimism draining away. I sensed my own natural sunniness, my "bright radiance" dimming.

But the typical hesitations and fears every parent has when they consider divorce felt all the more acute in my case, both because of my own experience as a child and because of the particular set of children and spouse I had. I could not bear to break a family, to do to my children what my parents had done to me and my sister; I could not bear the idea of causing such suffering myself. I never wanted my children to experience the disorientation, that protectiveness toward the vulnerability of their father, the sense of being responsible for a parent's well-being that had so weighed on me as a young child. And I had been an emotionally sophisticated and resilient ten-year-old with lots of friends and a plucky spirit. Benj was an odd, isolated, especially vulnerable child for whom novelty was the biggest challenge; he was a child who required stability and certainty and reliability much more than I had. He adored and needed his father desperately. Richard, moreover, was far more vulnerable than my father had been. My father was a gregarious, charming man with a wide social network; Richard was a loner, and our family was his entire social universe. His solitariness and his hurt were what I had come into his life to remedy. Now I would be thrusting him into solitude, inflicting hurt upon him. I was tormented by the idea of abandoning him. And I knew Richard would miss the children almost beyond his ability to bear it; his sons were "his Heart and his Heart's joy" (Wordsworth, "Michael").

As I agonized over what to do, I was haunted by a remark that Richard's mother had made on her deathbed. "I worry so much about leaving my boys," she'd said, "Anthony and Sam especially, they're so young, and I don't know what will become of them yet, I can't be sure they'll be okay. But I'm so relieved that I don't need to worry about Ricko," she'd said, squeezing my hand as hard as she could, "because he has YOU." Every time I remembered her words, it wrenched me. I knew now, so much more than I had known then, what a mother's love and concern for her son meant, and I felt an overwhelming desire to honor her wish as I would want my son to be cared for by his partner.

I felt, however illogically or misguidedly, that to reject or abandon Richard would be in some way also to reject or abandon Benj. For in many ways my son was someone who was going to be the man I could no longer be married to. Crippling perfectionism, social awkwardness, rigidity about routines, and difficulty with physical expressions of affection, emotional immediacy, cognitive flexibility—all of these traits and qualities Richard shared with Benj. I feared that divorcing Richard would be sending Benj a message, however obliquely, about his own undesirability. My own son would be very difficult to be in a romantic relationship with—would I want a woman to turn away from him? Wouldn't I, in effect, be saying that Richard and Benj were not worthy of someone holding on, hanging in there with them, being patient and forgiving and understanding of their quirks and their limitations? Wouldn't I be implying that they were not valuable despite their issues, that they were not deserving of unconditional and infinite love? Just as I had with Richard, I wanted a gentleness of heart and a gentle hand for Benj. I wanted Benj to have his spirit recognized in the tangled thicket of his difficulties and opacities. I wanted people to look beyond the superficial oddities and potentially frustrating and confusing behaviors, to work hard but with tenderness, patience, and perseverance to understand him and bring light to his shade. Would my "giving up on" Richard be in some way an acknowledgment that this work had been, was, or would be in vain?

The failure of the marriage, which had once held so much hope and promise as a balm, a restorative force, was devastating to acknowledge. The fantasy I'd harbored my entire life that I could make up for the feelings of vulnerability and pain that characterized my childhood with a secure, loving, intact family of my own was shattered. I felt as if everything I had counted on was in question, and there was a bewildering sense of everything falling away. I had deep qualms; I felt that I would be betraying my deepest values and intentionally causing three people I loved grave harm.

But that was one side. On the other side was my strong conviction that if Richard and I were ever to be able to love each other again and be the parents, and the people, we wanted and needed to be for our beloved children, we needed a dramatic change, a dramatic reconfiguration of our relationship. I needed to overcome the resentment, frustration, and disappointment and find the affection for Richard again. I knew that if he were not my husband, if I did not have any expectations for what he could or should give me, I would be able to appreciate and love him again. And so after years of pondering, agonizing, and hesitating, I finally made the decision to end the marriage once and for all. Richard said he was heartbroken, but he didn't cry or protest; he accepted my decision as final and he understood it.

Richard and I continued to live together in the Poughkeepsie house; he slept two flights down in his study. We told almost no one of our separation—if Vassar knew, they would have eliminated his teaching position. We made the decision to move to New York City in a year: because we'd have a larger and deeper support network of family and friends, because Richard would have many more job opportunities there, because the educational opportunities were better for Benj and James there. The plan was for me to commute three days a week to Vassar, but I was almost certain I wouldn't be able to sustain that over the long run; I didn't want to be too far from Benj that often, and I thought I'd probably need to take a job that paid better and would enable me to support the children on my own. Working at the literary agency was still a possibility for me, and while the prospect of giving up teaching was a very sad one, the opportunity to break free from the confines of academia was exhilarating. Increasingly, I was realizing that I didn't have to do things because my parents, or my surrogate parents (my professors), or my husband wanted me to do them, or because I had always done them, or because doing them felt easy or familiar to me.

I vowed to do everything in my power to protect both Richard and the children. We would share custody and continue to spend a great deal of time together as a family. The happiness and well-being of the children would always be our paramount concern. And we would continue our work together as parents, seeking the best life for our sons.

. . . a child, more than all other gifts
That earth can offer to declining man,
Brings hope with it, and forward-looking thoughts,
And stirrings of inquietude, when they
By tendency of nature needs must fail.
—Wordsworth, "Michael"

IN THE LATE SUMMER, we brought Benj to Dr. G, the same New York City speech therapist/psychologist who had first evaluated him when he was not yet three. After the initial celebration over Benj's admission to both Poughkeepsie-area private schools, we'd gone back and forth over whether the progressive school—which would be both more tolerant of him and more confusing for him—or the more structured but also more rigid traditional school would be the best setting for him. Eventually, we'd sidestepped the choice between two styles of education by deciding to keep him in his Vassar lab school for kindergarten; once we'd committed to going to the city in a year, we wanted to keep him where he was so as to remove the stress of two school transitions in one year. The question of whether progressive or traditional education was more appropriate for Benj still remained an open one. We hoped that Dr. G could help us figure out which type of school in general and which mainstream private school in New York City would be best for our brilliant but quirky son. But what happened was that the possibility of any regular school taking him seemed increasingly slim.

The visit got off to a good start. Benjamin remembered Dr. G from two and a half years earlier, and greeted her enthusiastically. But he soon began to exhibit extreme anxiety, expressing fear of noises outside, of her stopwatch, and of the situation in general. We left him in the room with her and went out to the waiting room, where we sat next to each other on hard wooden chairs and leafed through our books. Despite white-noise machines both inside and outside the door to the office, we could clearly hear Benjamin talking incessantly, periodically expostulating "Oh no!" or "I can't!" and weeping.

Hearing my child crying as I sat on the other side of the door, powerless to help, was a painful reminder of the limits on my ability to ensure Benj's well-being. He'd been having a great summer at camp and had been cheery and buoyant in the car on the way down to New York City, but in a new situation faced with new challenges he broke down and couldn't cope. Sitting in the waiting room and listening to him cry or protest or be unable to do things he was being asked to do, I saw Benj's great vulnerability in a very poignant way. I couldn't be in there with him and he was struggling, greatly, on his own.

"You heard that, right?" Dr. G said, somewhat grimly, when she opened the door at last, beckoning us into the room. She sent Benj out to the waiting room to play while she reported what had happened. We sat facing her on a couch as she outlined all the ways in which he was deficient or problematic. "Well, first off, he's extremely labile." "What do you mean by labile?" I asked. "He goes from one emotional pole to the other, he's fragile, he's anxious, he's rigid, he has catastrophic thinking."

"Catastrophic thinking?"

"He imagines the worst-case scenario; he can be paralyzed by anxiety if things aren't clear to him or if an outcome is uncertain."

She then briskly enumerated all the other problems she'd seen in him: "He didn't know how to begin telling a story." "He didn't know I was pretend-crying. He's very empathic, but he didn't get it that I wasn't really crying. He got very distressed by my crying and didn't see that we were pretending/role-playing." "You know he's terrible at puzzles, right?"

After listing all his weaknesses and issues, she sighed and said: "Well, I don't have to tell you, you already know all of this, right?" What could we say in response? We both did and we didn't.

Every once in a while Benj would poke his head in the door to show us a book or toy he'd found. He was always smiling and seemed oblivious to the tension and anxiety in the room. Dr. G would say, "Hi sweetheart, just a little longer," and he'd happily return to his activities outside. He had no idea how "badly" he'd just done. He just had no idea. The fact was that he hadn't performed or realized he had to make a positive impression or do his best. He'd just reacted. He'd had no idea that he was being judged and evaluated, whether he'd succeeded or failed. His cluelessness as to his own performance insulated him from embarrassment or shame, but his lack of perception throughout this process was painful for me.

"Okay, so how does this all affect your sense of what school would be right for him?" I asked.

"In terms of schools, Benjamin has two huge strikes against him. On the one hand, there's his emotional lability. On the other, there's his uneven neuropsychological profile. Because of his motor delays, he doesn't do well on many of the performance tasks. On some verbal tasks like vocabulary he gets 99 percent–plus but on others, like social reasoning, he's way below that. He's all over the map. He's going to have very scattered scores, and that can be a huge red flag to schools."

During the drive home, with Benj happily engrossed in a maze book in the back of the car, we sighed and worried. All the excuses we came up with to explain his poor performance—he was overwhelmed by the bustle and noise of New York City, the photo-taking at the beginning of the session had spooked him, the newness of the situation brought out the worst in him—didn't change the fact that she'd identified and given negative names and labels to behaviors and features of Benj that we recognized and acknowledged. She'd articulated in clinical language all the things we'd ourselves felt, suspected, guessed were real features of his temperament and being.

A day or two later, in a phone conversation, Dr. G was even more blunt. "You can't be average and you can't be difficult or problematic to get into a private school in New York City," she said. "Schools in New York City don't want average kids, and they also don't want kids who cry and break down, they don't want fragile kids. You have to have at least 84 percent composite score on the ERBs (the standardized test required for admission to private school in New York). You really might want to consider special schools. You need to get him some psychological help, and you need to get him into a social-skills group ASAP."

I began to research New York City special schools online. I could see how wonderful they might be for my darling boy. Looking at these schools and realizing how well Benj might do in them, I felt strongly that I might have failed him in the past. Should I have put Benj in a special-education preschool where he might have received more one-on-one attention and support of his specific issues? I thought of two children of family friends who'd struggled through mainstream schools and never had their specific learning issues identified. Both of these boys had gone to progressive, unstructured, nurturing schools, and both had felt adrift, unsupported, misunderstood. Only as adults had they been given labels (of Asperger's and bipolar disorder), which came as a relief to them and their parents. I hadn't sought out a clinician who would give Benj a label. We'd so wanted him to be taken for HIM, to be loved and appreciated for who he really was, to be delighted in and not viewed as someone who couldn't love and feel and empathize. "He's very empathic," I thought to myself. "He's very kind and loving. And he's so young—how do we know if he'll outgrow certain behaviors and overcome many of his 'weaknesses'? As long as he's getting services, why saddle him with a label that might stigmatize him, circumscribe his options, limit him in his life?" We'd been going along just fine, with people who knew him as Benj, who'd appreciated and supported him, but had he just been floating along? Was he developing as much as he could be? Was this the point where we'd have to face the fact that Benj would never ever be able to make it in, and perhaps that he would not be best served by, a mainstream school? Might one of these special schools be just the right home for Benj, a place where he could be properly supported and cherished? Where he wouldn't have to be the "weirdo" or the "difficult one"?

But I knew that the idea of putting Benj in a special school would be anathema to Richard, for whom much of the impetus behind therapy had always been to "bring Benj up to speed" so that he could attend a "normal" school as a "normal" child. Richard strongly resisted the idea that Benj might not be able to make it in a school like the ones we had gone to. In fact, his desire for Benj to attend a strong mainstream school was one of the primary reasons he kept details of Benj's situation secret and urged secrecy on me; he didn't want to bias people against Benj and hurt his chances of admission.

I asked Richard to check out the special schools online—"You'll be so pleasantly surprised and impressed, blown away, in fact!" I told him—but he was impassive. In the week since we'd seen Dr. G, he'd retreated from the worry we'd felt and back to his adamant stance that Benj could make it in a mainstream school. "I really don't think Benj needs to be in a special school. He's doing so well now. He got into both the regular schools here. Why shouldn't he get into similar schools like them in New York City?" "Well, the application process is much tougher in the city," I said. "But more than that, just because he was accepted doesn't mean he would actually have done well at those schools.

They saw him for half an hour. I'm not sure they'd really be able to support him through his unusual anxieties or make the accommodations he needs." "But he can do it," Richard said. "I know he can."

Every time Benj behaved oddly or problematically in a social situation or in school, Richard would say a version of the following: "It's so frustrating. He's so smart and capable and he's just a little odd. If he could just pull it together! Why can't he just do it/hack it? Why can't he just hold it in?" I knew that this frustration stemmed from his deep love of Benj and unwavering belief in Benj—his faith that Benj could do it. But I thought that Benj seemed increasingly to need the small class size, individualized attention, and acceptance of his quirks that only a special school could provide, and Dr. G's opinion held a great deal of weight with me. So over Richard's objections, I insisted that we add special schools to the list and requested the applications. Richard reluctantly agreed to sign them.

At a meeting with Dr. G six weeks later, Benj was markedly less anxious and more compliant, and she told us she thought there was, in fact, hope he could be accepted into and do well in a mainstream school. But, then, as she'd initially predicted, his ERB test came back with lots of scatter and a huge gap between his verbal and performance scores. So to maximize both his chances of acceptance and our chances of finding just the right fit for him, we cast an extremely wide net and applied to twenty public and private elementary schools (twelve mainstream and eight special) in the New York City area. Despite our marital separation, Richard and I went to almost every school and did every interview together. While teaching full-time at Vassar, I traveled in and out of the city at least forty times in three months for countless tours and interviews and "playdates."

This was my first foray back into the hypercompetitive world of New York schools since the earlier, painful disappointment with my preschool, and I was continually put off by the aggressive, cutthroat environment in which only "perfect," "easy," consistent kids were welcomed. This process was full of agonizing and often heartbreakingly hilarious moments. There was the time Benj came out of an "assessment" to meet us in the lobby and said loudly: "I didn't have fun at this school, Mommy." Or the time he blurted out in full earshot of the admissions director: "This school is number seven on my list." The tester at a supposedly relaxed and nurturing private school insisted that Benj's lowercase *J* was really a *U* and made him cry. At another school, the tester came out of the assessment room and told me bluntly: "I'm sorry, but he didn't copy the shapes quickly enough." And at one visit that seemed to be going wonderfully, everything fell apart after he got weepy when his team lost a game of pickup basketball and the teacher told me in a stern, disapproving voice: "He doesn't handle disappointment well enough for this school; we want tough, resilient kids."

Richard and I were especially attracted to a small, structured, nurturing school known to be open to kids with "uneven learning profiles." We loved its warmth, its diversity, its small classes and individualized attention. In a spirit of cautious optimism, we brought Benj there for a visit one Saturday morning in early December. There were about a hundred kids and parents and teachers gathered in the big lunchroom. The kids were divided into small groups, and led upstairs by a teacher into classrooms for their "playdate." I could see Benj getting revved up, flicking the hair out of his eyes, walking on his toes, turning a bit red, but he was smiling and enthusiastically followed his head teacher as she led the group out of the room.

We took our seats in semicircular rows arrayed behind the head of the school, who sat at the front of the room and asked the assembled parents to tell her why they were interested in the school. Overeager mothers laughed nervously as their husbands rambled on, dropped names, or cracked mildly inappropriate jokes. As a parent was rattling on about what a perfect fit with the school her child was, I heard an unmistakable familiar moan, almost a keening sound, at first faint, then louder and louder. A figure appeared in the doorway: the assistant admissions director. All heads swiveled in the same direction. She tried to gesture subtly to me. Ninety percent of the parents sighed in audible relief and some seemed to positively gloat. "One competitor down," I could see them thinking. A few kind souls gave me sympathetic glances.

I got up and walked to the door. Benj was sitting on a bench in the large entry hall, his face bright red, his cheeks tear-streaked, and his expression disconsolate. The teacher who had been his group leader was standing next to him, looking alternately apologetic and irritated. The story emerged in bits and pieces. It turned out that Benj hadn't wanted to walk up the stairs to the classroom because they were very steep and the railing ended suddenly, but the teacher had insisted that he walk in a certain way when he was feeling frightened. Then they made all the kids sit at desks and copy shapes—something Benj, with his fine motor delays, found an especially onerous task. The admissions staff had really bonded with me when I toured and they were willing to give him another chance, but I decided not to put him through it again. I just didn't feel that they'd be able to stretch to accommodate him and meet his needs.

So often during this difficult and painful school application process, I took solace in Wordsworth's accounts of his own school experiences, his resistance to conformity, his distaste for traditional modes of evaluation:

> Examinations, when the man was weighed
> As in the balance;
> . . . .
>   Things they were which then
> I did not love, nor do I love them now:
> Such glory was but little sought by me,
> And little won.
>   —*Prelude*, III

Perhaps because I taught students who especially needed the reassurance or corrective, perhaps because I myself needed these reminders, I had always been especially drawn to *Prelude* passages that reject narrow and conventional ideas of achievement, that celebrate the freedom of childhood play and the worth of seemingly random activities. This aspect of the *Prelude* had become especially powerful and poignant for me as I'd watched Benjamin be tested or evaluated countless times in countless ways by therapists and psychologists and now by teachers and school admissions committees. I found great comfort in Wordsworth's reminder that the essence of my child was not being measured in the balance and in his belief in his own value despite the fact that he was not a conventional student or a conventional person:

> Not of outward things
> Done visibly for other minds—words, signs,
> Symbols or actions—but of my own heart
> Have I been speaking, and my youthful mind.
> —*Prelude*, III

It was Benj's "own heart" and his "youthful mind" that mattered, I told myself, not his proficiency with "outward things."

Out of the twenty schools we applied to, Benj ended up being accepted at only one: a special-needs school that had only existed for two years and therefore had more spots and more openness to unusual, challenging kids. The school was designed for bright kids with all different sorts of issues—ADD, dyslexia, sensory disorders. It had a top-notch sensory gym and a developmentally sensitive, challenging, individualized curriculum. Benj would be in a classroom of twelve kids with two teachers and get occupational therapy, speech therapy, and social-skills training. We were so grateful to have this option, although Richard still lamented that Benj hadn't been admitted to a "regular school."

In contrast to our nerve-wracking saga with Benj's school admission process, two-and-a-half-year-old James was admitted early to the preschool I'd attended, the one that had been the first to alert me to serious concerns about Benj. Jamesie now said "me" and "I" and "my" all the time—amazing how effortless it was for him, compared to Benj who couldn't get it straight until he was four. Every morning after James watched *Sesame Street*, he would run to tell me everything that had happened: "I saw Elmo! Elmo dance with Mr. Noodle. Oscar close trash can and say, 'ARRRGGGHH!' Super Grover go to Africa and see elephant!" He didn't recite the skits or sing the songs; instead, he excitedly recounted, in his own broken baby talk, what he had seen. And James ripped books, chewed books, threw books—he did anything but read them. Every time I watched James running and jumping and skipping or listened to him talk to his stuffed animals, every time he cried "Mommy!" and threw his arms around me, I saw much more clearly how "abnormal" Benj had been and realized that I'd have worried so much earlier and so much more intensely had Benj been my second child.

I will call the *world* a School instituted for the purpose of teaching little children to read—I will call the *human heart* the *horn Book* used in that School—and I will call the *Child able to read, the Soul* made from that *school* and its *hornbook*. Do you not see how necessary a World of Pains and troubles is to school an Intelligence and make it a soul? A Place where the heart must feel and suffer in a thousand diverse ways!

—Keats

THAT SPRING, JUST AS Vassar classes were ending, I planned a trip to Japan to see my father, who hadn't spoken in over a year, whose level of consciousness was unclear, and who seemed unlikely to live much longer. I felt a bit nervous and very sad about leaving the children for so long and going so far away from them, but comforted by the fact that Benj was thriving in his nursery school and heartily enjoying his last few weeks there. I would return from Japan just in time for his kindergarten graduation after three wonderful years at the school.

The afternoon before I was scheduled to leave for Japan, I took a Metro-North train from Poughkeepsie to Manhattan, where I would stay the night at my mother's apartment before my early-morning flight. I sat curled up in a window seat, engrossed in a book, when I suddenly heard "Priscilla?" and looked up to see Benj's kindergarten teacher, Peter, sitting across the aisle from me. I'd never seen him outside the context of the school, and it felt both nice and strange to encounter him on the train. He introduced me to his son, a shaggy-haired teenager sitting beside him. "This is *Ben's* mother," Peter said to his son, who seemed to perk up at that news; he'd clearly heard a lot about Benj from his dad. He shook my hand, said a friendly hello, then put his headphones on and slouched down in his seat. I told Peter I was going to visit my father in Japan, and he told me that they were going to meet his older son in New York City. "We're going to the Brian Wilson concert tonight," he said excitedly. "You like Brian Wilson?" I cried. "*Pet Sounds* is one of my all-time favorite albums!" Peter and I agreed that Benj and Brian Wilson were similar in so many ways: both had perfect pitch, strange anxieties, beautiful singing voices, and an appealing fragility.

Peter was a musician himself. After a career in music, he'd gone back to school in his forties to get a dual degree in special education and early-childhood education. He played both guitar and banjo for the kids in his classroom and in all-school events, and Benj had always been fascinated by him. Since Benj had started at the school as a three-year-old, his especially powerful and accurate voice had soared above all others in the all-school events and sing-alongs, which Peter led. And Benj had made his presence known to Peter in other, less conventional or socially appropriate ways, as well. When Peter began to play, Benj would get out of his seat, or break away from his classroom group, and come forward to get a closer look and listen. Often he reached out curious fingers to touch Peter's guitar, and Peter patiently but firmly laid down rules for handling the guitar, clear and consistent rules that Benj respected. At the holiday concert during Benj's first year at the school, Peter had launched into a song he'd been practicing with the kids, and Benj, who was sitting on my lap, had yelled out: "Wrong key! F-sharp! F-sharp!" Peter thought for a second, looked down at the guitar, and said, "He's right. I've been practicing with them in F!" He began again, and this time Benj beamed his approval and sang his heart out. Benj's unself-conscious corrections of Peter—"Tune! Tune!" or "Wrong key!" or "Too fast!" he'd cry—became amusing and lovable staples of the group sing-alongs and performances. Benj would voice a protest or pipe up a concern; Peter would laugh—"Benj keeps me in line!" he'd say—and adjust his playing accordingly. This year, Peter was Benj's classroom teacher, and a few weeks after school began, he'd asked us for per-mission to administer some intelligence tests to Benj. Although we were usually very wary of anyone or anything that seemed to be fix-ated on Benj's precocity, because we trusted his intentions and knew Benj wouldn't mind doing the tests with him, we'd said yes. Peter had been astounded by Benj's proficiency. "I couldn't get a ceiling on him," he'd said. "When we got to the sixth-grade level for spelling, he said he wanted to stop. I could have kept pushing him to keep going but I didn't want to force him."

Peter not only marveled at Benj's abilities but also got a real kick out of Benj's funny ways. At pickup or drop-off, he'd often laughingly report to us on things Benj had said or done that day. Now, with a bit of train ride stretching before us, I looked forward to a more leisurely and detailed conversation sharing humorous and touching moments. But today Peter was in an unexpectedly reflective and serious mood.

"It must be so difficult for you, being Benj's mom," he said sym-pathetically. "You always seem so upbeat and energetic, but I know you must be tired. He'll just wear you out."

I nodded, and smiled politely, but inside I was discomfited and in turmoil. Was Benj really this difficult for his teachers? Was he wear-ing them out? I felt a fierce protectiveness of Benj, a desire to defend him against what felt, however good Peter's intentions were, like a criticism. "He doesn't wear me out!" I wanted to cry, even though sometimes he did.

Peter continued speaking, as if he were unburdening himself of thoughts he'd been carrying around and longing to share. "Ben just doesn't know how to hang out or relax. He lives life like he's playing

chess. He's twelve steps ahead of what's going on. He's always anticipating, always planning, making sure he's not caught off guard or
surprised. And that can be so exhausting for him, and for the people
around him."

Peter's words were intended to offer fellowship to me, but at first
I was so taken aback by the grim picture he was painting of Benj's
functioning that I couldn't take his gesture in the spirit in which it
was meant. "I'd thought he was having a great year. Is that not the
case?" I asked.

"He's increasingly inconsistent. He has a great day and then a very
off day—when his anxiety level is high and his frustration tolerance
low. There's just no way to predict. I always wonder: 'What's going
on in that little head?'"

"Yes, I know what you mean," I said. I really did.

"With some things, for instance, he's really improved." Peter continued his musings. "His handwriting is so much better, and he's doing much better with Friday class games. But he has such difficulty
with conversations. I'll ask him, 'What did you do last night?' and
he'll either ignore me or get worried when he can't think of an answer. His biggest difficulty is trouble with Circle Time—having to
sit still and pay attention in a sustained way is really tough for him.
His mind wanders and he hums or fidgets. Actually, he's started to
do things so that he'll get kicked out of Circle, but I won't let him
leave."

"Wow, I really had no idea things were this hard for him," I said.

"Well, we're more demanding with the kindergarten kids. We
have to be, to help get them ready for elementary school, especially
since so many of them will be going to public school. The expectations are so much higher for this age group. There's much more of an
emphasis on conformity as kids get into first grade. And as he gets
older, Benj's differences, and his difficulties, become more apparent."

I'd had no idea Benj was considered so difficult or so much work for his teachers. I'd had no idea he'd been hanging on by a thread. A year ago, he'd been doing wonderfully at the Vassar preschool and had been accepted to both of the mainstream private elementary schools in the Poughkeepsie area. But now, he was having a lot of trouble in that same Vassar preschool, the most accepting, flexible, supportive mainstream school imaginable, in a place I'd thought he had his best chance of success. "Thank goodness he'll be going to a special school next year, and he won't stick out so much as problematic or difficult," I thought. "Those teachers will be better equipped to handle him." I felt at once incredibly sad and incredibly relieved.

Peter mused on. "Benj needs to be challenged. You've got to expose him to things, let him live through things, although I know it's hard because novelty is so difficult for him."

"Yes, that's so true," I said. "And we're so grateful for your patience with and dedication to him. Really—he just loves you so much, Peter."

"You know, Priscilla, I end the days with Benj spent but exhilarated too. I've never taught a more perplexing, challenging child, one who tested me more. But I've also never taught a more brilliant or a more sweet child, a child who rewarded my efforts more."

The train pulled into Grand Central and as we stood up and made our way toward the doors, Peter put his arm around me. "You're on a journey with this child, Priscilla. That's true of every child, of course, but more so with this one."

> There is a comfort in the strength of love;
> 'Twill make a thing endurable, which else
> Would overset the brain, or break the heart.
> —Wordsworth, "Michael"

Early the next morning, I began the long trip (twenty-seven hours door-to-door) to Japan. I stayed in a nearby hotel, and in the mornings I would take the subway to my father's and stepmother's apartment building in a suburb of Kyoto. During the elevator ride to the twenty-third floor, I'd gear myself up to smile and comfort, not to break down or be overwhelmed by the truly horrifying sight of Daddy lying on the hospital bed that had been set up in the living room. My father had been an immensely charming, witty, and dynamic man, described as a "brilliant talker" by Anatole Broyard in his memoir *Kafka Was the Rage*, with the most mobile, expressive face imaginable. Now he was completely immobile, unable to eat or drink, unable to speak or indicate whether or not he heard others speaking to him. His levels of consciousness and awareness were uncertain; no X-rays or scans had been done in over a year, and my stepmother didn't want him moved out of the apartment to have them performed—such a transition might invite infection or illness. Yasuko was convinced my father could hear and understand us and that he responded to her, but there had been no indications so far as my sister or brother, both of whom had been to visit him in the past year, could tell that this was the case. His head was bald from the radiation treatments years earlier, his eyes a blazing blue-green, his face frozen into a mask of impassivity. A large tube went into a permanent opening cut into his throat and suctioned phlegm from his lungs— the sucking sounds were a perpetual soundtrack to our encounters.

Although the apartment smelled both stale and sterile, and medical supplies were everywhere, my stepmother had worked hard to create a tranquil and comforting environment for my father. Tubes were attached all over his body, but most were, thankfully, hidden beneath the blankets covering him; these bright and cheery red, white, and blue blankets had been crocheted by his mother for me and Claire when we were very young children, and had once adorned the twin beds in our shared bedroom in the Connecticut house. Bookcases filled with his beloved books were all around us, and lots of green plants and flowers hung from the ceiling and filled the living room's balcony. Paintings of my brother's were hung on the walls. A stuffed Super Grover that Claire and I had sent Daddy when he was first diagnosed with cancer hung from one of the metal posts of the bed, and all around the bed were photos of us as children and of my young children. There was Benj reading *The Runaway Bunny*, standing proudly in front of a series of alphabet blocks spelling out DE-LECTABLE, dressed in a New York Giants helmet, tentatively holding baby James on his lap.

My visits would always begin with me standing by my father's head and talking to him in an animated and happy tone, mustering that same cheer in my voice I'd summoned during those post-separation dinners and lunches so many years ago. I'd list all the good things that were happening (James was loving *Sesame Street*, would be attending our wonderful preschool, and was talking up a storm; Benj was a Mets and Giants fan and was graduating from kindergarten). I felt like I did when, as a young girl, I'd think of everything I could tell my father that might make him feel better, like the 100 on my math quiz or the good part I got in the class play. This time, however, I had no way of knowing if anything I was saying registered. At other times, my stepmother and I would sit at the dining-room table, just a few feet away from where my father lay, and chat in what seemed to me like falsely chipper tones.

One morning, she told me that he liked her to read to him, and asked if I would. I took an anthology of poetry off the shelf, and scanned through it. Oddly enough, my father had never loved Wordsworth—hadn't even read much of him—but as I chose poems, I realized that the poems he'd most loved, that he'd taught me to love, were all poems of paradise lost or paradise sought, and all deeply inspired by Wordsworth. I began with Gerard Manley Hopkins's "Spring and Fall: To a Young Child," in which the speaker addresses the grief of a young girl "for Goldengrove unleaving." I then chose Dylan Thomas's gorgeous, lyrical "Fern Hill," a poem celebrating the bliss of childhood on a farm in Wales, one that my father and I had exclaimed over together and passionately loved. I'd memorized it for a poetry recitation contest once and when I practiced it for him, he'd always teared up a bit. This time, I could barely get the words out, and as I came to the last three lines, my voice broke:

> Oh as I was young and easy in the mercy of his means,
> Time held me green and dying
> Though I sang in my chains like the sea.

His eyes seemed a little shinier. And then, as I read Yeats's "The Lake Isle of Innsifree" to him, I saw tears slipping out of his eyes. I wiped them away with small cotton squares that Yasuko handed me. I kissed him on his forehead. And when I rose to go on the last night of my stay, I feared I was leaving him forever.

TWO DAYS AFTER I returned from Japan was Benj's graduation from the Vassar preschool. It was a short ceremony, held in a Vassar auditorium with a small stage. The *Peanuts* theme song was playing as the parents filed in; we barely filled a few rows of the auditorium. The fourteen or so kids walked in to the song "Graduation Day," Benj at the front of the line, almost sprinting to his seat and grinning broadly. The director came up and welcomed the parents; in the middle of her speech, Benj called out, "Hi Julie!" and everyone laughed. Before each step of the graduation, Benj would read it aloud from the program in a dramatic voice, and before each song or piece of music, he'd begin to hum it. Some of the other parents, who knew Benj well, chuckled affectionately. The teacher they'd had sit next to him occasionally redirected or quieted him but never in a harsh or punitive way.

Then the children took the stage to perform some songs. Benj called out, "Oh Grams! Hi Grams!!!!" when he spotted his grandmother in the audience. She waved, her eyes shiny with tears. As the children began to sing, I suddenly noticed that there was a small line of tape on the stage in front of where Benj was standing proudly in his place. For some reason, it was seeing that tape they'd put there for him that brought on my own flow of tears. The tape seemed to symbolize the loving guidelines, the clear and comforting structure this extraordinary school had given him, the special care they'd paid to him in the most unobtrusive way possible. The director, the teachers, the other parents, most of whom had been our cohorts for the past three years, had done everything in their power to help Benj succeed, to integrate into the school and into the group of children. I thought of the kind mom who'd sent me a description of the birthday party she was planning for her child so I could run it by Benj in advance, the dad who'd always listen to Benj's disquisitions on clouds with unfeigned interest and make silly jokes to relax Benj at tense moments, the young teacher who'd helped Benj learn how to walk on a mini–balance beam despite his "I can't do it!" on the first day. The school allowed his therapists in the classroom, they welcomed our daily involvement, they had a very strong no-teasing policy. In this school, in this community, he'd been understood and treasured. He'd been safe.

And now we were stepping into the unknown. Would the next school make the same special efforts? Would Benj feel welcomed and at home there? How would he weather all the impending transitions to a new home, new city, new school, parents living apart? I looked at six-year-old Benj and thought of Wordsworth's fears for Coleridge's six-year-old son:

> O blessed vision! happy child!
> Thou art so exquisitely wild,
> I think of thee with many fears
> For what may be thy lot in future years.
> —Wordsworth, "To H. C., Six Years Old"

The children finished their songs and returned to their seats; now it was time for the diplomas to be given out. Each child's name was called in alphabetical order, and he or she would walk from his or her seat, go up one set of steps on the right side of the stage, cross to the middle of the stage, where the teachers would shake his or her hand and bestow the diploma, then complete the walk across the stage and go down the stairs left. When we saw that this was the procedure, Richard and I looked at each other, a little worried. I thought, "Uh-oh, two sets of stairs with no railings and all eyes upon him." Benj's name was called, and he leapt to his feet, but instead of walking toward the stage, he spun around to locate me and Richard in the audience; Richard gave him a thumbs-up and I waved and smiled at him. Reassured, he turned and walked to stage right, then made his way slowly and a little awkwardly up the stairs. When he got to the top, he smiled again, this time in relief, and walked over to Peter, who pulled Benj a bit closer to him and whispered something in his ear. Benj accepted his diploma from Peter with a beaming smile, and then I noticed one of his teachers stationed at the bottom of the stairs on the stage's left side. When Benj got to the top of the stairs, she stepped forward, smiled, and held her hand up to him, to assist him down the stairs. But Benj high-fived her instead, and walked down the stairs all by himself. When he got to the bottom, he took her hand in his, in a rather gallant gesture, and they walked together, jauntily, back to his seat.

Thou little Child, yet glorious in the might
Of heaven-born freedom on thy being's height,
Why with such earnest pains dost thou provoke
The years to bring the inevitable yoke,
Thus blindly with thy blessedness at strife?
Full soon thy Soul shall have her earthly freight,
And custom lie upon thee with a weight,
Heavy as frost, and deep almost as life!
　　—"Intimations Ode"

IN THE LATE SUMMER of 2005, I moved with my children from a large craftsman-style house in the woods of sleepy Poughkeepsie to a small apartment on the eighteenth floor of a glistening apartment tower on Manhattan's Upper West Side. Richard found a tiny apartment in Upper Manhattan but spent a lot of time at our apartment and saw the boys daily. I was determined to avoid acrimony and minimize stress for the children, so we began working with a social worker and a psychologist on a "collaborative divorce."

We decided that at least until James graduated from kindergarten, we would use an arrangement called nesting—in which the children stay in one place and the parents move in and out of the apartment so that the children don't have to travel back and forth between two houses. Richard spent two nights a week in "my" apartment (I stayed with my mom or a friend), and twice a month he would take the boys to my mom's country house in Connecticut for the weekend. The boys seemed remarkably accepting of this new arrangement, and, for once, Benj's disinclination to ask questions or probe emotional issues made things easier: he didn't ask why and he didn't blame himself.

I was living again, for the first time since I went to college, in the city of my childhood; our apartment was, in fact, just a few blocks from my childhood home. I walked the same streets, visited the same playgrounds, and James began at the preschool I'd attended. When Richard and I had first envisioned going to the city, we'd thought that this decision had promised a return, in some way, to the enchanted world of my childhood. But within a week of moving back to the city, a crucial figure of my romantic childhood, Grammy Peg, died, heartbroken since the death of my grandfather four months earlier. My father, the native New Yorker, was thousands of miles away, and as I passed familiar spots, I'd often find myself overcome with longing for him. The Upper West Side itself was so different; much more glittering and wealthy, with most of the old neighborhood stores closed and replaced with upscale clothing boutiques or chain stores. With the world of my childhood irrevocably gone, I felt like a grownup, in a negative sense, for the first time. I felt as Wordsworth, looking back as an adult on his childhood, felt:

> so wide appears
> The vacancy between me and those days,
> Which yet have such self-presence in my mind,
> That musing on them, often do I seem
> Two consciousnesses, conscious of myself
> And of some other Being.
> —*Prelude*, II

And I was living with a very different child than I had been. I saw the city anew through Benjamin's eyes—he was fascinated by the elevators, the subways, the streets and avenues, the logic and rationality of the city's grid, the signs and billboards, entirely different things than those that had captivated me.

I had worried about my country boys' adjustment to dazzling, loud, and potentially overwhelming New York City, but to my great relief, both boys seemed to embrace their new surroundings. James romped around the Hippo Playground in Riverside Park, and looked forward to the arrival of the Mr. Softee ice-cream truck that stopped on our corner every afternoon. Benj loved going up and down in our building's elevator (he fought with James over who got to press the buttons) and watching helicopters, blimps, and boats through our living-room windows. He liked to take the Broadway bus down to my sister and brother-in-law's apartment and enjoyed bagel-and-cream-cheese brunches with them. And he especially loved having visitors to our apartment. He made elevator charts and asked each visitor which elevator they'd taken so he could record it on his chart. He gave each person who visited an extensive tour, in which he pointed out the special features of each room ("My room has three windows"; "The circuit breaker is on this wall in James's room") and each closet ("Our winter coats are kept here"; "In this closet we put the messy stuff Mommy doesn't want people to see!"). It felt so good to be living close to my family, and to have old friends visiting almost daily and getting to know my children.

And it felt good to write to the head of the Vassar English Department and tell him that I'd decided to leave academia after the coming year's teaching responsibilities were over; the father of a special-needs child himself, he accepted my decision with great graciousness and understanding. Stepping off that tenure track felt like an enormous liberation, and I looked forward to beginning at the literary agency the following summer.

...

> Shades of the prison-house begin to close
> Upon the growing Boy . . .
> —"Intimations Ode"

A FEW WEEKS AFTER we moved to New York City, Benjamin entered his new school, as a first-grader. The adjustment period was agonizingly difficult. During these first weeks of school, his anxiety was extreme, manifested in tics of various kinds: throat-clearing, tossing his hair out of his eyes, humming, tapping on surfaces, walking on his toes, and blinking rapidly. He had difficulty following directions, completing tasks, and staying calm. His characteristic worries—of new demands, of fire drills, of making mistakes, of losing games, strange and unexpected sounds—were ratcheted up to an unprecedented level. His perfectionism was greatly exacerbated by the behavioral system implemented in his classroom— one that doled out numbers (essentially demerits) to students who "called out" or "fidgeted," and handed out "super student" awards to the calmer, more compliant students. According to his teachers, Benj was doing a lot of "calling out"—interrupting, asking lots of questions, many of which he knew or could read the answers to, repeating instructions unnecessarily, repeatedly asking for reassurance, giggling uncontrollably, physically touching or hugging others without their permission.

Those first months, I spent hours every day either e-mailing or on the phone with the teachers and therapists, or at the school observing Benj and having "urgent" meetings with the school psychologist, or taking Benj to therapy sessions. And just when it looked to me as if he was finally adjusting, one day in mid-October, as I was on my way into school to pick up Benj, the school psychologist appeared seemingly out of nowhere, and grabbed me by the arm. "I need to talk to you," she said sternly, pulling me down the hall and into a windowless conference room. She sat me down in a leather swivel chair, sighed, and told me: "Patience is running thin" with Benj; "Things are getting worse rather than better"; "He is continuing to struggle"; and "You need to get a child psychiatrist on board yesterday." She then hurried to speak sweetly of what a "nice kid" he was, but the impression had been made. It was hard for me to believe that even in this special school, presumably meant to handle kids with anxiety, sensory issues, and language problems, Benj was doing so poorly, but the school psychologist was intransigent in her insistence that he was. Now I feared that every single day Benj would be running the gauntlet and his placement in the school was precarious at best. And where would he go if he couldn't stay there? I had exhausted every other option; I'd applied to every conceivable school and this was our only chance. And how could I possibly keep up this level of involvement once I was back at work (I was on sabbatical from Vassar that semester but would be teaching a full load in January and then beginning at the literary agency in June)?

That night, at home, after putting the boys to bed, I sat at my desk collating copies of reports that dated back three years to when Benj was first evaluated. I was gearing up for a big Committee on Special Education meeting for Benj and for child psychiatrist visits the new school had insisted on. Reading through three years' worth of Benj's school and occupational and speech therapy reports, I was struck by the number of references to how happy and enthusiastic Benj was, and I felt so acutely how these early months at the new school had dampened Benj's natural enthusiasm and dimmed his joy. These reports were also brimming with affection and fondness for Benj, and I wondered: do any of the teachers or staff members at his new school feel even close to this way about Benji? The message I was getting from the new school was: "We're fed up with him." Given this, the hope expressed in these reports, the conviction that Benj would continue to make amazing progress and flourish in school seemed Pollyanna-ish to me now. But at the same time, I knew that if only this new school would give Benj time and make the effort to understand him, he would be okay. I believed in him so strongly, and I wanted the school to see this potential, to appreciate his beauty, to have faith in him. And some lines from Wordsworth kept running through my head:

> Fair seed-time had my soul, and I grew up
> Fostered alike by beauty and by fear.
>   —*Prelude*, I

Wordsworth's words exemplified everything I felt Benj wasn't being given at his school. He needed fairness, he needed seed-time, he needed flexibility, patience, and understanding, he needed room to develop at his own pace. He needed people who cared for and about his soul.

A few days later, I wrote an e-mail to close family and friends, summarizing all of the goings-on at school and ended it:

> Life is a wild roller-coaster right now and I am hanging on for dear life. To think that after all the work and time I invested into finding this school for Benj it may not work out is extremely dispiriting and scary. Is there ANY school that can handle Benj? How can I do the best by Benj? How very much I love him, how much I want him to be happy, how agonizing it is to think of him suffering and unable to express his anxiety verbally because of his language issues. There is nothing I wouldn't do for him but I'm not sure what to do, and that is the most frustrating thing of all.
>
> In the last month, I've realized in a way I never had before that this is and will be my life—this day-to-day work on and for and with Benj. He will improve and develop and there will be many

rewarding moments. But he has a lifelong disability and he will always need loads of effort on his behalf, both in every single interaction with him and with his teachers and therapists. It can be extremely exhausting and overwhelming . . . But the blessings of being his mother far outweigh the worry and stress and fatigue. Truly he has made me an infinitely stronger, more patient and compassionate person. I can do this. But I will need all your support and love behind me, and I know I have them!

This was the first time I'd ever admitted to anyone other than my mother, sister, and brother-in-law that being Benj's mom could be exhausting and overwhelming. I had begun, at last, to share the details of my life with him, in regular e-mails to my closest friends and family members, and to lean on them for support and strength.

Meanwhile, three-year-old James was having his own difficult time, but for entirely different reasons. Unlike Benj, who'd always smiled at everyone, surprised visitors with a hearty "Hi Benj!," and never had any trouble separating from us, James had never wanted to be held by people he didn't know well, buried his face in my chest or hid behind my legs when guests came over, and was shy in large groups, unfamiliar settings, or around new people. And now, as one of the youngest children in a large, loud, mixed-age classroom, James was feeling overwhelmed and suffering from terrible separation anxiety, crying in heaving sobs and clinging to our legs when we tried to leave. For the first two months, the school required that a parent stay either in the classroom or in the building for the entire four hours that he was at school. But slowly he acclimated and became more comfortable.

As time went on, Benj, too, began to settle down. He looked forward to school, adapted to its routines, and grew closer to his teachers. In early November, however, he missed almost an entire week of school due to a severe double ear infection, and on the morning he was supposed to return to school after the long absence, he seemed a little shaky. He complained that the Silk soy milk on his Cheerios tasted unsweetened, dragged his feet getting his socks and shoes on, and expressed his worry that cloudy skies meant that his class wouldn't get to have the usual Tuesday "park time" (I was scheduled to be a parent "park volunteer," and that might have made him especially on edge about the possible cancellation). Then, I accidentally sent him off to school with the wrong lunch-box (I mixed up his and James's). Things weren't looking particularly propitious at this point.

Although the skies stayed overcast, no rain fell, so I arrived at the school a little before one p.m. for my park volunteer duties. Walking in the front door to the building, I bumped into one of the two regular gym teachers. Benj had been having particular trouble in gym; he almost always got a time-out in gym, and in the last week or so I'd been e-mailing back and forth with the gym teachers, brainstorming ways to make the gym experience more positive for him. Benj absolutely loved sports, both to watch and to play, but because his biggest area of anxiety was about losing, making a mistake, doing the wrong thing, sports were especially difficult for him. The teachers had told me that he tended to cry easily when he thought he was losing, and sometimes thought he was losing when he wasn't. He would visibly tense up, slip into his rigid black-and-white and catastrophic thinking ("If I am tagged then I will lose"; "Oh no! If I am in the squirrel house now"—in a game of fox/squirrel tag—"I am here forever!"), and become distraught and weepy. A few days ago, they'd e-mailed to tell me about difficulties he'd been having with a yoga game that involved making a pose representing his own version of an image (animal, plant, bridge, building) from a card. He would say, "I can't do it, I don't know how!" and the teachers guessed that because it was such an open-ended activity (with no "right answer"), he was unsure of what was expected of him. Sometimes, they told me, he would be in the middle of making an interesting pose and cry "I can't do it!" even as he *was* doing it. They'd noticed that when they gave him a card with a photo of someone doing an *actual* yoga pose, Benj had an easier time; the clear parameters of what needed to be done made him feel more secure.

I wanted Benj to really grasp the ideas that the teachers had no "right answer" in mind, thought what he was doing was interesting even when he thought he was doing something "wrong," and wanted more than anything for him to have fun in class. Since the best way, still, to enable him to understand something was to give it to him in writing, I showed him the teacher's e-mail and wrote out a "yoga story" for him. Now, standing outside the school, the gym teacher told me that Benj had done really well the previous day in yoga. According to her, as he was contorting his little body into various poses, he called out: "Mommy says I can do it even when I feel like I am not doing it!" and "You think my poses are interesting so I will keep trying, Ms. R!" At the end of the class, he went up to her, hugged her, and said: "I felt better today, Ms. R."

After my conversation with Ms. R, I walked to Benj's classroom to meet his class; as a parent park volunteer, I would hold his and one other child's hand on the five-block walk to and from the park and help supervise the twelve children as they raced around the playground. During our hour in the park, I played football with him and two other little boys, and Benj threw some spectacular touchdowns and kicked a mean extra point. He engaged with one little boy in a way I'd never seen him do before: they actually had a lengthy conversation about their favorite sports teams, and Benj patiently explained to Aidan what "blow-out" and "shut-out" meant for football games. As we were walking back to the school building, Benj said: "Mommy, I have twelve stars for the day already, and there's only one more period. So if I get a star in Afternoon Meeting, that means I get thirteen stars for the day!" Thirteen was the maximum number of stars a child could earn according to the new positive-reinforcement system the school had implemented a few weeks earlier after speaking with his previous nursery school's director and me about Benj's need for positive feedback and support. I hugged him good-bye and told him I'd see him in forty-five minutes.

As soon as I walked into the classroom at dismissal time, Benj came bounding up to me with his irrepressible Benj smile. Of course I knew before he told me: "Oh Mommy, I got thirteen stars!" His head classroom teacher and occupational therapist were standing behind him, smiling proudly. "That face, that face!" his teacher said affectionately. I took Benj on my lap and told him how proud I was of him for accomplishing something he'd repeatedly told me he could never do because "it is too hard to get thirteen stars." "Remember, Benj, how you said you could never ever get thirteen stars? You see, Benj, you CAN do things you don't think at first you can! You are amazing, Benji!"

We left school and proceeded to the pediatrician's office to have the ear infection assessed. He was delighted when the doctor told him: "Benjamin, your ears look great!" "That means the medicine is working, Mommy!" he exclaimed. The doctor then told me that we could stop the antibiotics the next day if they were bothering him or he was resisting them, but Benj interjected: "No, no, Dr. H, the bottle says to take this medicine twice daily for ten days and today is only day eight, so I need to take the medicine for two more days." Dr. H replied: "Well, with a patient as responsible and meticulous as you, Benjamin, I certainly agree!"

We then went to see Dr. G for Benj's regular Tuesday appointment. At one point during the session, I could hear the classic Benj "Oh no!" and a bit of weepiness, but within a few minutes I heard giggles and the excited Benj voice instead. The door opened at six and Dr. G and Benj emerged, her arms wrapped around him from behind. They walked toward me with big smiles on both of their faces and when they got to me, Benj broke free from Dr. G and grabbed my hands in his. "Okay, Mommy, we can go home and have supper now," he said. But Dr. G wouldn't let him go quite yet. "Before you go, Benj, I have to tell your mommy something." She then pulled me close in a long, warm embrace, and said: "I am so so proud of this boy." "Did you hear that, Benj?" I said. "Do you think maybe it's because you recovered so wonderfully from your moment of worry?" "Did you hear me playing tic-tac-toe, Mommy?" he asked. "She won the first game, and I was upset, but then I remembered to say 'Oh well, better luck next time!' and I recovered!" A day like this more than made up for all the stress and worry of the last few months, perhaps the most difficult of my life and of Benj's as well. I was so grateful for this day, and more than anything, I was simply filled with happiness that my dearest Benj was happy:

> A temper known to those, who, after long
> And weary expectation, have been blest
> With sudden happiness beyond all hope.
> —Wordsworth, "Nutting"

THIS, HOWEVER, WAS JUST that—one great day—and in general, the message we were still getting from the school was: "He is too anxious," "He is disruptive," "He is not adjusting quickly enough." And so, at the urging of his school psychologist and a child psychiatrist we consulted with at the school's insistence, we made the wrenching decision to try a course of medication. I wasn't dogmatically opposed to medications, but I worried that Benj was so young, and I feared the inevitable side effects and the slippery slope of one medication, then another, and another. I also suspected that Benj had inherited my sensitive nervous system—the one time I'd taken a quarter of a prescription sleeping pill, I'd been knocked flat for a good twenty-four hours. But most of all I resisted the idea that a pill could be a quick fix to make Benj more manageable and docile; I felt the school psychologist wanted him to "fit in" too quickly and wasn't being patient with his transition process. It was only when the director of the Vassar preschool, with whom I continued to consult, said she had seen good results in kids Benj's age, and that sometimes medications could help anxious kids live their lives with greater happiness and peace and be more fully themselves, that I finally relented. Even Richard, who had violently resisted the idea of medicating Benj, had some hopeful curiosity about what might happen. And so, with nervousness but also a bit of optimism, we started Benj on a very low dose of an antihypertensive drug used to treat tics, hyperactivity, and anxiety in children. That first night, I wrote to friends and family:

> I hope that this drug will help take the edge off his anxiety, allow him to get unstuck from his obsessions, and relax into his life. He is such a fundamentally joyful, optimistic, buoyant little person, and it just KILLS me to see him anguished by worry (his wrenching moan of despair when he gets a three or loses a game is just heartbreaking), or tuned out in a dull haze of perseveration, or revved up by a tormenting obsession. The most important thing I want for him is the chance to express his beautiful spirit with ease and fluidity, to laugh that great Benj belly laugh with abandon, to enjoy his amazing talents and gifts. We all love that gorgeous Benj smile of sheer delight; let's hope we see much more of it in the weeks to come!

Unfortunately, however, we noticed no positive changes and, increasingly, some regression in terms of his "irrelevant talk"—reciting the subway schedule, reading phrases out loud—an increase in tics, and a considerable amount of whininess and weepiness—all three of these things seemed associated with an increased sleepiness/irritability. Oddly enough, the drug seemed to intensify and even bring on just the kinds of behaviors it was intended to counteract or suppress: he was less able to control his body (more leaning on people, more fidgety), less able to control his voice (more vocal tics, endless repetition of silly words and phrases, louder voice), and less able to engage socially and participate in life with ease and joy. After a week of no improvement and increasingly clear deterioration, I made the decision to call the psychiatrist the next morning. I was almost certain that the medication wasn't doing what it should be doing and was probably aggravating rather than alleviating Benj's issues. In a few days, we would leave for Christmas celebrations at my mother's house, and I wanted Benj off the medication in time to enjoy the holiday.

That night, around three a.m., I was woken by the sound of Benj's calling, "Mommy! Mommy!" When I went into his room, he told me he was seeing colored bubbles and worms in the air in his room. He didn't seem agitated, just interested. I chalked this up to a dream, tucked him back in, and went back to sleep. But the next morning, I came into his room to wake him up, and saw Benj sitting on the edge of his bed, blinking rapid-fire, rolling his eyes from side to side and back in his head, pointing to corners of his room and to the air and to the ceiling and smiling to himself. Trying to disguise my worry, I asked him what was going on and he said he was pointing to all the bubbles in the air. Again he wasn't distressed or agitated; instead he seemed lost in a trance state. He smiled sleepily and laughed gently as he pointed to various parts of his room where he saw "worms" and "bubbles." "Look, Mommy, there's a pink one!" he'd say. "Are you pretending, Benj?" I asked, trying as hard as I could to keep my tone light and not betray the intense fear I was feeling. "No, I'm not pretending" was all he would say. I took him to the table for breakfast and, as he ate his cereal, retreated to my bedroom where in hushed tones I left an urgent message on the psychiatrist's voice-mail.

That morning, Benj continued to say that he was seeing things in the air. I'd ask him, "Do you see anything now?" and he'd say, "Just one blue bubble over there," or "I only see the bubbles on the white wall." When his guitar teacher arrived for a lesson, she told me that she had noticed alarming changes in his attention and focus over the past week—he'd seemed spacey and goofy and had been having a lot of difficulty keeping the measures, getting the right notes, and following the scores they used. She was quite disconcerted by what she was seeing—the loss of his energy and drive and ability to focus and feel things deeply. "That's what makes Benjamin so much fun," she said. "He's such a *real* person, and he feels things so intensely." She pressed hard on her chest to demonstrate how Benj feels and experiences things deep down at his core. "I would hate to see that spirit tamped down." I thought, how right she is about Benj's intensity and vulnerability to experience. He can remind all of us what pain and pleasure and joy and fear really mean, because he experiences them in their purest forms.

Finally, hours later, the psychiatrist called back. He told me that although he had never seen a child with the "visual field disturbance" Benj demonstrated, he did think that the drug was having a "negative effect on Benj's nervous system." He advised me to start tapering off the medication, since stopping it abruptly could cause life-threatening blood-pressure swings. Then he calmly announced: "The next drug we should go to is a minor tranquilizer, and if that doesn't work we'll try a major tranquilizer, but I'd rather avoid it since it has a slight potential for permanent neurologic side effects." Horrified, I told him that I was feeling very unsettled by Benj's reaction to the current medication and didn't feel ready to put him on another one just yet. However, he insisted on mailing the prescription for the minor tranquilizer to my mother's country house and urged me to start Benj on it as soon as possible.

The next day I spoke with Dr. G, who had never felt medications would be a good idea for Benj. She was insistent that she'd seen a really dramatic turn for the worse in Benj's behavior since he'd been on the medication: she reported that he had seemed very tired and more irritable and impatient than usual, that something funny had been going on with his eyes, and that he'd been at times aggressive, even angry, in an uncharacteristic way. "I'm actually frightened," this normally unflappable woman told me, "by what I see as a significant and odd change in the quality of his demeanor, his state of consciousness." She noted an increased sadness, a distant look in his eyes, a turning inward away from social engagement, a dissociative quality. "Something neurological is going on," she insisted. She was relieved to hear that we were tapering off the medication and supported me wholeheartedly in my decision not to try another one. "I would wait on medications till he's older and his nervous system has developed a bit more," she told me. "Right now he's making such progress with the cognitive therapy techniques, he's settling in, he's adjusting. I know he can do it."

And so, over the next few days we tapered off the drug. Although he was obviously better the first day off the medication—brighter eyes, more energy, happier—it was a day-to-day process getting him back to baseline. I wrote to my friends and family: "Keep your fingers crossed that he keeps coming back to us. Richard actually got teary last night with worry that we have 'lost' Benj." The day after Christmas, I walked down my mother's long, snowy driveway, lifted the latch on the mailbox, and saw a small white envelope addressed to me, with the psychiatrist's return address. I knew what it contained, and without any hesitation I ripped it into pieces and stuffed the fragments into my pocket.

Even though I was certain I'd made the right decision, I worried about how the school would react to the news that I'd taken him off the medication and had no plans to start another one. I wrote a three-page e-mail to his entire school team (teachers, therapists, psychologist), describing how he'd responded to the medication and making the case for why he shouldn't be medicated, why it was wrong for him, why I didn't want to try anything else right then. I did everything I could to convince them that we'd made the right decision, but I wasn't at all sure they'd accept it.

Benj's first day back at school after the holiday break was a nail-biter for me. How would he do after two weeks away? I went to pick him up from school with a great deal of trepidation. Although the school psychologist seemed clearly discouraged by the fact that we didn't plan to medicate Benj, I could tell that he'd done reasonably well that day and, more important, he ran to greet me with such spring in his step and delight on his face, and before we left, he insisted on tracking each and every one of his teachers down in the corridors and hugging them with great affection and warmth. He then went up to the head of the school, with whom he'd developed a sweet bond due to his fear of fire drills (she always told him in advance when there would be one so he wouldn't have to worry), exclaimed "Good-bye, Ms. S!," and threw his arms around her. She looked at him with fondness, and then said to me: "He has the most wonderful smile I have ever seen!"

After school, I took him to his regular psychologist appointment. I sat in the waiting room, supposedly reading a novel but really listening as hard as I could to what was going on behind the door. I heard him telling Dr. G, who was weeping and whining when she lost their game of tic-tac-toe (she role-played bad losing and good losing for him): "Oh, but Dr. G, you don't need to cry. You win some, you lose some." At another point, I heard him say: "Dr. G, you can be a gracious loser and just shake my hand now, okay?"

Being back in the routine of school and homework and therapy and back in his old body with his old neurological system was clearly an enormous relief to Benj, but January was still quite rough. The school made a change to the behavioral system, so just as Benj had gotten a handle on the old one—what he had to do or avoid doing to earn stars and super-student awards—there was a new wrinkle and his anxiety flared again. He was still having an especially hard time in gym class; the teacher was one tough cookie, and I wrote many e-mails to her, urging her to see what might look like defiance as anxiety, explaining Benj's behavior to her, offering suggestions for how to avoid his melting down or withdrawing. I heard that the school psychologist was pressing other parents to medicate their kids, but she never again said a word to me; I think she knew I'd be unyielding on this issue. I had almost daily exchanges of lengthy e-mails about Benj with his classroom teachers and his reading teacher; in these, I tried to strike a delicate balance between honoring their feelings, expressing solidarity with their frustrations, and advocating fiercely for Benj, showing them how to understand and support him in the best possible way.

And despite the continuing difficulties in school, Benj was making such great progress in coping with situations he never would have been able to handle in the past. That winter, Claire and I took both boys to the Big Apple Circus. Three years earlier, Benj wouldn't have been able to make it through one minute. A year earlier, he would have cried at points. But on that cold January day, he went in with a slight bit of apprehension ("Is it going to be very dark?") but then, using his coping strategies of self-talk and self-preparation very effectively, he said, "Mommy, if it gets dark, I can just hold your hand until it gets light again" and "If it gets too loud I can just cover my ears." It was a very loud, very hectic, very sensory-overloaded scene—loads of young kids, many of whom were screaming, laughing loudly, whining, or crying, nonstop action, frequent near-blackness (lights going off almost totally in between acts), loud band music, pistol shots—but there was only one moment during the entire show when Benj covered his ears (when some high-pitched bells kept ringing for a good minute), and Claire covered her ears at that point at well! And Benj didn't just tolerate the situation; he clapped with such enthusiasm after each performer, pointed out the neat things he saw, cheered and nudged James to clap at the end when everyone took their bows. What a pleasure for him and a victory for him and a joy to witness.

Also that January my mother took Benj to one of Claire's and my favorite childhood places, the American Museum of Natural History, for the first time. From the age of eight on, we'd lived in a building across the street from the museum, and Claire and I had spent countless hours wandering through it. When my mother had suggested she take Benj to the Natural History Museum, I'd wondered whether he would be able to take the huge space and the crowds, but the outing was a complete success. My mother reported that he'd shown little anxiety even in the dark exhibit halls, cavernous spaces, and crowded and noisy cafeteria, and had a fantastic time. He came back clutching a map of the museum in his hand and exclaiming: "We saw the dinosaur skeletons! They were on the fourth floor. We took the elevator to get there, and we also saw discovery machines! They can be used to discover the information about a dinosaur. Next time we're going to go see the giant whale!" He and Grams began to have regular weekend lunches at local restaurants and museum dates; he looked forward to these all week and proudly described them to us when he returned.

Because being able to refer to written documents helped Benj so much, I tried to put everything in writing for him. I wrote a lot of "social stories" (little narratives about making mistakes, acting like the teacher, interrupting, silly repeating/copying, computer talk, handling loss), and after revising them in accordance with his speech therapist's, Dr. G's, and his occupational therapist's recommendations, printed and bound them in *Benj's Social Stories Book*. Every night, I wrote out "Benj's Note for the Morning," sentences that I left at his place at the table for him to read before leaving for school. The notes reported what had happened in sports games while he was asleep, reassured him about something potentially scary that might happen that day, told him how proud I was of him for his accomplishments, or sent him off to school with good cheer; he kept each and every one in a large box in his room. In coordination with his speech therapist and with Benj's own participation (this was crucial), we devised a list of "School Rules," a "Personal Space" chart (keep your hands and feet to yourself; whom it's okay and not okay to hug, kiss, and hold hands with), a "Cool Down" chart (essentially a list of relaxation techniques: take deep breaths, give yourself a hug), a "Calling Out" chart (when it was appropriate and when it wasn't); he carried these with him on laminated note cards. Richard came up with "Benj Homework Goals"—a checklist that helped Benj stay focused and cooperative. And if Benj had had a rough day or a rough time with one particular class, I would encourage him to write an e-mail to the teacher in question. He'd dictate to me, often haltingly, but once we got something—anything—down, he would often pour forth ideas and feelings to me. Figuring out what to say and how to say it helped him to figure out what had gone wrong and what he could do differently next time:

> Dear Mrs. D,
>
> I will try hard not to do chess talk tomorrow. I know that when I do chess talk, I do not listen as well and I do not learn as much. I want to learn a lot in school so I must try not to do chess talk. But I love chess, so it is hard! But I can talk about chess with Daddy or Mommy or have conversations about chess with people. When other kids do chess talk, I should just ignore them and not copy them. Will you help me?
>
> I love you.
>
> Love,
>
> Benjamin (and Mommy the typist)

We also addressed his anxiety on a sensory level. I consulted with a nutritionist, who recommended calcium supplements and Omega-

3-rich fish oil (which I snuck into his applesauce every night). I increased his occupational therapy sessions and made sure he got outdoor playtime every day. His wonderful occupational therapist came up with all sorts of things for him to use in the classroom—a chewy necklace (made out of rubber Thera-Tubing) for oral input to increase his concentration and help with fidgeting, a weighted vest to wear at certain times of the day (this gave him a greater sense of body awareness and security about his position in space and had a calming effect on him), a half-deflated beach ball for him to sit on, a squeeze ball to squeeze when he was feeling frustrated, to release anxiety, or focus his energy. She gave Benj and his teachers a list of physical activities he could do if he was feeling antsy or anxious: twenty-five jumping jacks in the hall, stretches, or even walking up and down the corridor. And all this seemed to be helping, as Benj was calmer, more attentive, and, most important, happier.

In early February, I received a letter officially offering Benj a place in the school for the following year. This was enormously reassuring; up until that point I'd always felt he was "on the bubble" and on the verge of being "counseled out," especially after we'd chosen to not proceed with medications. And though there were still bumps, with vigilance and attentiveness to every detail of his daily life, with daily e-mailing and strategizing with his teachers and therapists, and with time and increased familiarity, he continued to settle down and settle in. Benj was invited on his first real playdate since starting school: a Super Bowl party for two at fellow football fan Aidan's house; they watched a tape of the game (so they could do so at a reasonable hour and minus commercials) and feasted on game-appropriate food including potato chips, mini hot dogs, and chocolate chip cookies.

Just a week later, however, I got the results of allergy testing I'd had done on Benj; that he had severe allergies to gluten, dairy, and eggs was both distressing and exciting news. His diet would have to radically change, and Benj hated change. I thought how ironic it was that we had tried so hard to make it possible for him to chew pretzels, crackers, and goldfish so he could eat the school snack and get comfortable with the cold and stickiness of ice cream and cupcakes so he could partake in birthday party food, and now it all had to go. He wouldn't be able to enjoy the meals and treats he so loved, and taking away an easy source of happiness for Benj was a difficult thing to consider. But at the same time, this discovery opened the possibility of affecting great changes in Benj's behavior, mood, and attention without the need for drugs. I immediately began to research palatable and yummy substitutes for his favorite foods (spaghetti, waffles, bread), and Benj was remarkably accepting of the changes, reminding his teachers that he needed a different snack than the other children ("Mrs. D, I can't eat *those* pretzels, but I can eat *these*!" he'd say, holding up the gluten-free version I'd sent to school in his backpack), checking the labels of any packaged food at his grandmother's house for "things I'm allergic to," and happily eating the gluten-, dairy-, and sugar-free chocolate cupcakes I sent to school on his birthday.

One day, when I came to pick him up from school, I noticed how kind the school's admissions director was with him. Her office was located directly across from Benj's classroom, and he wandered in to look at the New York Giants memorabilia on her desk and walls. She smiled and took him on her lap, listening patiently to the Giants facts and figures he shared with her. I found out that, like me, she'd grown up on the Giants. That night, I e-mailed her a *New York Times* article my father had written about me and him and the Giants. She wrote, "This is fantastic, magical, music to my ears . . . sounds like my childhood with my dad!" and I responded, "My father is extremely ill with lung cancer, and not conscious—oh how I wish I could tell him that his words meant so much to you! And by the way, your sweetness with Benj the other day really touched my heart.

I thank the powers that be every single day that we found this school for him!" Her response was just one sentence:

> Let me just say, I LOVE HIM, ALL of him—his ways are just amazing—he makes me (and many others) smile!!!!!

This was all I'd ever wanted for Benj. I sat at my computer smiling through tears:

> And they such joyful tidings were,
> The joy was more than he could bear!—
> He melted into tears.
>
> Sweet tears of hope and tenderness!
> And fast they fell a plenteous shower! . . .
> A gentle, a relaxing, power!
> —Wordsworth, "Peter Bell"

WITH THE HELP OF scripts and prompts, Benj continued to learn how to manage his anxieties by expressing them verbally. He had rarely said anything like "I'm hurt," "I'm worried," "I feel bad," until he was about six years old, and doing so spontaneously was a huge struggle for him. One night in early June, as his first year in Manhattan and at his new school were drawing to a close, there were terrible, loud thunderstorms in New York City. The sky turned pitch-black about seven p.m., and the thunder and lightning were very dramatic. Benj's two greatest fears throughout his life had been loud, unexpected sounds and thunderstorms.

That night, as I was getting him ready for bed, he said in a worried voice, "Mommy, I'm afraid. I don't know if I can stand to sleep tonight because I just hate this thunder." I then told him: "You know what, sweetie? Sometimes it helps to think of the sounds of a thunderstorm as music, like crashing cymbals or loud drums." Benj instantly perked up, smiled at me, and looked both intrigued and relieved. Then a spark came into his eye. "Or you know what else, Mommy?" he said. "What, Benji?" I asked. "The thunder sounds like giants bowling." He went to bed smiling.

Benj's ability to articulate his emotions in a clear and open way without giving in to them, his capacity to overcome two intense and inveterate fears of his, and his use of figurative language—his biggest linguistic hurdles had always been flexibility and nonliteral meaning—in such a playful and imaginative way took my breath away.

This little exchange between us both reminded me of my experience with my father and the lightning at the big window in Spain and underscored so powerfully just how far Benj had come. I sent a jubilant e-mail to family and friends describing it, and most wrote back to say how moved they were: "Benj is sheer poetry!" one especially romantic and dramatic friend (and a lover of Keats) wrote. Another, however, gently pointed out that thunder sounding like giants bowling was a common image and that Benj must have read it in a book. I didn't want to believe her, but of course I did, and it was so disappointing. My belief in Benj's metaphor-making abilities, his originality, had been misguided, I thought to myself; it was just the old echolalia. But then I realized: even if the phrase I'd thought was his own was lifted from a book, he was using what he'd learned to help cope with anxiety, he was applying his knowledge in a useful way, and he was learning how to comfort himself.

And it was hugely reassuring and gratifying when, a few days later, I learned that the school psychologist who had been so impatient with Benj's transition process and who had so strenuously pushed medications would not be returning to the school the following year. With her departure, the school's behavioral system was definitively being modified to reward good behavior rather than punish inappropriate behavior. Even more important, Benj was much calmer, and as a result much more able to enjoy school. He loved the structure and all the little rituals of the day; the morning meeting, calendar, checking the outside temperature, and Question of the Day. He still needed a good deal of teacher support, especially in negotiating peer interactions and in navigating Free Choice time. He proudly shared his guitar in "show and share," explaining frets, capos, and tuning to his admiring classmates. The gentle and encouraging "coaches" in his after-school gym class called him Benny Hoops and Kid Benj, and Benj, who'd always fiercely resisted any kind of nickname, now not only tolerated but reveled in these nicknames, because they made him feel like "a real athlete!" He loved the trip on a sightseeing bus around Manhattan that his class took, even stepping in to elaborate on the tour guide's commentary and answering his classmates' questions about buildings (how high they were, when they were built, and in what style), streets, and neighborhoods. He was ever more passionate about his new city and began to collect books about and maps of New York; he especially loved its transportation system. One day I came home from work to find that Benj had turned our apartment into a subway station; he'd made signs and taped them to the furniture (one sofa was the 1 train, another the 2, the bench in the entryway the shuttle to Times Square), and he was leading James through the station. A few days after school ended, accompanied by their fathers, he and his classmate Aidan, both relatively frail little boys with histories of motor delays and challenges, walked triumphantly across the Brooklyn Bridge together. "Five thousand nine hundred and eighty-nine feet long!" Benj proudly told me later.

He had a great summer at the school's camp, whose theme was the very un-Benj "Fairy Tales." He won the Fairy Tale Trivia contest and dressed as a prince in homemade crown and cape on Dress Like Your Favorite Fairy Tale Character Day. With his classroom teacher right there next to him in the pool, he put his face in the water for the first time during one heroic swimming lesson.

And the fall of Benj's second-grade year was like night and day compared to what we'd experienced the year before. He had the same teachers, who'd come to know him well and love him, and was in the same classroom with roughly the same group of kids. He now felt comfortable and was able to relax and enjoy the many pleasures of school. A school that had started off as an uncertain default choice, and become a terrifying place of judgment and anxiety, eventually adjusted its system, in part because of us, and ended up becoming the right school for him.

> Land and Sea, weakness and decline are great seperators, but death is the great divorcer for ever.
> —John Keats, to Charles Brown, 30 September 1820

ONE AFTERNOON THAT FALL, I got an e-mail from my stepmother saying that my father had taken a sudden turn for the worse and would probably only have a few more months to live. Although we'd been given this kind of warning many times before, I began to make plans to travel to Japan to see him. The boys left for a weekend at Grams's house with their father, and the following night I attended the wedding of a close childhood friend. I danced up a storm with my school friends; we were all so happy that this wonderful woman had finally found the right guy and the love she deserved. I returned from the wedding a bit giddy; I scrolled through my e-mail and opened one with no subject from my stepmother. It began:

> Dear Nick, Priscilla, and Claire,
>   Your Daddy passed away last night (12:12 a.m., Oct. 29). No struggle, no pain. Suddenly he stopped breathing, without any sign of doing so. In peace. He had reached the limit and decided to leave.

I called Claire at a hotel in DC where she was staying that weekend and woke her up. I lay in bed all night in a state of shock. I was stunned by the extent of my grief. I felt as if I couldn't breathe. I had been separated from Daddy by land and sea for many years. His weakness and decline had rendered him unable to speak, unable to communicate with us at all. But this was the great separator, forever. The finality of it was devastating to me.

I spent Sunday talking to Claire, my brother, my stepmother, e-mailing and calling my dad's friends to tell them the news, talking to a reporter at the *New York Times*. At various points during the day, whenever I wasn't in a conversation with someone, I would moan involuntarily, put my head down on my desk, and sob uncontrollably. And then, at six p.m., the doorbell rang. Even though Richard had a key to the apartment, the boys always insisted on ringing the doorbell so I'd come running and fling the door open with a big smile on my face and a warm happy hello in my voice. I knew my mom had told them what had happened, and I didn't know what reactions to expect from them. I opened the door to find them standing in front of Richard with hesitant looks on their faces. "Hi guys," I said, clenching my fists hard to keep from crying, and four-year-old Jamesie just buried his face in my stomach and hugged me tight. Benj said, somewhat awkwardly, "Mommy, Grams told us that your daddy died. Are you okay, Mommy?" I said: "I'm very sad, but I'm okay, honey." "You can sleep in my bed to make you less sad, Mommy," James quickly interjected. "That might be a bit uncomfortable," Benj said. "Your bed is kind of small, James." "Thank you, sweethearts," I said. "I'm so happy you're home."

In the days that followed, I tried to shield them from my grief—crying (as I had right after the discovery of Benj's hyperlexia) in the bathroom with the water running, falling to my knees as soon as I could get the door locked. I'd been so prepared for my father to die when he was first diagnosed nine years earlier and given ten months to live, but as time went on, I thought less and less about his illness in terms of what it meant ultimately and more in terms of the day-to-day details of care and my stepmother's well-being. Now that he really was gone, irrevocably, I was finally able to miss him as he was for most of his life rather than as he was in his decline. I'd missed him dreadfully for many years and I was just realizing the depth and breadth of that missing now.

The next night, someone from the *New York Times* came to our apartment to photograph a photo of my father that they wanted to use in his obituary. I spread the large black-and-white photo on our dining-room table's flat surface. It was taken in the mid-1970s in the living room of my childhood apartment, and in it, my father looked ruggedly handsome in jeans and a denim shirt, his hair long and curly, his black-rimmed glasses in one hand as he gazed off over his shoulder with an expectant, intense look on his face. I looked for nearby books to weigh down the photo's curled edges, and grabbed two of Benj's favorites, children's books called *Game Day* and *Teammates* by the New York Giants running back Tiki Barber. The *New York Times* sports section, open to an article on the Giants, just happened to be right above the photo. As the photographer zoomed in for the photo, I photographed it myself in its contexts—my father surrounded on all sides by writing about the New York Giants, a team now loved by his grandson with the same fervor that he and I had loved them.

The following night was Halloween. Benj dressed as a mailman (after Mr. Rogers's Mr. McFeeley) and James as a lion in a big furry suit with a wild hood and long, bushy tail; gentle, decorous Benj and fiery, passionate James made quite a funny, sweet pair. After the costumes were off, I took them to their room to get them settled down. We had a game of opposites and then one of synonyms, just as my father had played with me. "Hot," I'd say; "Cold!" James would delightedly cry. "Rrrroasting . . . ," I'd offer; "Freeeezing!" Benj would reply. As I was singing to them, as my father had done with me, my voice broke, and James, always so tuned into my moods, wiped his little hands across my wet cheeks. "Mommy," he said, "you're crying!" "I'm just very very sad, honey." "Do you need some nuzzling, Mommy?" he asked. And then, "Oh Mommy, can I hug you?" Benj cried. "I need to make you feel better." I leaned down for his hug, which was still a little brittle, but so so welcome to me. "Mommy, why did your daddy die?" James suddenly asked. "Oh, he was old and he'd been so sick, guys," I said, "and you know, for many years he smoked cigarettes and he just couldn't stop in time." "But he's in heaven now, Mommy," James piped up. "So he's happy." I'd never talked about heaven or even God with the boys before. "Do you think your daddy has a computer in heaven?" Benj asked. "I'm sure he has anything he wants, including a computer, Benj," I answered. Jamesie looked dreamy for a moment, and said: "He's having fun there, Benj! He's floating on a cloud!" Benj asked, somewhat worried, "What if he falls off the cloud?" "He'll be okay, sweetie," I answered, "there's no falling in heaven." "Because now he can fly," said James.

> with an eye made quiet by the power
> Of harmony, and the deep power of joy,
> We see into the life of things.
> —"Tintern Abbey"

THAT DECEMBER, SEVEN-YEAR-OLD BENJ was scheduled to play a guitar solo in his school's holiday concert, a simultaneously exciting and nerve-wracking prospect. When his guitar teacher had first told us of the plan for Benj to play "Jingle Bells" on the guitar with her accompanying him, Richard and I were both encouraged and apprehensive. Although he'd been taking classical guitar lessons for about a year, he'd only been practicing for the last few months, and he'd never performed in public. Benj had demonstrated extraordinary musical talent (perfect pitch, exquisite sense of rhythm, ability to sound out tunes on a glockenspiel, xylophone, or piano from a very young age), but I'd been reluctant to start him on an instrument until his motor skills were strong enough that he could play with minimal frustration. I also didn't want to push him or put too much pressure on him; I wanted music to be a joy and not a source of anxiety for him. Once he began, Benj's proficiency on the guitar had amazed us—his history of severe fine-motor delays made each strum a little triumph—but as all beginners do, he made lots of mistakes, and he'd resisted practicing. Although he was now regularly practicing, I worried he might break down in tears of frustration if he made a mistake in his performance or that he might get overloaded in the cramped and pressure-filled concert setting.

Benj, however, seemed only excited, and looked forward to the event with great anticipation. He counted down the days (crossing out each day on his desk calendar, telling me every night "only six/five/four more days till the holiday concert!"), sang and hummed the songs around the house, and threw himself into the dress rehearsal with gusto. The night before the concert, he was surprisingly calm. Every night, when I put Benj to bed, I'd sing a few songs to him (since we'd moved to New York City, his favorite was Cole Porter's "Take Me Back to Manhattan," although he insisted on substituting James Taylor's "Country Road" when we were at Grams's Connecticut house) and afterward, we'd run through a few questions that he'd come up with and answers I'd devised to help him cope with anxieties. The questions were: "How do I stop a bad dream from coming?" "How do I stop a bad daydream from coming?" and "What do you do when the lights go out?" I gave long, elaborate answers to these questions.

This December night, however, Benj stopped me before the third question. "Mommy, I want to add a new question to the sequence.

Can I?" "Well, sweetie, I have to hear it first before I make any promises. What is it?" "Okay," he said, and his face lit up with eagerness and delight, "how do you keep a *good* dream from *leaving*?" I broke into a huge smile, and he said laughingly, "Mommy, do you accept or decline?" "I accept, Benj!" "Well, how do you do it?" he asked. "Keep a good dream from leaving, I mean." I was so surprised and amazed by this unexpected question from Benj, who so rarely changed his routines, that at first I didn't know what to say or how to respond. Then, all of a sudden, I blurted out: "Oh Benj, you think hard about what you were dreaming about, imagine it, remember how wonderful it was, and try to hold on to it in your mind." Benj smiled and nodded and happily snuggled under his covers for sleep. Walking out of his room, I shook my head in amazement. From keeping anxiety at bay, we'd come to summoning and fostering and sustaining happiness, from managing worry, we'd gotten to holding on to joy. And in helping Benj learn how to hold on to Wordsworth's "celestial light . . . the glory and the freshness of a dream," I recovered my dream of a child capable of dreaminess, strong feeling, intense appreciation of beauty and wonder. Benj was beginning to access a little of the wonder of my childhood perspective, and in mothering him, I was discovering a whole new kind of wonder, a whole new sense of what wonder could be.

The next morning, when I saw him in the lobby of school, Benj was just so full of joy, absolutely radiant from the minute his class traipsed past the waiting parents—"Mommy!!!" he cried, "there's only two minutes left until the holiday concert!!"—and into the small school gym, where the concert was to be held. Glancing over the program, I saw that the concert would consist of group numbers that involved all the kids, a performance by each classroom, and four "solos": three classical violinists, all a few years older than Benj, and Benj on guitar. Richard and I stood side by side in the back of the crowded gym; we glanced nervously at each other when a group number ended and it was Benj's turn. The room was dead-silent, the atmosphere one of hushed expectancy. He got up quietly, walked to the two chairs set up at the front of the room, and calmly took his guitar from his teacher. They took their seats, she looked at him, and counted under her breath one, two, three, four. And then the jaunty little tune began: a Christmas song I'd never particularly liked, not one of the really poignant or stirring ones, but played by Benj that day, it moved me deeper than anything ever has. I felt that I was witnessing the effortless easy pure expression of his little spirit, unthwarted despite all the convolutions and complications that his mind and body so often threw in his way. In the minute and a half it took to play the song, his soul was so transparent, so palpable.

He played beautifully, and when he made one tiny "mistake" toward the end, he smiled, strummed again, and continued on to the end with aplomb. He was unfazed by all the flashing lights of cameras, the loud and rowdy audience, and the close quarters. When he did the final strum, the crowd went wild—he got a standing ovation! Hearing the burst of applause, the cheers and whistles, he looked out at the audience with an expression of delighted surprise, stood up, and took an awkward but very enthusiastic bow, and went back to his seat with a huge smile.

Watching him up there playing guitar, so poised, confident, and happy, I couldn't stop the tears from coming, and when I looked at his teachers and therapists lining the gym walls, I saw that they were almost all tearing up as well. His math teacher later told me that the school custodian, a big, burly, muscled guy in his thirties, had told her the day before: "Wait till you see Benj play the guitar in the concert. It will make you cry!" Benj's team of therapists and teachers and family members had collectively held their breath as Benj began to play, let it out as he proceeded without a hitch, and finally applauded not only his talent but, much more important, his courage, his triumph over his anxiety and fine-motor issues, and the flowering of his expressivity. On this day, he was the personification of joy. When I remembered that a year ago to the day he had been in the grip of a hallucinatory reaction to psychiatric medication, I felt all the more blessed.

And whereas, a year earlier, Benj's very placement in the school had seemed so precarious, we'd recently learned that the founder and director of his K-5 school would open a middle and high school just in time for Benj. How overwhelmingly relieved I'd been to hear that there would be a safe harbor for him throughout his childhood and adolescence, a place where he would be accepted on his own terms, supported through his challenges, given the therapies he needed, encouraged to grow, take risks, and develop his unique gifts. Financially, too, I was feeling far less anxious, as so far both years we had prevailed in our fight to win partial tuition reimbursement and coverage for his many therapies from the New York City Board of Education, who could not come up with an appropriate public school placement for Benj. Standing in that gym, I felt an overpowering sense of relief and gratitude. Benj had found a safe place in the world at this wonderful school and an appropriate and inspiring vehicle—music—to express his feelings and connect with others.

> O joy! that in our embers
> Is something that doth live,
> That nature yet remembers
> What was so fugitive!
> The thought of our past years in me doth breed
> Perpetual benediction
> . . . .
> for those first affections,

Those shadowy recollections,
Which, be they what they may,
Are yet the fountain light of all our day,
Are yet a master light of all our seeing;
Uphold us, cherish

. . . .

truths that wake,
To perish never;
Which neither listlessness, nor mad endeavour,
Nor Man nor Boy,
Nor all that is at enmity with joy,
Can utterly abolish or destroy!
—"Intimations Ode"

A FEW MONTHS LATER, my father's memorial service at long last took place. Yale Drama School organized the event in collaboration with me and Claire, and it was held at Symphony Space on the Upper West Side, in the auditorium next to the movie theater where my dad had so often taken us as little girls. I sat through the eulogies and listened to my father described as a "delirious romantic" with a "divine innocence" and "a vulnerability, and . . . otherworldliness which could be almost childlike," and to have, at the end, the face of a "boy-sage, a combination of innocence and serene dignity." I watched a slideshow of my father's life that Claire and I had put together: it began with a photo of him as a quizzical and sweet-faced young boy of about six or seven, and then there were shots of him as a young man sitting in front of a typewriter, sitting on a porch swing engrossed in a book, grinning ecstatically at me and Claire and Nick as babies, reading to us as little girls, throwing a football to me, at his wedding to Yasuko, at Claire's college graduation, and then, finally, in a wheelchair, bald and gaunt, gazing out a hospital window at a cherry tree in bloom. I began my eulogy with the opening lines of the

"Intimations Ode" and ended them with the closing lines of my father's *New York Times* article on me and the New York Giants, which
told of my writing the consolatory letter to Harry Carson, dejected
after a bitter defeat, and was published on the day of the Giants' first
Super Bowl win in 1987:

> This afternoon several of us will gather in my apartment [to
> watch the Giants] . . . Priscilla will of course be there . . . She'll
> be on edge, agog, scared sometimes, but finally, I predict, ec-
> static. Tomorrow she may even want to write another letter to
> Harry Carson, saying some such thing as this: "Didn't I tell
> you! I still love you. More than ever."
>
> So Daddy, I say to you today: "Didn't I tell you? I still love
> you. More than ever."

After the service, I returned home to my Giants fan, my little
boy who was learning to love with the whole of his being, to comfort and protect. Upon my arrival at the apartment, Benj ran to the
door and held his arms out to me. "Mommy," he cried, "How are
you? I love you!" I showed him the program from the event and he
insisted that I give him two from the large stack I'd brought home.
One went into his "Benj's Special Things" box and the other was
pinned onto his bulletin board. "He's my grandfather, I need to
have this," he told me.

AROUND THE TIME OF my father's service, a few weeks after his
eighth birthday, Benj composed a full-length song on the guitar
with verses, chorus, and bridge. But there were no words to the
song until one night when I suggested he begin with "My name
is Benjamin . . ." and he took it from there, writing all the lyrics by himself in the space of five minutes. As it had been with

everything from play therapy to homework, I gave him a starting point, a place to begin, a little structure to anchor him, and then stood back and watched him take off by himself. In its composition and its lyrics, this song exemplified both Benj's increasingly secure sense of identity and his growing openness to and solicitation of others:

My name is Benjamin . . .
I'm eight years old and I play guitar
I live on the 18th floor, in New York City
And I play guitar
So many presents from friends all over town
I love to ride in elevators going up and down
I love the music player that Daddy gave me
Although it's small, it plays so much; why don't you come and
    see-e-e-e-e?

My name is Benjamin . . .
I'm eight years old and I play guitar
I live on the 18th floor, in New York City
And I play guitar

> . . . here I stand, not only with the sense
> Of present pleasure, but with pleasing thoughts
> That in this moment there is life and food
> For future years. And so I dare to hope,
> Though changed, no doubt, from what I was when first
> I came among these hills . . .
> —"Tintern Abbey"

BY THE TIME BENJ turned eight, Richard and I had worked things out so that we had a very amicable co-parenting relationship and a lovely, supportive friendship. We'd spent six months in mediation and, in consultation with Benj's psychologist, drafted a fifteen-page parenting plan that covered everything from financial responsibilities to our philosophy of parenting and designed a flexible joint custody and co-parenting arrangement. We made a huge effort to get beyond recrimination and pettiness and to respect each other's irreplaceable significance to the children. We remained close to each other's extended families and often socialized together. We attended every conference and meeting together, stood or sat side by side at every school event and cheered our kids on together, and spent holidays together as a family. We were united, always, in our love for and devotion to our children. In the act of parenting, when soaring and when it was laborious, in moments of elation and moments of despair, we were still together, in the words of the Frost poem we printed on our wedding program, "Wing to wing, and oar to oar."

As Richard's fortieth birthday approached, I suggested that Benj write a song as a gift for Daddy. "I don't think so, Mommy," he said, "a song is not a gift." "Oh, but it can be," I said, "it can be a wonderful gift." He still demurred, but when I told him there would be no gift Daddy would like better, he said with alacrity: "I have to do it then." A moment later, he added: "But only if you help me, Mommy."

Benj and I worked on his song for a good week; the tune came quickly and easily, but he needed help with the lyrics. After writing two songs in quick succession about eight months earlier—the "Benjamin Song" was followed a month or so later by the "Connecticut Song" for a States Presentation at school—Benj didn't write another for a while. The "Benjamin Song" had been about himself; the "Connecticut Song" a series of facts strung together and engagingly presented with clever rhymes and turns of phrase ("Connecticut is our fifth state / Connecticut joined this country in 1788"; "Its hero is Nathan Hale . . . / Its great university is Yale.") But this "Daddy Song," as we came to call it, involved another person, someone he knew intimately and loved dearly, and it involved the expression of emotion and gratitude. "I don't know how, I don't know what to say," he'd always cry when faced with a creative writing assignment at school, and this was a really tough creative task. So, to help, I asked leading questions: "What does he look like?" "I don't know, he needs to be here, I have to look at him." "Well, is he tall or short?" "Tall, of course; are you crazy?" he said disbelievingly. "We want different sorts of things he does with you, Benji." "Different times of day, too, right?" he asked. "Yes," I said. "Think about the song as a way of thanking Daddy and letting him know how much you love him." "Well of course I love him," he said. "Why don't I just say that?" Our work continued.

One night, as we brainstormed ideas for the lyrics, James suddenly wanted in on the action. "Mommy, write this down!" he insisted, and this is what I wrote, dictated by James in less than a minute:

JAMES'S DADDY SONG IDEAS:

He's tall and handsome
He has great eyes
He is very strong
He reads to me
He knows how to play games
He knows how to love people
He has a very big heart

James was as different from Benjamin as could possibly be imagined; a friend of mine once remarked that "Benj and James are two halves of one person." Both boys had a great enthusiasm for life, a wonderful capacity to be thrilled, and shone with excitement when doing something they really enjoyed. Both had dark-blond hair and bright blue eyes. But there the similarities ended. Physically adept and aggressive, with an especially loud voice, James was now a rambunctious, inquisitive, emotionally expressive and loving five-year-old. He wasn't reading yet and didn't seem especially academically-minded. He'd always had lots of buddies and many playdates. One of his favorite activities was listening to stories; unlike Benj, he'd always eagerly asked why characters behaved certain ways and commented on the events. Also unlike Benj, and much to his father's delight, James's books of choice were myths, legends, romances, adventure stories: *Peter Pan*, the Arthurian legends, the *Swallows and Amazons* series, *The Jungle Book*. Zeus and Odin, Hermes and Freya, were central to the adventures James was constantly creating with his Playmobil people. One of his teachers accurately referred to James as "Mr. Imaginative Play." He was a theatrical impresario at his nursery school, conceiving, casting, directing, and starring in numerous plays. His imagination was limitless; he was continually inventing pretend scenarios, using words in innovative ways, seeing many sides to situations. He was acutely sensitive to others' moods and feelings, and he was a hugger.

I didn't want James ever to feel compelled to make up for his brother's lapses or deficiencies or to feel it was his role to be the emotionally attuned and loving one. I didn't want Benj's difficulties or his own strengths to be a burden on James. And at the same time I didn't want James to feel intimidated or daunted by Benj's precocity and "specialness."

I never wanted to think of James as the "normal" one and Benj as the "special" one. It had always been such a temptation to do this, in part because we so desperately wanted one child we didn't have to worry so intensely about. When I began to sense that three-year-old James's fine-motor development was a little off, Richard had resisted getting an occupational therapy evaluation for James—"He's nothing like Benj!" he'd said—but I stuck to my guns, insisted on it, and it turned out that James had even more severe fine-motor delays than Benj had and needed his own occupational therapy. They were both special, and they had unique sets of needs, but it was difficult managing the two of them when their interests, temperaments, and needs were so diametrically opposed.

Coping with a brother who was so mercurial and so bafflingly other had been hard on James. He simply adored Benj, but he couldn't understand why Benj imposed rules on him in supposedly free-form games, cried in frustration when he missed a basketball shot, or insisted on doing things in a certain order that made no sense to happy-go-lucky and impetuous James. How much confusion and disappointment had Benj's impenetrability and non-responsiveness caused my extremely warm and affectionate younger son? "Benj, why don't you *listen* to me?" James would cry in utter frustration. And James's insatiable desire for pretending ran up against a very literal barrier in the person of Benj, who stubbornly insisted on bringing things back down to earth. "Mommy you're the princess and I'm the prince coming to save you!" James would cry, "and Benj you be the dragon." Meanwhile Benj would either disregard him completely or, when James came lunging at him with a "sword," back up, horrified, crying: "I don't want to be a dragon!" Playing board games was even harder. Benj would criticize James's decisions—"Why did you do that, James?" he'd ask reprovingly—and James would blithely plow ahead, oblivious to his brother's disapproval, just happy to be sharing an activity with Benj. And for poor Benj, James's physical exuberance, his hastiness, his volubility and volume, could be very difficult to take.

These differences notwithstanding, they were deeply bonded to each other. And as they grew, that bond grew stronger and stronger. I always take a lot of photos of the boys on Halloween; one in particular taken just a few months before Richard's fortieth birthday perfectly captured the romantic/anti-romantic dichotomy they exemplified and the poignancy of their relationship. Benj is dressed as his hero, the New York Giants quarterback Eli Manning, James as a medieval knight complete with sword, breastplate, shield, and headpiece. Benj is Mr. Realism, James Mr. Romance. They're standing in front of a bookshelf in our living room, and volumes of Shakespeare, poetry, and the complete *Wizard of Oz* series are visible behind them. James is tenderly holding one of Benj's hands in both of his and gazing at it with adoration as if he's about to propose marriage. Benj stands tall and straight, the Giants pants barely covering his knobby knees, his skinny legs stretching long till his bare feet. He's for the moment patiently tolerating James's loving touch and smiling gently at me, but looking as if he wants to run off and throw the football he's holding in his other hand. When I e-mailed this photo to friends, I called it "Warriors of Two Eras Unite in Friendship."

On the day of Richard's birthday, the two friendly warriors were playing with Richard in James's room as I laid the tablecloth and set the table with the *Star Wars*–themed birthday plates, cups, and napkins. We'd wrapped his gifts in sports-ball wrapping paper (picked out by Benj) and there were handmade cards from both boys. James's was a sheet of white paper covered in haphazardly distributed Spider-man stickers and enthusiastic, vibrant-colored scribbles. Benj's was a drawing of a man with dark black hair, blue eyes, and a huge, glowing, yellow heart. Under the picture, he'd written: "Daddy, you have a heart of gold. Happy 40th Birthday! Love Benj." His neat handwriting, his perfectly plausible drawing, his deft deployment of one of his favorite idioms were so gratifying and delightful to see.

Then I called out, "Time for the party!"—but Benj came running in, looking a bit perturbed. "Oh no, not yet Mommy, first I have to put on my party clothes," he said. "You don't have to change your clothes, honey," I replied, "you look nice." Benj would have none of it. "Yes I do, Mommy, see my pants have a rip,"—he pointed to a tiny tear in one knee—"and I need a fancier shirt." He went to his room—while he was gone, James bounced around impatiently, periodically calling out, "Let's go, Benj!"—and a few minutes later emerged in a striped oxford shirt and khaki pants. I helped him with the buttons—still difficult for him at almost nine years old.

"Daddy, each of the boys has a song for you." I put on my "ringmaster" voice: "Intro-ducing James!" While I read his words about Daddy, James danced frenetically, sang impromptu phrases ("I love Daddy, he never gets maddie") and banged wildly on one of his kiddie bongos. It had always been so hard for Benj to bear out-of-tune singing, unrhythmic drumming, and out-of-control movements, but he sat through James's show with a big smile on his face and when it was over he cheered: "Yay, James!" "Thank you, Jamesie," Richard said, and James leapt up onto his lap.

Benj took his guitar out of its case, I took a seat next to Benj, and Richard and James sat opposite us. Richard held James tight in an attempt to calm and settle him and Benj strummed and tuned his guitar, taking his time before beginning. James cried: "Hit it, Benj!" "I need to get used to it," Benj said, but James was impatient and didn't understand Benj's hesitations. "Let's go, Benji!" he shouted again. "He's getting ready, Jamesie," I said. "I know it's very hard to wait." Benj continued to strum his guitar softly. "I'm a little nervous," he said to me. "Sing it with me, Mommy."

As soon as Benj and I began to sing, James, who had been squirming around with excitement and eagerness, sat completely rapt, and Richard was very still, solemn almost, listening intently:

Daddy is nice
Daddy is tall
Daddy is smart
He plays ball

I love Daddy
He is the best
Daddy tucks me in
Before I take a rest

Happy birthday
I sing and play
I love Daddy
Hip hip hooray!

Daddy has black hair
He has blue eyes
Daddy reads books
He is wise

He helps with homework
I play with him
We play games of chess
He takes me to Coach Mike's gym

Happy birthday
I sing and play
I love Daddy
Hip hip hooray!

Happy birthday
I sing and play
I love Daddy
Hip hip hooray!

As we sang, James would periodically nod enthusiastically, expostulate "Yes!," or simply smile an even broader smile. Richard, on the other hand, had tears brimming in his eyes. On the last chorus, Benj improvised a harmony with me, and after we ended the last "hip hip hooray!" I couldn't help myself from letting out a loud whoop, then hugging Benj tight. "Why did you scream, Mommy?" Benj asked smilingly. "I screamed with joy," I said. "I knew that," he replied.

> . . . that best portion of a good man's life,
> His little, nameless, unremembered, acts
> Of kindness and of love.
> —"Tintern Abbey"

A FEW WEEKS AFTER Richard's birthday we had a parent-teacher conference at Benj's school. From dreading these when he first began, we now actually looked forward to them. We were in such frequent contact with the teachers via e-mail, brief conversations at drop-off and pickup, and interactions during park time and field trips, that we knew there would be no unpleasant surprises, no rug pulled out from under us. And Benj, now a third-grader, was doing so well. We knew that.

It was a buoyant and exciting conference. The teachers told us that everyone saw a great improvement in Benj's ability to come down quickly from a moment of frustration or anxiety and in his relationships with his peers. "He's become such a lovely, supportive friend," his speech therapist told me, "he rushes to his classmates' sides when they're hurt or worried, he high-fives or exclaims 'Yay so-and-so!' when they do well." His biggest challenges remained "difficulties with cognitive flexibility"—accepting changes in routine, performing novel tasks, handling open-ended situations where there wasn't a clear right or wrong answer—and anything that required him to be imaginative or creative: writing a story, drawing a picture that wasn't copying. But he was learning to manage his own anxiety much more effectively. The teachers emphasized "flexibility" as a personal goal for Benj, and they'd noticed that when he started to get anxious, he would say to himself or to them: "Okay, I will try to be flexible now." I told them that I'd seen an instance of this the previous weekend when his computer broke—a very traumatic thing for him—and he was getting all worked up and beginning to cry and then he took a deep breath and said: "Okay, Mommy, okay, I will try to be flexible; there are several things we can do to fix this problem: we can unplug it and try again; we can send it to a repair shop; and if that doesn't work we can get a new computer, and that might be very expensive but I have money in my ATM machine so I can give you some. So this won't wreck my life, and besides, I can just read in the morning instead of working on the computer."

The teachers were dedicated to helping Benj become more flexible. When he'd say things like "On Thursday, we don't eat peanut butter" or "Why are we doing computer today? Computer is only for Mondays" (we and the teachers called these "silly Benj rules"), the teachers jokingly and lovingly reminded him: "You're making up your own rules, Benj, and don't worry, we're the teachers and we know what's okay or not okay to do." But they also celebrated the sweet rituals he'd created: one example was Friday Hugs—he gave them both huge hugs every Friday before leaving school. They laughingly told us that the previous day, when the whole class made and ate their own ice cream sundaes for one of the teacher's birthdays, Benjamin cheerfully set to making a sundae for his teacher himself, since "I can't eat ice cream because I'm allergic." He sat there beaming with pride as she exclaimed over her great sundae and he didn't mind a bit that he couldn't enjoy what everyone else was eating. His rules-based thinking made some things, like giving up "treats," easier for him than they would be for other children.

The teachers told us that Benj had developed a special fondness for a little girl in his class, named Anitra; he cheered vociferously for her whenever she got an answer right or climbed up the ladder in gym class, and they often sat together at lunch. And so I made an effort to encourage the development of a real friendship outside of school between Benj and Anitra. At first they had "music playdates" at her apartment; their music teacher led them through duets (she on piano, he on guitar) and sing-alongs. Then we graduated to a space show in the Natural History Museum's Planetarium, and in the following months, Benj took Anitra as his "date" to a few concerts and Anitra took Benj as her guest to a Rangers game and a Yankees game. They both had occasional meltdowns during these playdates, when things went in unexpected directions or they lost at games, but their mutual interests drew them together and a genuine and deep fondness was flowering between the two of them.

Benj was also beginning to demonstrate much more affection and caring for James, always generously sharing his gifts or treats with James, not wanting to watch his favorite TV show, *Cyberchase*, unless James watched with him, and even, on rare occasions, expressing fervent love for James. "It *kills* me to see him sad!" Benj said once when James was crying after bumping his leg on the bookcase, his own eyes filling with tears as he watched his brother cry. One afternoon, when I told James he'd lost his TV privileges because he'd thrown a toy, Benj implored: "Don't punish him, Mommy, it was just a mistake!" A few minutes later, however, Benj, always a stickler for rules and standards, acknowledged: "Well, I just hate to see him sad, Mommy, but I guess he does need the consequence." Another night, when James was very sick with a high fever, Benj cried: "Is he going to be okay, Mommy? Because I couldn't live without James!" He brought James a pile of books and stood next to his bed, gently stroking his hot forehead. "I'm nothing without James," Benj cried, "I just love him so so much!" I jokingly told my mother that he must have heard those lines in a book or television show—he was channeling *Wuthering Heights*' Heathcliff and Cathy!

And his relationship with his Grams continued to deepen. My mother's impatience with dreamy idealism, her need for structure, her pragmatic nature meshed perfectly with Benj's personality and temperament. After two outgoing, verbal, emotionally expressive daughters who would chat into the wee hours of the morning with her if she'd let us, she was relieved by Benj, who'd say, "Uh-oh, seven fifty-seven, three minutes till bedtime," and abruptly stop whatever activity he was engaged in. She saw his practical, rational, literal bent as refreshing in a family of dreamers and idealists. She encouraged his interest in the stock market and accounting; "Maybe someone in this family will actually go into business!" she'd say smilingly. She relied on Benj for technological and technical assistance; he fixed her BlackBerry and computer for her, and always knew how to get the television working again and which kind of battery each remote needed. She loved the fact that he leaned toward the pragmatic rather than the imaginative; "We need this in our family!" she'd often say.

Benj's insistence on and pleasure in routine and ritual both gratified and delighted my mother. Arriving at her country house for the weekend, he always called attention to each detail of the evening to unfold: "Suppertime with Grams's special salad dressing!" "Grams, time for you to give me my special chocolate treat!" and "Time for reading!" he'd happily cry. At Christmas, he was always the most enthusiastic singer of carols, decorator of cookies, and hanger of stockings. He loved to hand out presents to all assembled—reading names off the tags and trotting over to cheerfully hand off the package to its recipient. "He's got Grammy's spirit of Christmas," my mother would sigh.

My mom is not a soft person at all, not a cuddler, but, paradoxically, Benj's lack of cuddliness has enabled her to be more tender with him than she ever was with me. While she never took my sister and me to the movies when we were children, she had frequent movie dates with Benj, and sat uncomplainingly through such mainstream fare as *Hotel for Dogs*, *Ice Age 2*, and *The Tale of Despereaux*, because he wanted to. It was my father who'd taken us to see the dollhouses and historical exhibits at the Museum of the City of New York and the mummies at the Met, but it was my mother who now introduced Benj to all these New York City gems. She also loved to take Benj to concerts (Little Orchestra Society, the family music series at the 92nd Street Y, Jazz for Young People at Lincoln Center) and to restaurants for lunch. "Benj has impeccable table manners!" she'd exclaim; his careful observance of rules and conventions made him the perfect fancy-restaurant dining companion for her, because he knew just what fork to use, always put his napkin on his lap, and ordered in the most polite way. Moreover, he always tried new foods when she was the one offering them or encouraging him; "My Benj is such a good eater!" she'd say happily. While my mother never watched sports when I was a child, she'd recently become interested in following tennis, and she and Benj shared a love for Roger Federer; Benj kept her posted on Roger's progress through tournaments. Benj came to love the *Nancy Drew* series my mother had adored as a young girl and they discussed the books together animatedly. Benj could make my mom get misty-eyed in a way we never did. She frequently said that Benj would be her escort to her hundredth birthday party. "He's the love of my life, you know," she'd tell me.

> All good poetry is the spontaneous overflow of powerful feel-
> ings: it takes its origin from emotion recollected in tranquility.
> —Wordsworth, Preface to *Lyrical Ballads* (1800)

IN THE LATE FALL of Benj's fourth-grade year, I received an e-mail from his classroom teacher announcing an upcoming "Poetry Publication Party" at the school. She told us that the class had spent the past several months reading poems, learning about different poetic forms, and writing original poetry, and the party was to celebrate the completion of the unit. After his immersion in poetry as a toddler, I'd never seen Benj read or recite poetry, and I wasn't sure I'd ever discussed it with him. I'd heard very little about this poetry unit; most of the work had been done in class. I was very curious about what would happen.

The small classroom was packed that morning, the parents ringed outside the desks arrayed in a semicircle, the children grouped in a somewhat fidgety cluster on the floor inside. Benj was slated to go first; Richard and I watched as he walked up to the front of the room, cleared his throat a bit nervously, and began to read:

> Can be updated
> Often come preloaded with DirectX
> Memory is space available for programs and processes
> Play sounds when events occur
> Use user accounts to separate people's files
> The brain is the CPU
> Easy to use to manage files
> Restart in "Safe Mode"
> Store personal information

As Benj read quickly in a rather monotone voice, glancing up and out between every few lines, my initial reaction was: "This doesn't sound like poetry! How could this be considered a poem?" Sensing my befuddlement, Richard leaned over and whispered to me: "It's an acrostic!" (a poem in which the first letters of the lines together form a word). I nodded and smiled. While the computer acrostic wasn't very "poetic," it was very Benj, and it was a great example of him dipping his toe into something unfamiliar or uncomfortable (being creative, reading aloud to a group, sharing his work) while anchoring it in something very familiar and comfortable.

After the computer acrostic, Benj read a "cinquain" (a five-line poem) about sledding and a "clerihew" (a witty four-line poem that pokes fun at well-known people) about the Boxcar Children. I, a former literature professor, didn't even know what a cinquain or a clerihew were, and had to have Richard explain them to me! I thought to myself: in a way, Benj was especially well suited to these assignments; the logic and tightness of the formal structures probably appealed to him and gave him safe, circumscribed, relatively predictable outlets for his emotions, ideas, and sense of humor. Ironically, little anti-romantic Benj was now a poet!

The other eleven kids in Benj's class then each took his or her turn. Some stuttered, others made odd remarks, exhibited tics, or stumbled over the words on the page, but the children all encouraged each other with reassuring phrases—"You can do it!" "Go, Joe!"—and congratulatory high-fives. The teachers graciously accommodated each child's unique set of needs: one especially nervous boy was allowed to read from his place on the floor, and another stood with a teacher's comforting arm draped around his shoulder in order to get through his turn. When another child with whom Benj had never particularly connected read a very clever and funny poem and hammed it up with dramatic flourishes and gestures, Benj laughed and cheered exuberantly; the boy grinned with pride, and his father looked at Benj gratefully. I smiled, thinking how wonderful that a poem was bringing together our very different children. However dissimilar we might be in superficial ways, we parents shared an abiding gratitude for this school, an understanding and respect for each other, and a great affection for each other's children, whom we'd come to know well over the past few years. Every kid here was "odd," every kid had challenges, but they all supported each other in coping with their difficulties. This was a community where you didn't have to be conventional or "typical" to be appreciated, and a cohort of parents who had all been humbled and softened by their experience with their "unusual" or "difficult" child. And watching our mostly unromantic children read poetry they had created brought tears to many eyes.

After all the children had read three poems, each child brought his poetry book to his or her guests to share. Benj proudly handed me his "book"—a stapled together stack of 8 ½ × 11 pages titled *Benjamin's Book of Poems*. I opened it and read: "This Book is dedicated to my parents and Anitra." And then I read:

ACROSTIC

Born on March 16th
Every day I take the subway or car home
New things I like
Janowsky teaches me OT
Art is hard for me
Miniclip.com is my favorite game website
Is 9 years old
Never teases classmates

One of the most moving aspects of parenting Benj had always been watching his careful, painstaking, steady consolidation of his own identity, and this "Benjamin" poem, which "stored his personal information," seemed to distill Benj's progress, his growth, how far he'd come over the past six years. In this poem, he answered the questions—when is your birthday, how old are you?—we'd taught him in those first days of speech therapy. His need for routines was still strong—"every day," but so was his increasing openness to different approaches and options: "I take the subway or car." "New things I like": how great was this! Benj still had trouble with novelty, but the help he'd gotten had made him increasingly able to follow his natural curiosity and pursue his love of learning and experiencing new things. Just being able to say "is hard for me" was so huge for him, as was the simple announcement of "my favorite": Benj couldn't have told you what his favorite anything was just two years earlier.

The juxtaposition of "computer" and "Benjamin" acrostics particularly struck me, because what had concerned us most initially was that Benj was somehow robotic, mechanical, unable to feel deeply or be responsive to others. Richard had been especially bothered by his "computer talk." At one point, early in Benj's work with Dr. G, as she patiently coaxed him through expressing a complicated emotion, he'd sighed in frustration and said: "It would be so much easier to be a computer." And now, though he still loved computers with a passion, he also had close and loving relationships to his family members and teachers (Ms. J, his occupational therapist, had been his stalwart supporter since first grade) and was aware of the ethics of social relating. His being teased had always been one of my greatest fears, and his poem's line "Never teases classmates" summed up the school's guiding ethic, which protected Benj and all the other children.

I hugged Benj to me and told him how proud I was of him. And then I turned the page of *Benjamin's Book of Poems* and read:

TWO HAIKUS:

In winter it snows
Water freezes to cold ice
Trees are bare from leaves

Birch trees in winter
White bark against the white snow
Alone with myself

I was stunned. How could Benj have come up with such evocative, such poetic images? And then I realized that these poems were reminding me of the Frost children's collection, *A Swinger of Birches*, that Benj had so adored as a two- and three-year-old. *A Swinger of Birches* was filled with poems about and drawings of trees, snow and winter, ice and cold, and Benj had especially loved "Fire and Ice," "Stopping by Woods on a Snowy Evening," "Looking for a Sunset Bird in Winter," and "Birches." The last two poems I'd first encountered during my first semester of teaching, as a section leader for Yale's Modern Poetry lecture, a few weeks after we'd returned to school following Richard's mother's death. The wonderful professor and these Frost poems had sustained me in my sorrow and helped me feel reconnected to Yale and the graduate program in English, and later, Benj's delight in these poems had connected my personal and professional lives in such a nourishing way.

In those first days after we discovered his hyperlexia, I'd listened to Benj's lisping "swing-ah ah birches!" as he took *A Swinger of Birches* from the shelf and wondered whether Benj could ever be a swinger of birches, in both a literal and figurative sense. Could Benj ever be the playful and adventurous child Wordsworth and Frost describe? Could fearful Benj ever swing, would cautious Benj ever climb? Could he ever dare, risk, aspire? Would he ever seek transcendence or experience rapturous joy? I'd think of these lines from "Birches":

> So was I once myself a swinger of birches.
> And so I dream of going back to be.
> It's when I'm weary of considerations,
> And life is too much like a pathless wood . . .

Often in those early days, I'd felt so "weary of considerations"—not wanting to have to think and plan and consider so much—wanting to just BE. At times, I'd felt lost in a "pathless wood"—not knowing which way to go, trying to sort through the often conflicting advice, wondering at each point along the way what was the right approach, the right school, the right therapist, the right choice to make.

And now, Benj could climb and swing, he was more comfortable taking risks, he had strong and deep connections to the people in his life, he was in a wonderful, and clearly the *right*, school for him, he was happy. When I first realized Benj was hyperlexic, I'd feared that the beauty and significance of the poems he'd seemed to love might have been utterly lost on him. But now, to my amazement, he was writing haikus about birches in winter, using similar images, moods, and attitudes in his own writing; they'd been stored in him, they'd influenced and shaped him. Poetry mattered to him; it seemed to help him make sense of his experience.

One line from Benj's haiku—"alone with myself"—reminded me of a poem I myself had written when I was nine years old, the same age Benj was when he wrote these poems. Although, as a young girl, I'd written countless stories and songs, and even a novel (a rewriting of *The Phantom Tollbooth*), I never wrote much poetry, but there was one poem that had come effortlessly and that my father had especially loved. I'd recovered it a year earlier, when my stepmother sent me the contents of a box labeled GIRLS that my dad had brought with him to Japan from his apartment in New York City. In the mailer from Japan, there were envelopes marked GIRLS' HAIR, with long, blond strands visible through the thin paper, there were report cards, letters and postcards we'd sent him from sleepaway camp, drawings, "feel better soon" notes (one I'd written just a few months after my parents' separation read: "Do not worry, Daddy, I will see you soon! Try to keep yourself busy and remember I am thinking of you all the time and love you so so much!"), and then there was this poem, carefully written out in my neat print on a piece of my father's typing paper.

Loneliness

Loneliness is when no one listens,
When no one seems to know who you are.
Loneliness is a grey sky no one looks at,
A balloon when no one's holding the string.
Loneliness is strange to me,
  A distant thought.
    —Priscilla Gilman, age 9

Just a year after I'd written this, my father was plunged into extreme loneliness with the loss of our family, and I'd spent the rest of his life trying to assuage that loneliness.

When I was a young child with close, loving relationships to my family and friends, loneliness had been strange to me, a distant thought. But in those first months after my parents' separation and with the loss of my father as a regular presence in my daily life, in the early years as Benj's mother, in the later part of my marriage, I'd come to know loneliness all too well. I had felt so lonely, in a disconcerting, frightening way in those first weeks after Benj was born, in those first days after we realized he was hyperlexic, during the second half of my marriage. Utterly and completely alone. Both he and Richard seemed so far from me and I didn't know how to reach them. Little Benj was the balloon whose string I couldn't properly grasp; he floated away from me and didn't want me to hold him or lead him or guide him. And then as my connection to him deepened, I worried about his ability to connect to others, about his social isolation, his oddness. Would he ever have a real bosom buddy? A deep relationship to his brother? A romantic partner?

Loneliness was what I'd wanted to keep Benj from ever experiencing. I was terrified of his being lonely and desolate as a result of his differences. So afraid, in fact, that at first I didn't understand that he wasn't me or my father or anyone but himself. When I first read his birch haiku, I thought it was stark and bleak. But then I recognized that it wasn't a sad poem at all, because for Benj, being alone with himself isn't the same thing as loneliness; in fact, it's a pleasure and a source of strength.

Both Wordsworth and Benj have felt "perhaps too much, / The self-sufficing power of solitude" (*Prelude*, II); both also hone that "inward eye / Which is the bliss of solitude" ("I Wandered Lonely as a Cloud"). Like young Wordsworth, Benj has his own private universe where he likes to go:

> So it was with me in my solitude . . .
> Unknown, unthought of, yet I was most rich,
> I had a world about me—'twas my own . . .
> —*Prelude*, III

This was a world that we both had to force our way into and draw him out of. But it was also a world we'd had to learn to understand and respect. And with his poems, Benj had both reminded me of the importance and beauty of solitude and shown me how far from loneliness he was.

With Benj's book of poems in my hand and my entire experience with him flashing through my mind, I thought of Wordsworth's famous lines about how poetry "takes its origin" from powerful emotion and painful experiences recollected in grateful tranquility:

> The mind of man is framed even like the breath
> And harmony of music. There is a dark
> Invisible workmanship that reconciles
> Discordant elements, and makes them move
> In one society. Ah me, that all
> The terrors, all the early miseries,
> Regrets, vexations, lassitudes, that all
> The thoughts and feelings which have been infused
> Into my mind, should ever have made up
> The calm existence that is mine when I
> Am worthy of myself.
> —*Prelude*, I

A poem begins . . . as a lump in the throat, a sense of wrong, a homesickness, a lovesickness . . . It finds the thought and the thought finds the words.
— Robert Frost

NOW, ALMOST A YEAR after that poetry publication party, there are still occasional moments when I feel lonely as Benj's mother. Moments when I still get that "lump in the throat" feeling, that sense of wrong, of homesickness and lovesickness. Seemingly simple things like watching him struggle to integrate and manage a flood of confusing emotions, his "spontaneous overflow of powerful feelings." His uneasy relationships with his peers and lack of social flexibility. His anxiety. His occasional unresponsiveness to a question, kind word, or compliment from another person. His "inappropriateness" in certain situations.

But usually the "lump in the throat" feeling comes from a very different place: a feeling of awe, a palpable charge of connectedness and love that I feel with this uncanny child. Watching his progress. Receiving a hand-drawn Mother's Day card a few months after the poetry publication party, another acrostic, which read:

Mom I love you!
Our time together is fun
Takes me to concerts
Hugs me

Every night she sings to me.
Really my friend!

Below the text he'd drawn a picture of two figures clearly meant
to be him and me, our bodies separated by inches of space but connected by an arc of red hearts, like a rainbow, between our heads.
When I glanced over it, I began to cry; he tenderly hugged me
and patted me comfortingly on the back. His picture seemed to
literalize an idea from the German poet Rilke that I'd always loved
and that I'd only really come to understand through being Benj's
mother:

> Once the realization is accepted that even between the closest
> human beings infinite distances continue to exist, a wonderful
> living side by side can grow up, if they succeed in loving the
> distance between them which makes it possible for each to see
> the other whole against the sky.
> —Rainer Maria Rilke, *Letters*

What initially felt to me like a bewildering distance now feels
like a beneficent space. Of course all the work of the past years has
been designed to bring me closer to Benj and Benj closer to the normal world, but it has also been about learning to love the distance
between Benj and me. The distance, space, gap between me and my
child is no longer a terrifying void, an unbridgeable gulf, a yawning
emptiness, but rather a capacious and blessed opening, an aperture of
respect and marvel. Being at arm's length from Benj is what's enabled
me to see him truly, to accept and appreciate his irreducible other-
ness. Benj had taught me both how to be alone with myself and to
recognize that the space between us is something to cherish.

Measuring the space or distance between Wordsworth's radiant visions and the reality of my experience with Benjamin initially

heightened my "sense of wrong" and my feelings of betrayal and disillusionment. I had an image in my mind, a sense of what my child and my experience of parenting him would be like, that had both drawn me to and been intensified by Wordsworth. As a lover of Wordsworth, I was more vulnerable to experiencing the situation as poignant, heartbreaking, even tragic, because I was invested in a certain mythology of childhood.

But while on the one hand, I felt the loss of what I'd dreamed and hoped for more strongly because of Wordsworth, on the other, I found in Wordsworth a language with which to express both the depth and breadth of my loss and the possibility of its recompense. Wordsworth gave me the thought and the words for the lump in my throat. He gave me an elegiac vocabulary. His words housed my thoughts and gave shape and contour to my feelings. He assuaged my sickness, my sense of wrong. He gave me solace and comfort. So while my heartbreak may have been greater because of my attachment to the "splendor in the grass," the romantic dream, my consolation was also stronger because I had Wordsworth to help me recognize and celebrate "what remained behind."

At the same time that Wordsworth so powerfully depicts the "romantic child"—his poetry contains some of literature's most iconic images of blessed infants and cavorting, carefree children full of imaginative play—his work is also imbued with a respect and fondness for unromantic, anti-romantic, different children. So many times, I'd read Wordsworth and think, that reminds me of Benj! In poem after poem, Wordsworth presents children *like* Benj: odd children, with strange obsessions, who frustrate adult expectations, who see the world in a unique and uncanny way, who exist in many ways at odds with their culture, who are unusual, vulnerable, and solitary, and who long to escape from the confines of conventional society. I'd read or write about or teach his "Lucy" poems and feel more poignantly than ever how they affirm the value of every life, no matter how seemingly insignificant from the perspective of conventional standards or worldly success. In moments of worry or sadness about Benj, I'd think of how *The Prelude* celebrates the integrity and value of the self regardless of how one appears to others, of one's performance on tests or choice of profession. Wordsworth's poetry argues passionately for the worth and value of society's forgotten, excluded, or less powerful ones, eccentrics and outcasts, beggars, radicals, old people, butterflies, and children. I'd always loved Wordsworth because he is one of the greatest and most eloquent champions of individuality and respect for all beings, no matter how odd, humble, or different, and then I had a kid who especially needed this kind of defense, this kind of understanding and advocacy, and Wordsworth comforted and emboldened, inspired and heartened me again and again.

Wordsworth has guided me in understanding the limitations of my own inherited ideas of achievement. As a high school, college, and graduate student, I had been a superachiever who cared about grades, degrees, awards, and jobs, but the irony is that by the time I had Benj, I'd come to a place where I genuinely didn't care how talented or "gifted" my children were: I just wanted them to be happy and to have loving relationships. And this was precisely the problem area for Benj: he was intellectually precocious in ways that made other parents envious ("How did you teach him to read? Did you use flashcards?"), but he lacked the ability to make meaningful friendships. To be compelled to think of my child in terms of how much he could do, how many items on a checklist he had performed or shown mastery of, in terms of his "skills," "aptitudes," his deficits, how much he deviated from norms—was absolutely antithetical to where I was as a parent. I didn't want to think of Benj in terms of syndromes and categories and labels and diagnoses, in terms of his performance on tests and evaluations, in terms of his differences from a perceived norm or imagined ideal. One of the questions my experience with

Benj has insistently raised for me is: how do you value your child in a culture whose benchmarks for achievement and whose standards for evaluating and assessing kids are so out of line with your own values and who your child is?

As various deficits or issues have been identified, I've often asked myself: does the deficit really represent something meaningful? At different points, Benj has been asked to string beads, unscrew a nut and bolt, identify pictures of a 1950s-style woman's purse and television with antennae (he got no points on the test, because he called the purse a backpack and the television first a rabbit and then an alien). It has at times seemed ridiculous that he would be expected to know what these things were, or to be able to perform certain actions or possess certain skills that often seem completely irrelevant to his daily life. In my experiences as first a high-achieving student, then as a professor of high-achieving students, and later as a mother navigating the intensely competitive New York City private-school-admission circus, I've had to confront such artificial benchmarks of progress and achievement over and over again. And while on the one hand, I've often been saddened to learn that Benj is falling short of a norm, on the other I've often felt a strong resistance to the idea that he must conform to that norm.

Just as I have worked to keep Benj "nursed at happy distance from the cares / Of a too-anxious world" (Wordsworth, "Ode," 1817), so he has helped me to distance myself from that too-anxious world whose values I once shared. The German Romantic Heine's remark—"What the world seeks and hopes for has now become utterly foreign to my heart"—perfectly describes where I am vis-à-vis my child. What many people desire for their children—and what I myself once desired—has become utterly foreign to my heart. A partial list of the milestones and moments of triumph that have mattered most to me: Benj pats his crying baby brother on the head and says "It's okay, James"; drinks from an open cup without spilling all over himself or screaming in frustration as the juice dribbles down his chin; says "yes" for the first time at three and a half years old; refers to himself as "I" for the first time at a little over four; says "I love you" for the first time at four and a half; sits in a darkened theater without panicking to watch a local holiday concert; dances as a Mouse in his kindergarten's production of *The Nutcracker*; says, "Don't worry, Mommy, I'm just fine," after he's fallen and hit his chin; swims the length of a pool unassisted, his little head bobbing determinedly above the water; cheers James on in a game; says, "Oh thank you, Mommy—I am so pleased with and proud of you for buying me this bowling book!" I can't imagine obsessing over first-, second-, or third-tier private schools, the perfect birthday party, sports ability. How prestigious the schools he'll attend, how high his scores will be, how many degrees he'll get, how many grandchildren he'll give me—I can't give any of these things a moment's thought. As Wordsworth says in the "Intimations Ode": "Another race hath been, and other palms are won."

Wordsworth has strengthened my commitment to simultaneously helping Benj integrate into society and honoring his differences. Our therapeutic efforts have been, of course, designed to help Benj be more "romantic": more spontaneous, imaginative, intrepid, playful, connected to others. But even while striving so hard to help Benj become more romantic, I always wanted to remember that Benj's anti-romantic traits are valuable and wonderful and an essential part of who he is. They are strengths and gifts. I never want them denigrated or dismissed as "splinter skills." Both my reading of Wordsworth and my experiences with Benj have taught me the danger of the very idea of "normalcy." I will always resist mightily any orientation or approach that sees Benj as a problem or somehow "broken" rather than as simply and profoundly himself.

Over and over again, I've found that even ostensibly supportive and sympathetic advocates for special-needs children subtly privilege some minds, some learning styles, some disabilities over others.

In particular, in depreciating rote learning, esoteric obsessions, and memorization, they favor the dyslexic over the hyperlexic mind. The winter Benj was applying to kindergarten, I read two articles about dyslexia and hyperlexia, which together struck me in a kind of eureka moment. The first was a *Washington Post* article about a study from Georgetown, which showed—using brain scans—that hyperlexia was the "true opposite" of dyslexia. Yes, that's right, I thought: Benj's memory, mathematical gifts, rhyming ability, mimicry ability are all the strengths that are deficient in dyslexia. The second, an article in the *Yale Alumni Magazine* about renowned dyslexia expert Sally Shaywitz, encapsulated the way dyslexia is celebrated in an essentially romantic way. Shaywitz described dyslexia as "an island of weakness in a sea of strengths." Dyslexia is a significant learning disability, but it does not fundamentally affect a person's social interactions, ability to form relationships, or experience joy. In fact, the emphasis is always that dyslexia is accompanied by striking strengths, gifts, and abilities, particularly in critical and creative thinking. Reading Shaywitz's claim that "in many cases, dyslexia seems to be associated with an ability to solve problems in original ways, to think not rotely but intuitively and holistically," I thought to myself: the dyslexic here sounds like the quintessentially creative self, the romantic poet.

In contrast with this, the implication in almost everything I'd read, from Web sites to academic articles, was that hyperlexia is an island of strength in a sea of weaknesses. All the things that are excellent in dyslexia—verbal fluency and spontaneity, cognitive flexibility, people skills—are deficient in hyperlexia. Hyperlexia is typically described as a splinter or savant skill, and the reading that defines it as automatic, rote, meaningful only because basic skills can be taught more easily to an autistic-spectrum child with hyperlexia, since they can be reached through the written word. One expert described the reading hyperlexic kids do as "barking at text," the implication being that it's animalistic, unreflective, compulsive, and unappreciative.

It's true that Benj's drive to read, his ability to memorize and imitate, have all turned out to be the crucial building blocks for the amazing progress he's made. But it's also true that Benj has always taken genuine, extravagant, passionate delight in the sounds and intonations and rhythms of language. Since the age of two, he's loved poems and nursery rhymes and rhyming story books for their rhythmic qualities, their cadences, their formal intricacy, and their linguistic inventiveness, as well as neat-sounding words, repetition, onomatopoeia, alliteration, consonance—all those things his English-professor parents love. Moreover, his experience of numbers and letters was quite close to fantasy play. It's true that the fantasy took unorthodox objects, but imagination was nonetheless playing a role. So while in those first days of realizing that Benj had serious developmental problems it might have seemed that he lacked a "poetic spirit," I know now that he never really did. My experience with Benj has, in fact, exploded all kinds of stereotypes and misperceptions I had about what it means to be poetic, about imagination, about romanticism. Watching him write his own songs and poems has changed the way I think about inspiration and the creative process.

Benj was recently given a homework assignment to write a poem of at least eight rhyming lines using as many suffixes and spelling words as possible. I sat with him while he pieced it together—tapping out rhythms, looking up synonyms and words in his rhyming dictionary—and there wasn't one moment of panic. For him, it was like fitting the pieces of a puzzle together—a creative task he saw as challenging and fun. And this is what he came up with:

The Reading Boy

There once was a boy who was good,
And on a big ladder he stood.
He pulled a small book off the shelf,

And started to read it himself.
The boy enjoyed reading the stories
That were full of excitement and glories.
And after the reading he spent
All his money to buy a play tent
Where he could enjoy a good book
Alone in his own private nook.

As a two-year-old, Benj would take his books off the shelf and make little havens or nooks with them, happily engrossed in a world that lived to him alone. In the wake of the discovery that Benj was hyperlexic, I'd been made to feel that his reading wasn't a blissful act either of solitude or emotional engagement, and that the private nook of our family was being invaded by outside judgments. But now I'd recovered my sense of the integrity and sacredness of our family, reorganized as it was, and Benj again had that happy space of contemplation and immersion in books; reading had been reclaimed for him as an act of pleasure, learning, joy. In addition to the nonfiction books he'd always loved, he was actually enjoying the "excitement and glories" of novels like *From the Mixed-Up Files of Mrs. Basil E. Frankweiler, The Phantom Tollbooth, Charlie and the Chocolate Factory, Mrs. Frisby and the Rats of NIMH,* the *Lightning Thief* series. Benj had that "dear nook unvisited" Wordsworth celebrates in "Nutting" and I had learned both how to let him be "alone in his own private nook" and to encourage him to experience things and take risks in the world outside his nook.

Wordsworth has also helped me to let go of my impulse to overprotect Benj and my larger tendency to protect my loved ones from sadness or disappointment. One of the biggest challenges of parenting Benj has been letting him fall and letting him fail; it's even harder than for most parents, because making mistakes and losing are so excruciating for him and because he has genuinely needed so much help. At our first appointment with Dr. G, when Benj was not quite three years old, she'd said to Richard, somewhat reprovingly: "You're carrying him like a baby." But in that same meeting, she'd told us that his speech was at a fourteen-month level. He *was* vulnerable and he did need our special protection, but we also needed always to work extra hard to develop his independence and to allow and encourage him to experience fear, pain, disappointment—the full range of human emotion.

One summer day when Benj was five, he was having one of those "terrible horrible no-good very bad days." He'd woken up that morning with a wet bed, lost his favorite marble under the fridge, and at lunch he spilled his yogurt on his feet, lap, and chair. As the cold yogurt splattered everywhere, he yelped in frustration and screwed up his face as if he were about to break down. "Mommy, can you make life just right?" he implored. "I can't, honey, I wish I could, but I can't. Life can't always be the way you want it to be," I told him. I've always wanted to make life just right for those I loved, but through my experience with Benj, I've learned of both the impossibility and the undesirability of insulating loved ones from fear and pain. I want Benj to be:

> A Creature not too bright or good
> For human nature's daily food;
> For transient sorrows, simple wiles,
> Praise, blame, love, kisses, tears, and smiles.
> —Wordsworth, "She Was a Phantom of Delight"

With a child as brilliant as Benj, the temptation will always exist to push or accelerate him. There have been music teachers who wanted to put him in serious Suzuki training at five, teachers and administrators who've placed him in reading and math groups four years beyond his grade level—they took him out at my insistence, because emotionally he wasn't ready. I've never wanted Benj to be "too bright or good," locked away and lonely in his specialness and giftedness. I've never wanted his intellectual or artistic talents to be privileged over his emotional well-being. And so we have worked to develop his emotional range and sensitivity, to cultivate his empathy, to improve his ability to express his feelings and receive the feelings of others. All along, our implicit goal has been to help Benj join Wordsworth's "race of real children":

> A race of real children; not too wise,
> Too learned, or too good; but wanton, fresh,
> And bandied up and down by love and hate;
> Not unresentful where self-justified;
> Fierce, moody, patient, venturous, modest, shy;
> Mad at their sports like withered leaves in winds;
> Though doing wrong and suffering, and full oft
> Bending beneath our life's mysterious weight
> Of pain, and doubt, and fear, yet yielding not
> In happiness to the happiest upon earth.
> —*Prelude*, V

Given Benj's intense anxiety about getting things just right, one of my most important tasks as a parent has been helping him to accept "good enough," become comfortable with making mistakes as part of the learning process, and not be so hard on himself. But even as I work to relieve the pressure he puts on himself, I am constantly revising my understanding of what best motivates him, comforts him, and triggers his productivity and best, most satisfying work. It took Benj himself to help me realize that his needs are not always what I think they are.

In the spring of Benj's fourth-grade year, he didn't want to participate in an upcoming music recital because he was afraid to perform

alone, and the only way his guitar teacher and I could convince him
to consider doing it was if I sang and he played. We decided on John
Denver's "Leaving on a Jet Plane"; it was in his *Folk Pop* guitar book,
it was a song I'd sung so many times to baby Benj, and it was one his
father often played in the car during drives to and from the country.
During our practice sessions, he began to harmonize with me on the
chorus (singing different and eerily beautiful harmonies each time)
and eventually he asked if we could split the verses—I sang the first
half and he the second of each verse and on the chorus we harmo-
nized. The performance was a triumph; he sang with such freedom
and joy, and he was ecstatic while playing and afterward, asking,
"Can we do it again?" a minute after we finished to thunderous applause.

For the past year and a half, almost every night we're together,
Benj and I sing duets—of songs by the Beatles, Cat Stevens, the
Grateful Dead, Simon and Garfunkel, Neil Young, and James Taylor—while he plays guitar. All the nuances of our complex dance of
relationship appear in our singing together. We have to make decisions together—about what song to do first, which key to sing in,
what tempo, who will sing what part. We have to cope with differences of opinion, disagreement, and each other's falterings. We
have moments of tension ("You missed your cue, Mommy!"), delight
in each other ("Mommy, that was so cool what you did!" "Benj, I
loved how you sang that!"), humor, transport. Our singing together
is about compromise and collaboration, attentiveness and abandon,
coming together and honoring the space between us. Our duets
highlight how far we've come—now it's not only me singing to him,
it's not him playing alone, it's us making music together and com-
municating with each other in ways we can't with words alone.

One night this past December, we were sitting in Benj's room, recording ourselves playing and singing songs for a CD we planned to
give his grandmother as a Christmas gift. He was making mistakes

and getting frustrated. "Oh Benji, don't worry, it's not a big deal," I told him. "We have enough songs already—we can just use the ones we have." That did calm him down momentarily, but when he continued to make little mistakes, he stopped, sighed, and looked at me somewhat accusingly. "I think it's because you told me it's not a big deal, Mommy," he said, "you made it not important enough." "But sweetheart," I stammered, "I just don't want you to be too worried about how well we sing or perform. Grams will love whatever we do." "I think Grams would prefer it if we had the harmonies better than we do right now, Mommy," he said. "We have to think it's important and we have to try our very best. In the concert (a school holiday concert a few days earlier) I played well because I knew it was important." What could I do but laugh? Here I'd been trying to protect him from anxiety, trying to relax him and relieve the pressure on him, but he was telling me, in no uncertain terms, that he needs the pressure, that he excels under pressure, and doesn't do as well when he doesn't feel an imperative to get something right. He was turning the tables on me, and asking me to push him.

Thinking about it later, I had to concede that to a great extent he was right. As a musician, he needs that perfectionist ear, he needs to be willing to practice long and hard, to be able to notice and correct his own errors, and he may need even more pressure, both from within and without, to become a truly great player. I'd never pushed him with an aggressive teacher or demanded that he practice long hours; I'd always downplayed any sense of his precocity as a musician. But if music is his bridge to the world, why not make it as strong as possible? I'd thought performance pressure would inhibit his flight, but in certain situations and at certain moments it's actually what enables it.

Even as I've always tried to situate Benj outside a competitive culture of hoop jumping and gold stars, I've had to respect and honor his need for tangible markers of achievement (certificates, trophies,

"Good Job!" stickers). He loves worksheets, does workbooks in bed to help himself fall asleep at night, and actually finds spelling and math quizzes relaxing. Some of his favorite books are the Guinness and Scholastic Books of World Records, and he loves sports teams with perfect records, even rooting for the Patriots over his beloved Giants in the Super Bowl a few years ago because he believed the best team should win and he wanted the perfect-so-far Patriots to set a record for consecutive victories and remain unbeaten. Even as I myself have moved away from a culture of kudos and recognition for high achieving, I've got a son who craves clear markers of achievement, and I have to listen attentively to him, at every moment. I have to always make sure I'm giving him what he, Benjamin, needs, and not what I would have needed or wanted or what I think a "typical" kid would need or want.

Whenever I've been tempted either to overprotect or to accelerate Benj, whenever I've caught myself projecting my own dreams or fears, desires or issues, onto him, I've remembered Wordsworth's scathing critique of overzealous educators and parents who try to control and micromanage children's lives:

> These mighty workmen of our later age,
> Who, with a broad highway, have overbridged
> The froward chaos of futurity,
> Tamed to their bidding; they who have the skill
> To manage books, and things, and make them act
> On infant minds as surely as the sun
> Deals with a flower; the keepers of our time,
> The guides and wardens of our faculties,
> Sages who in their prescience would control
> All accidents, and to the very road
> Which they have fashioned would confine us down,
> Like engines; when will their presumption learn,

That in the unreasoning progress of the world
A wiser spirit is at work for us,
A better eye than theirs, most prodigal
Of blessings, and most studious of our good,
Even in what seem our most unfruitful hours?
   —*Prelude*, V

One question I have grappled with since those first days of real-izing that Benj had special needs was how I could be the "guard and warden of [his] faculties" while still remaining "prodigal of blessings" that came in unexpected ways. How, in other words, could I adopt the mentality of intervention while still retaining an enchanted, romantic, magical sense of childhood, of the mystery and wonder of development, of the uniqueness and beautiful odd quirkiness of my child? Wordsworth expresses a similar difficulty in a famous question from Book III of *The Prelude*: "Whether to work or to feel?" Mothering Benj, to borrow another classic Words-worthian phrase, is truly "passionate work." One of the large chal-lenges of my relationship with Benj has been integrating working and feeling into one act of dedicated devotion: figuring out how to rise above the relentless daily demands, the need for predictable schedules and structured tasks and meticulous planning and hold on to a sense of boundless possibility and exuberant unpredictabil-ity. How could I as a parent be both pragmatic and romantic, real-istic and visionary, precise and focused in my attention to his needs and yet able to be "surprised by joy" (Wordsworth). The epigraph to the "Intimations Ode" begins: "My heart leaps up when I behold / A rainbow in the sky," and it is just this capacity for leaps, for surprise, for being carried away by strong feeling that I have striven so hard to preserve.

Despite numerous evaluations over the past seven years by de-velopmental pediatricians, psychologists, speech and language therapists, occupational therapists, and psychiatrists, Benj has never received an official label or diagnosis. He clearly has shades of obsessive-compulsive disorder, and could be grouped under the headings of sensory-integration disorder and social-pragmatic language disorder; now, as he gets older, I often describe him as "borderline Asperger's," usually as a kind of shorthand when I need to succinctly explain why he's in a special school. I've always been ambivalent about the idea of labels. They're undeniably useful for securing the much-needed therapies and special services, but I've often wondered how a label would be helpful in understanding Benj. Would a label make people more sympathetic to him? Or would it get in the way of appreciating the complex, intricate person Benj is? How much detail, nuance, subtlety do we lose when we slap labels on people, and especially on still-developing kids? Reducing Benj to a label would mean the loss of mystery, romance, respect for the idea of identity as something that can never be precisely defined or fully known and mastered.

At the same time that I've always possessed an unshakeable faith in my knowledge of who Benj essentially is, I'm continually reminded of the limits of my ability or desire to fully understand him. In this, I am a true Wordsworthian; Wordsworth repeatedly resists the impulse to solve mystery and affirms the value of mystery itself:

> Points have we all of us within our souls
> Where all stand single; this I feel, and make
> Breathings for incommunicable powers.
> —*Prelude*, III

To recognize Benj's singleness and make breathings for Benj's powers have always been my primary aspirations as a mother.

People often ask me: What are your goals and hopes and dreams for Benj? And the answer is so simple: That he be seen whole against the sky. That he not suffer beyond his and my capacity to bear it. That he be allowed to enjoy the pleasures of "his own private nook" and come out of that nook for joyful engagement with others. That he always hold on to his visionary gleam, his bright radiance. I think of the following wonderful lines from e. e. cummings:

> To be nobody but yourself in a world which is doing its best,
> night and day, to make you everybody else means to fight
> the hardest battle which any human can fight and never stop
> fighting.

My goal as a mother is to never stop fighting that battle for Benj's essential self and to teach him how to fight it on his own behalf.

Above all, this book is a story about identity—its fragility, its poignancy, its difficult forging, its flowering, its ultimate ineffability. Wordsworth's poetry repeatedly laments scientific and scholarly reductiveness about notions of identity, and celebrates what remains unknowable, unexplainable, unmeasurable:

> Sweet is the lore which Nature brings;
> Our meddling intellect
> Mis-shapes the beauteous forms of things:—
> We murder to dissect.
> —"The Tables Turned"

The meddling intellect Wordsworth deplores could describe both the academics who identify themselves according to camps and theories and dissect rather than genuinely appreciate literature and the clinicians and approaches that see children in terms of their deficits, their labels, their categories rather than their inimitable beings and unique souls. In both cases, a sense of mystery and of beauty is sacrificed. I think of Keats on negative capability:

Negative Capability, that is when man is capable of being in
uncertainties, Mysteries, doubts, without any irritable reaching
after fact & reason . . .

Benj, of course, has had such difficulty with uncertainty, and has
so often irritably reached after fact and reason, but in parenting him,
I've attained a negative capability I never had as a student or a scholar
and teacher of romantic poetry. I've become capable of being in uncertainties.

A few months ago, as part of a homework assignment, Benj wrote
this letter to his teacher:

> Dear Mrs. M,
> I am writing to say that my favorite part of school is
> math. The cardinal reason why is that I like working with
> numbers. I also enjoy the remarkable process of figuring out
> the problems. And I especially like reaching the definite, hard
> conclusion of the problems. For these reasons, I really enjoy
> math.
> Love,
>
> Benjamin

Benj has special difficulty tolerating doubt and not-knowing (if
I say, "I don't know" in response to a question he asks me, he'll
cry indignantly, "But you HAVE to know!!") and he always wants
to figure out the solutions to problems. It's a funny paradox: Benj
wants and needs definite hard conclusions more than most people
do, but it's via him that I've learned not to search for them, that
they're impossible and undesirable. There have been no easy solutions to the problems Benj and I have faced, and there is no "definite hard conclusion" to our story. Benj still has many challenges.

He hasn't ever had unsupervised time with a peer, an unstructured playdate, a phone call to or from a friend, a sleepover. He can melt down if he loses a game, he has odd and obsessive anxieties, and tics like reciting, clearing his throat, or humming surface during times of stress. He continues to struggle with open-ended situations, abstract language, and unexpected events. He's not mainstreamed, and he still has lots of therapists and needs a good deal of support and many accommodations. I'm sure there are obstacles, hurdles, things I can't even envision yet. What I do have is an abiding faith that we can ride out anything that is thrown at us. I think often of a line from Toni Morrison's *Song of Solomon*: "If you surrendered to the air, you could ride it." In one of the wonderful ironies of my experience, little controlling rigid Benj has helped me to let go of my desire to follow a predetermined path and taught me how to surrender.

Through my experience with Benj, I've finally both come to terms with my nostalgia for a "romantic" childhood and to understand, truly, Wordsworth's notion of abundant recompense:

> That time is past,
> And all its aching joys are now no more,
> And all its dizzy raptures. Not for this
> Faint I, nor mourn nor murmur; other gifts
> Have followed; for such loss, I would believe,
> Abundant recompense.
> —"Tintern Abbey"

One of the essay questions on our final exam for "Major English Poets" read simply: "Discuss Wordsworth's notion of abundant recompense as it appears in three of the four poets we have studied," and many years later, as a professor myself, I gave a version of this question to my own students on an exam. But while I'd read and written about abundant recompense, while I'd meditated on it, I didn't know what it really meant, in a deep sense, until I became Benj's mother. Benj has taught me so much more than any professor, or class, ever has. As someone who has lived to learn, I have, in Benj, been given my greatest and most meaningful coursework. In many unexpected ways, Benj has turned out to be what those onesies proclaimed him to be: a "Mighty Prophet, . . . Seer Blest / On whom those truths do rest, / Which we are toiling all our lives to find."

In my experience with Benj, I have had to come to terms with the loss of my romantic vision, my idea of how my child, and my life, were going to be. But out of the death of that dream has come a flourishing of amazing life. Being Benj's mother has changed me profoundly, has made me more, rather than less, idealistic; more, rather than less, passionate; more, rather than less, creative:

> For I have learned
> To look on nature, not as in the hour
> Of thoughtless youth; but hearing oftentimes
> The still, sad music of humanity . . .
> And I have felt
> A presence that disturbs me with the joy
> Of elevated thoughts; a sense sublime
> Of something far more deeply interfused . . .
> —"Tintern Abbey"

In parenting Benj, I have gotten more in touch with a profound kind of romanticism; I have been given access to a transcendent sense of mystery and awe and wonder.

One night very recently, as I was spreading peanut butter on his waffle and he was standing at the kitchen window looking out at the New Jersey skyline, I suddenly heard Benj cry:

"Don't the lights look beautiful out there?"

"Yes, honey," I said, somewhat surprised.

Benj, in a rush: "And that relates to the love between you and me?"

I almost couldn't believe what I'd heard. I stammered: "What a beautiful thing to say, sweetheart!"

Benj ran up to me and wrapped his arms around me, exclaiming: "I love you more than anything in the world!"

While initially Benj presented as the contradiction of romantic ideas of childhood—he defied and rebuffed every expectation I had—ultimately he has reaffirmed, in a deeper and truer way, my romantic ideals and given me "more than all other gifts":

> [He] gave me eyes, [he] gave me ears;
> And humble cares, and delicate fears;
> A heart, the fountain of sweet tears;
>   And love, and thought, and joy.
> —Wordsworth, "The Sparrow's Nest"

FULL TEXT OF WORDSWORTH POEMS:

Lines Composed a Few Miles Above Tintern Abbey, on Revisiting the Banks of the Wye During a Tour, July 13, 1798

Five years have past; five summers, with the length
Of five long winters! and again I hear
These waters, rolling from their mountain-springs
With a soft inland murmur.—Once again
Do I behold these steep and lofty cliffs,
That on a wild secluded scene impress
Thoughts of more deep seclusion; and connect
The landscape with the quiet of the sky.
The day is come when I again repose
Here, under this dark sycamore, and view   *10*
These plots of cottage-ground, these orchard-tufts,
Which at this season, with their unripe fruits,
Are clad in one green hue, and lose themselves
'Mid groves and copses. Once again I see
These hedge-rows, hardly hedge-rows, little lines
Of sportive wood run wild: these pastoral farms,
Green to the very door; and wreaths of smoke

Sent up, in silence, from among the trees!
With some uncertain notice, as might seem
Of vagrant dwellers in the houseless woods,   *20*
Or of some Hermit's cave, where by his fire
The Hermit sits alone.

                         These beauteous forms,
Through a long absence, have not been to me
As is a landscape to a blind man's eye:
But oft, in lonely rooms, and 'mid the din
Of towns and cities, I have owed to them
In hours of weariness, sensations sweet,
Felt in the blood, and felt along the heart;
And passing even into my purer mind,
With tranquil restoration:—feelings too   *30*
Of unremembered pleasure: such, perhaps,
As have no slight or trivial influence
On that best portion of a good man's life,
His little, nameless, unremembered, acts
Of kindness and of love. Nor less, I trust,
To them I may have owed another gift,
Of aspect more sublime; that blessed mood,
In which the burthen of the mystery,
In which the heavy and the weary weight
Of all this unintelligible world,   *40*
Is lightened:—that serene and blessed mood,
In which the affections gently lead us on,—
Until, the breath of this corporeal frame
And even the motion of our human blood
Almost suspended, we are laid asleep
In body, and become a living soul:
While with an eye made quiet by the power

Of harmony, and the deep power of joy,
We see into the life of things.

                                    If this
Be but a vain belief, yet, oh! how oft—   50
In darkness and amid the many shapes
Of joyless daylight; when the fretful stir
Unprofitable, and the fever of the world,
Have hung upon the beatings of my heart—
How oft, in spirit, have I turned to thee,
O sylvan Wye! thou wanderer thro' the woods,
How often has my spirit turned to thee!

   And now, with gleams of half-extinguished thought,
With many recognitions dim and faint,
And somewhat of a sad perplexity,   60
The picture of the mind revives again:
While here I stand, not only with the sense
Of present pleasure, but with pleasing thoughts
That in this moment there is life and food
For future years. And so I dare to hope,
Though changed, no doubt, from what I was when first
I came among these hills; when like a roe
I bounded o'er the mountains, by the sides
Of the deep rivers, and the lonely streams,
Wherever nature led: more like a man   70
Flying from something that he dreads, than one
Who sought the thing he loved. For nature then
(The coarser pleasures of my boyish days,
And their glad animal movements all gone by)
To me was all in all.—I cannot paint
What then I was. The sounding cataract
Haunted me like a passion: the tall rock,

The mountain, and the deep and gloomy wood,
Their colours and their forms, were then to me
An appetite; a feeling and a love,   *80*
That had no need of a remoter charm,
By thought supplied, nor any interest
Unborrowed from the eye.—That time is past,
And all its aching joys are now no more,
And all its dizzy raptures. Not for this
Faint I, nor mourn nor murmur; other gifts
Have followed; for such loss, I would believe,
Abundant recompense. For I have learned
To look on nature, not as in the hour
Of thoughtless youth; but hearing oftentimes   *90*
The still, sad music of humanity,
Nor harsh nor grating, though of ample power
To chasten and subdue. And I have felt
A presence that disturbs me with the joy
Of elevated thoughts; a sense sublime
Of something far more deeply interfused,
Whose dwelling is the light of setting suns,
And the round ocean and the living air,
And the blue sky, and in the mind of man:
A motion and a spirit, that impels   *100*
All thinking things, all objects of all thought,
And rolls through all things. Therefore am I still
A lover of the meadows and the woods,
And mountains; and of all that we behold
From this green earth; of all the mighty world
Of eye, and ear,—both what they half create,
And what perceive; well pleased to recognise
In nature and the language of the sense,
The anchor of my purest thoughts, the nurse,

The guide, the guardian of my heart, and soul   *110*
Of all my moral being.
                        Nor perchance,
If I were not thus taught, should I the more
Suffer my genial spirits to decay:
For thou art with me here upon the banks
Of this fair river; thou my dearest Friend,
My dear, dear Friend; and in thy voice I catch
The language of my former heart, and read
My former pleasures in the shooting lights
Of thy wild eyes. Oh! yet a little while
May I behold in thee what I was once,   *120*
My dear, dear Sister! and this prayer I make,
Knowing that Nature never did betray
The heart that loved her; 'tis her privilege,
Through all the years of this our life, to lead
From joy to joy: for she can so inform
The mind that is within us, so impress
With quietness and beauty, and so feed
With lofty thoughts, that neither evil tongues,
Rash judgments, nor the sneers of selfish men,
Nor greetings where no kindness is, nor all   *130*
The dreary intercourse of daily life,
Shall e'er prevail against us, or disturb
Our cheerful faith, that all which we behold
Is full of blessings. Therefore let the moon
Shine on thee in thy solitary walk;
And let the misty mountain-winds be free
To blow against thee: and, in after years,
When these wild ecstasies shall be matured
Into a sober pleasure; when thy mind
Shall be a mansion for all lovely forms,   *140*

Thy memory be as a dwelling-place
For all sweet sounds and harmonies; oh! then,
If solitude, or fear, or pain, or grief,
Should be thy portion, with what healing thoughts
Of tender joy wilt thou remember me,
And these my exhortations! Nor, perchance—
If I should be where I no more can hear
Thy voice, nor catch from thy wild eyes these gleams
Of past existence—wilt thou then forget
That on the banks of this delightful stream   150
We stood together; and that I, so long
A worshipper of Nature, hither came
Unwearied in that service; rather say
With warmer love—oh! with far deeper zeal
Of holier love. Nor wilt thou then forget,
That after many wanderings, many years
Of absence, these steep woods and lofty cliffs,
And this green pastoral landscape, were to me
More dear, both for themselves and for thy sake!

Nutting

————————————It seems a day
(I speak of one from many singled out)
One of those heavenly days that cannot die;
When, in the eagerness of boyish hope,
I left our cottage-threshold, sallying forth
With a huge wallet o'er my shoulder slung,

A nutting-crook in hand; and turned my steps
Tow'rd some far-distant wood, a Figure quaint,
Tricked out in proud disguise of cast-off weeds
Which for that service had been husbanded,   *10*
By exhortation of my frugal Dame—
Motley accoutrement, of power to smile
At thorns, and brakes, and brambles,—and, in truth,
More ragged than need was! O'er pathless rocks,
Through beds of matted fern, and tangled thickets,
Forcing my way, I came to one dear nook
Unvisited, where not a broken bough
Drooped with its withered leaves, ungracious sign
Of devastation; but the hazels rose
Tall and erect, with tempting clusters hung,   *20*
A virgin scene!—A little while I stood,
Breathing with such suppression of the heart
As joy delights in; and, with wise restraint
Voluptuous, fearless of a rival, eyed
The banquet;—or beneath the trees I sate
Among the flowers, and with the flowers I played;
A temper known to those, who, after long
And weary expectation, have been blest
With sudden happiness beyond all hope.
Perhaps it was a bower beneath whose leaves   *30*
The violets of five seasons re-appear
And fade, unseen by any human eye;
Where fairy water-breaks do murmur on
For ever; and I saw the sparkling foam,
And—with my cheek on one of those green stones
That, fleeced with moss, under the shady trees,
Lay round me, scattered like a flock of sheep—
I heard the murmur and the murmuring sound,

In that sweet mood when pleasure loves to pay
Tribute to ease; and, of its joy secure,   *40*
The heart luxuriates with indifferent things,
Wasting its kindliness on stocks and stones,
And on the vacant air. Then up I rose,
And dragged to earth both branch and bough, with crash
And merciless ravage: and the shady nook
Of hazels, and the green and mossy bower,
Deformed and sullied, patiently gave up
Their quiet being: and, unless I now
Confound my present feelings with the past;
Ere from the mutilated bower I turned   *50*
Exulting, rich beyond the wealth of kings,
I felt a sense of pain when I beheld
The silent trees, and saw the intruding sky.—
Then, dearest Maiden, move along these shades
In gentleness of heart; with gentle hand
Touch—for there is a spirit in the woods.

The Tables Turned

Up! up! my Friend, and quit your books;
Or surely you'll grow double:
Up! up! my Friend, and clear your looks;
Why all this toil and trouble?

The sun, above the mountain's head,
A freshening lustre mellow
Through all the long green fields has spread,
His first sweet evening yellow.

Books! 'tis a dull and endless strife:
Come, hear the woodland linnet,   10
How sweet his music! on my life,
There's more of wisdom in it.

And hark! how blithe the throstle sings!
He, too, is no mean preacher:
Come forth into the light of things,
Let Nature be your Teacher.

She has a world of ready wealth,
Our minds and hearts to bless—
Spontaneous wisdom breathed by health,
Truth breathed by cheerfulness.   20

One impulse from a vernal wood
May teach you more of man,
Of moral evil and of good,
Than all the sages can.

Sweet is the lore which Nature brings;
Our meddling intellect
Mis-shapes the beauteous forms of things:—
We murder to dissect.

Enough of Science and of Art;
Close up those barren leaves;   30
Come forth, and bring with you a heart
That watches and receives.

Ode: Intimations of Immortality from Recollections of Early Childhood

I

There was a time when meadow, grove, and stream,
The earth, and every common sight,
    To me did seem
    Apparelled in celestial light,
The glory and the freshness of a dream.   5
It is not now as it hath been of yore;—
    Turn wheresoe'er I may,
      By night or day,
The things which I have seen I now can see no more.

II

    The Rainbow comes and goes,   10
    And lovely is the Rose,
    The Moon doth with delight
Look round her when the heavens are bare,
    Waters on a starry night
    Are beautiful and fair;   15
  The sunshine is a glorious birth;
  But yet I know, where'er I go,
That there hath past away a glory from the earth.

III

Now, while the birds thus sing a joyous song,
  And while the young lambs bound   20
    As to the tabor's sound,
To me alone there came a thought of grief:

A timely utterance gave that thought relief,
    And I again am strong:
The cataracts blow their trumpets from the steep;   25
No more shall grief of mine the season wrong;
I hear the Echoes through the mountains throng,
The Winds come to me from the fields of sleep,
    And all the earth is gay;
        Land and sea   30
  Give themselves up to jollity,
        And with the heart of May
Doth every Beast keep holiday;—
        Thou Child of Joy,
Shout round me, let me hear thy shouts, thou happy   35
Shepherd-boy!

                        IV

Ye blessed Creatures, I have heard the call
  Ye to each other make; I see
The heavens laugh with you in your jubilee;
  My heart is at your festival,
        My head hath its coronal,   40
The fulness of your bliss, I feel—I feel it all.
        Oh evil day! if I were sullen
        While Earth herself is adorning,
            This sweet May-morning,
        And the Children are culling   45
            On every side,
    In a thousand valleys far and wide,
    Fresh flowers; while the sun shines warm,
And the Babe leaps up on his Mother's arm:—
        I hear, I hear, with joy I hear!   50

—But there's a Tree, of many, one,
A single Field which I have looked upon,
Both of them speak of something that is gone:
    The Pansy at my feet
    Doth the same tale repeat:
Whither is fled the visionary gleam?
Where is it now, the glory and the dream?

v

Our birth is but a sleep and a forgetting:
The Soul that rises with us, our life's Star,
    Hath had elsewhere its setting,   *60*
      And cometh from afar:
    Not in entire forgetfulness,
    And not in utter nakedness,
But trailing clouds of glory do we come
    From God, who is our home: *65*
Heaven lies about us in our infancy!
Shades of the prison-house begin to close
    Upon the growing Boy,
But He beholds the light, and whence it flows,
    He sees it in his joy;   *70*
The Youth, who daily farther from the east
    Must travel, still is Nature's Priest,
    And by the vision splendid
    Is on his way attended;
At length the Man perceives it die away,   *75*
And fade into the light of common day.

VI

Earth fills her lap with pleasures of her own;
Yearnings she hath in her own natural kind,
And, even with something of a Mother's mind,
    And no unworthy aim,   80
    The homely Nurse doth all she can
To make her Foster-child, her Inmate Man,
    Forget the glories he hath known,
And that imperial palace whence he came.

VII

Behold the Child among his new-born blisses,   85
A six years' Darling of a pigmy size!
See, where 'mid work of his own hand he lies,
Fretted by sallies of his mother's kisses,
With light upon him from his father's eyes!
See, at his feet, some little plan or chart,   90
Some fragment from his dream of human life,
Shaped by himself with newly-learned art;
    A wedding or a festival,
    A mourning or a funeral;
      And this hath now his heart,   95
    And unto this he frames his song:
      Then will he fit his tongue
To dialogues of business, love, or strife;
    But it will not be long
    Ere this be thrown aside,   100
    And with new joy and pride
The little Actor cons another part;
Filling from time to time his "humorous stage"

With all the Persons, down to palsied Age,
That Life brings with her in her equipage;   *105*
      As if his whole vocation
      Were endless imitation.

VIII

Thou, whose exterior semblance doth belie
      Thy Soul's immensity;
Thou best Philosopher, who yet dost keep   *110*
Thy heritage, thou Eye among the blind,
That, deaf and silent, read'st the eternal deep,
Haunted for ever by the eternal mind,—
      Mighty Prophet! Seer blest!
      On whom those truths do rest,   *115*
Which we are toiling all our lives to find,
In darkness lost, the darkness of the grave;
Thou, over whom thy Immortality
Broods like the Day, a Master o'er a Slave,
A Presence which is not to be put by;   *120*
Thou little Child, yet glorious in the might
Of heaven-born freedom on thy being's height,
Why with such earnest pains dost thou provoke
The years to bring the inevitable yoke,
Thus blindly with thy blessedness at strife?   *125*
Full soon thy Soul shall have her earthly freight,
And custom lie upon thee with a weight,
Heavy as frost, and deep almost as life!

IX

      O joy! that in our embers
      Is something that doth live,   *130*
      That nature yet remembers
      What was so fugitive!
The thought of our past years in me doth breed
Perpetual benediction: not indeed
For that which is most worthy to be blest;   *135*
Delight and liberty, the simple creed
Of Childhood, whether busy or at rest,
With new-fledged hope still fluttering in his breast:—
      Not for these I raise
      The song of thanks and praise;   *140*
  But for those obstinate questionings
  Of sense and outward things,
  Fallings from us, vanishings;
  Blank misgivings of a Creature
Moving about in worlds not realised,   *145*
High instincts before which our mortal Nature
Did tremble like a guilty Thing surprised:
      But for those first affections,
      Those shadowy recollections,
  Which, be they what they may,   *150*
Are yet the fountain light of all our day,
Are yet a master light of all our seeing;
  Uphold us, cherish, and have power to make
Our noisy years seem moments in the being
Of the eternal Silence: truths that wake,   *155*
      To perish never;
Which neither listlessness, nor mad endeavour,
      Nor Man nor Boy,

Nor all that is at enmity with joy,
Can utterly abolish or destroy!   160
  Hence in a season of calm weather
    Though inland far we be,
Our Souls have sight of that immortal sea
    Which brought us hither,
  Can in a moment travel thither,   165
And see the Children sport upon the shore,
And hear the mighty waters rolling evermore.

X

Then sing, ye Birds, sing, sing a joyous song!
    And let the young Lambs bound
    As to the tabor's sound!   170
We in thought will join your throng,
    Ye that pipe and ye that play,
    Ye that through your hearts to-day
    Feel the gladness of the May!
What though the radiance which was once so bright   175
Be now for ever taken from my sight,
  Though nothing can bring back the hour
Of splendour in the grass, of glory in the flower;
    We will grieve not, rather find
    Strength in what remains behind;   180
    In the primal sympathy
    Which having been must ever be;
    In the soothing thoughts that spring
    Out of human suffering;
    In the faith that looks through death,   185
In years that bring the philosophic mind.

XI

And O, ye Fountains, Meadows, Hills, and Groves,
Forebode not any severing of our loves!
Yet in my heart of hearts I feel your might;
I only have relinquished one delight   190
To live beneath your more habitual sway.
I love the Brooks which down their channels fret,
Even more than when I tripped lightly as they;
The innocent brightness of a new-born Day
     Is lovely yet;   195
The Clouds that gather round the setting sun
Do take a sober colouring from an eye
That hath kept watch o'er man's mortality;
Another race hath been, and other palms are won.
Thanks to the human heart by which we live,   200
Thanks to its tenderness, its joys, and fears,
To me the meanest flower that blows can give
Thoughts that do often lie too deep for tears.

ACKNOWLEDGMENTS

WILLIAM BLAKE WROTE: "GRATITUDE is heaven itself." My heartfelt gratitude goes to:

The truly remarkable Tina Bennett, my dear friend since the first days of Yale graduate school and now my indomitable agent, for scintillating and hilarious conversations, for her tireless work on behalf of this book, her penetrating insights, her no-nonsense straightforwardness, her brilliant mind and huge heart.

My extraordinary editors: Claire Wachtel, for her passion and unshakeable commitment to this project, her wonderful combination of warmth and toughness, intuition and shrewdness, for pushing me hard and caring so deeply; and Jonathan Burnham, for the book of poems at the eleventh hour, for believing in this story's universality, for his flair and literary sensitivity.

Tina Andreadis and Suzanne Williams, for being such unwavering, compassionate, and congenial advocates.

All the wonderful people at HarperCollins: Kathy Schneider, Archie Ferguson, Elizabeth Perrella, Shannon Ceci, William Ruoto, Samantha Choy, Jamie Brickhouse, Caitlin McCaskey, Angie Lee,

Leah Wasielewski, and Mark Ferguson, for their creativity and dedication, their zeal and graciousness.

Ivonne Rojas, Dot Vincent, and Stefanie Lieberman, for their enthusiasm.

Svetlana Katz, for her unerring eye, her wry humor, and good dark chocolate.

Chris Rovee, Alan Richardson, David Rosen, Libby Fay, Natalie Friedman, Elisabeth Schmitz, Chris Miller, Karen Lower, Zoltan Markus, Kristi Carter, Sunny Schwartz, and Nancy Kim for their interest in my work and their useful comments.

Eyal Press, for his brilliant, compassionate, and extremely helpful read of the entire manuscript.

Erik Lawrence, for his creative inspiration and his embracing love of my boys.

Jamie Leonhart, who helped me find my voice and improved the book immensely with her empathetic discernment, gentle prodding, and loving faith in me.

Jordin Ruderman, who brings a magical combination of solidity and effervescence, practical, down-to-earth goodness and unruly and wild imagination and creative energy to her friendship with me and her godmothering of Benj.

Audette Louis, for adoring Benj from the moment she first held him in his fairy-tale Baby Gap onesie.

Julie Riess, for being Benj's staunchest advocate and a kindred spirit for his mom.

The many teachers, professors, and colleagues at Brearley, Yale, and Vassar, who enlightened, supported, and inspired me.

My students, from Yale to Vassar, the San Bruno County Jail to PS 101Q, for teaching me so much.

The numerous therapists, teachers, psychologists, coaches, and family friends whose love and care, wisdom and insight, generosity and ingenuity have made Benj's happy life possible—I give thanks for each and every one of you every single day.

Aunt P, Nicky, Yasuko, and Richard's family, who provide a nourishing and supportive larger circle of loving relatives for the boys.

Chris Jennings, for bringing out the best in me, renewing me, making me feel free.

Clairey, Toad to my Frog, Martha to my George, Tacy to my Betsy, Cinderella to my Prince, for her stalwart comradeship through bright days and darker ones, for being my dearest confidante and friend, for "streaks of love."

Sasha, for his insight, common sense, and protectiveness, for being the best brother-in-law a girl and the best uncle two boys could ask for.

Three children I adore: Sanja and Sebastian, for their ebullience, tenderness, and sweetness; and Rafaella, for her spunk, spirit, and "radical innocence."

Grampy Merle and Grammy Peg, the tutelary spirits of my romantic childhood.

My mother, for her fierce devotion to the well-being of her daughters and grandchildren, her tenacity, and her abiding and sustaining love. No one else could have gotten Benj to eat broccoli or hit the ball back over the net.

My father, who taught me how to see, how to read, and how to love.

Richard, for being an incredible father to our boys. They are blessed beyond measure to have you.

My dearest Jamesie, for his warm and affectionate nature, his kindness, and his purity of heart. As Wordsworth's Michael tells his son: "All thy life hast been my daily joy."

And, of course, my beloved Benj, to whom this book is dedicated.

© Elena Seibert

PRISCILLA GILMAN grew up in New York City and received her BA and PhD in English and American literature from Yale University. She spent two years as an assistant professor of English at Yale and four years as an assistant professor of English at Vassar College before leaving academia in 2006. She has taught poetry appreciation to inmates in a restorative justice program and to New York City public school students. *The Anti-Romantic Child*, her first book, was excerpted in *Newsweek* magazine and featured on the cover of its international edition; it was also nominated for a Books for a Better Life award for Best First Book. Gilman writes regularly for such publications as the *Daily Beast*, the *New York Times*, and the *Huffington Post*, speaks frequently at schools, conferences, and organizations about parenting, education, and the arts, and is a Scholar/Facilitator for the New York Council for the Humanities. She lives in New York City with her family.

www.priscillagilman.com
www.facebook.com/priscillagilmanauthor